Troikanomics

Ray Kinsella • Maurice Kinsella

# Troikanomics

## Austerity, Autonomy and Existential Crisis in the European Union

palgrave
macmillan

Ray Kinsella
Michael Smurfit Graduate School of Business (Formerly)
Co Dublin, Ireland

Maurice Kinsella
The Galilee House of Studies
Athy, Kildare, Ireland

ISBN 978-3-030-40432-1 ISBN 978-3-319-97070-7 (eBook)
https://doi.org/10.1007/978-3-319-97070-7

Library of Congress Control Number: 2018954348



Cover illustration: Getty Images/ altmodern

This Palgrave Macmillan imprint is published by the registered company Springer Nature Switzerland AG
The registered company address is: Gewerbestrasse 11, 6330 Cham, Switzerland

# Acknowledgements

To Carmel who brought us all together.

Our thanks to our family for always being there for us while we were writing this book—and to Ita, Michael, and Thomas for their input.

Our colleagues, past and present, in University College Dublin including the Michael Smurfit Graduate School of Business, the Galilee House of Studies, the University of Ulster, and in the Central Bank of Ireland, helped shape our ideas in Economics and Philosophy.

Special thanks to Dr Bruce Arnold, Michael Clarke, formerly of the Department of Industry and Commerce, and Professor Antony Coughlan of the University of Dublin Trinity College. Each of them have made distinctive contributions to articulating themes explored in this book.

We are grateful to Palgrave Macmillan for providing us with the opportunity to make our ideas available to a wider audience. It is always about individuals, of course, and the individuals that we would like to thank are Clara Heathcock and Laura Pacey. They instantly saw the relevance of the ideas we were putting forward to a Europe in crisis—they were always positive and extremely accommodating.

The experience of working together has been hugely enriching. It has reinforced the conviction with which each of us began this project. Namely, that a perspective on political economy that is not informed by philosophical critique is a poor and incomplete one.

# Contents

# List of Figures

# 1

# Foundations of the Argument

## An Inflection Point in the European Union

*Troikanomics (from 'Troika', a triumvirate charged with the task of mitigating against the European Banking and Debt Crisis; and 'nomics' from the Greek 'nomos', meaning 'law of'). This concept represents the extent to which, in its structural and operational characteristics, the Troika was a 'law-unto-itself'. It existed outside of established European Union (EU) mandates and was not accountable to the national governments over which it exercised control, nor to their citizens. It is indicative of a deeper undermining of national autonomy within the EU that is iteratively expressing itself in numerous individual existential crises.*

The European Banking and Debt Crisis has been an existential milestone in the history of the EU and the Eurozone. Not only has it threatened to upend their obdurately protected status quo, but its consequences have brought their longer-term survival into question. The Troika, and its *modus operandi* 'Troikanomics', has scorched itself into the ongoing narrative of this crisis. It was a rogue form of austerity which, in subjugating member nations' national autonomy, prefigured something deeper. It is one among the most visible of multiple forms of existential crises that have spread across different domains of the EU. The Troika was a trium-



R. Kinsella, M. Kinsella, *Troikanomics*, https://doi.org/10.1007/978-3-319-97070-7_1

virate established in 2010, from the capabilities of the European Central Bank (ECB), the European Commission (EC), and the International Monetary Fund (IMF). Its purpose was to provide a 'firewall' against contagion in highly indebted EU peripheral countries by developing, coordinating, and overseeing a programme of conditional funding to them. Troikanomics expressed itself in the unprecedentedly severe fiscal and structural adjustments that were allied with the provision of this funding—imposed through an economic programme of austerity that was deeply oppressive in its political oversight.[1] This process exacerbated the single greatest sociopolitical and economic dislocation in the EU's recent history by transposing the primary burden of adjustment onto debtor countries, corroding their autonomous capacities and enfeebling their national sovereignty.[2]

In 2018 the European Council formally decided to replace the Troika with a new institutional mechanism, the European Monetary Fund—crafted around the European Stability Mechanism.[3] This has been designed to provide mutual assistance to EU member nations which have been impacted by external (often asymmetric) 'shocks' and are in need of short-term financial assistance. It draws to a close the *formal* activity of the mechanisms underpinning this highly contentious initiative, but by no means concludes their deeper ramifications—including negative social fallout. What makes this decision all the more substantial is that it overlaps with the formal exit of Greece from its interminable Bailouts, albeit that it remains under 'enhanced surveillance' for the foreseeable future.[4] The demise of the Troika has in fact been evident since 2014, and was one of the key recommendations of the European Parliament's Report (2014) on its workings—in which they

---

[1] The European Parliament (2014) notes that the Troika 'originated in the decision of 25 March 2010 by euro area Heads of State and Government to establish a joint programme and to provide conditional bilateral loans to Greece, thereby also building on recommendations from the Ecofin Council'.

[2] See, for example, Hall (2012) for a discussion on the onerous adjustment requirements imposed on these countries.

[3] See Berschens (2017).

[4] Greece's experiences of the Debt Crisis, and its subsequent dealings with the Troika, are discussed in greater detail in Chap. 7.

identified multiple failings in the manner in which it had engaged with Greece, Ireland, Portugal, Cyprus, and Spain.[5]

The rapid proliferation of the crisis across the Eurozone increasingly threatened to manifest itself in *political* contagion (which has largely been pejoratively dismissed as 'Populism'—belying its deeper existential legitimacy).[6] This threat, coupled with inadequacies in the architecture of the Eurozone (e.g. a lack of institutional or regulatory fail-safes), meant that the EU's response to the crisis was primarily ad hoc—with the Troika being a demonstrable example. At the heart of the matter, therefore, is the reality that, like the institutional structure of the Eurozone itself, the substance and mode of the Troika's engagement with 'debtor' countries was not adequately thought through.

The need for emergency financial assistance to support the rebalancing and stabilisation of highly indebted countries became increasingly evident as the crisis unfolded. So too did the aligned need to apply some form of conditionality to financing arrangements—a well-established characteristic of IMF Programmes. Consequently, the real issue was not *the principle* of conditional funding per se, but rather the manner in which it was implemented. Namely, the scale and scope of this conditionality subverted domestic political governance and catalysed nihilistic economic repression—all the while challenging the democratic legitimacy of both individual member nations and the EU itself. This process, including the imposition of macroeconomic adjustment and 'reforms', impelled these countries into a decisive inflection point in their histories by deeply subverting their national autonomy. These events contravened the community-rooted principles of solidarity and subsidiarity that the EU continued to proffer as being indispensable aspirations.

The mind-set and motivations that the EU exemplified in its attempts to resolve the crisis reflected a profound failure to recognise national autonomy's status as both intrinsic and relational: a capacity possessed by member nations *prior* to their accession to the EU (expressed in the principle of subsidiarity) and fostered through healthy transnational rela-

[5] All of these countries, except for Greece, subsequently exited the Bailout arrangements with the Troika: Ireland in December 2013, Spain in January 2014, Portugal in May 2014, and Cyprus in March 2016.

[6] For further discussion, see Kinsella (2012).

tionships within the EU (expressed in the principle of solidarity). This is *in particular* the case within a community such as the EU, where members are bound together in reciprocal relationships through a number of multilateral mechanisms, such as the Economic and Monetary Union (EMU). What the EU *was meant to be* became increasingly opaque—cast into darkness by the shadow of what it *had become*. Troikanomics continues to demonstrate the costs, at multiple levels and in multiple arenas, of this discrepancy and the consequences of the EU's default into a hegemonistic and technocratic orthodoxy.

There have been extensive discussions on what structural and functional form that the Troika's replacement should take, over and above its foundations in the European Stability Mechanism. More important than the mechanisms through which it operates is the *mind-set* that it possesses in attempting to carve out a new paradigm for the EU's intra-community relationships. With the EU now facing into a period of transformational changes (by design, e.g. the 2019 European Elections, and by circumstance, e.g. policy responses to the ongoing Migration Crisis), these kinds of issues, and their deeper existential corollaries, require reflecting upon. The lessons we can glean from the burden of Troikanomics, and the wider existential crisis within which it was embedded, can help to inform us in deciding on the content and character of the path that the EU chooses to adopt as it faces into a new political and administrative regime—a new European Commission—beyond the 2019 European Parliamentary elections. In this regard, the path ahead should use this existential crisis as an opportunity for honest and reflective critique so as to reaffirm its foundational vision and values, and the role it hopes to play within wider geopolitical narratives.

## Navigating the Narrative of the Crisis

Reflecting on the ever-proliferating books, reports, and academic studies on the European Banking and Debt Crisis, it is easy to become both fatigued and frustrated. Fatigued at the sheer volume of expert perspectives that have produced compelling analyses on this existential epoch and the legacy it has left both on countries and on individual lives.

Frustrated at the difficulties that they have faced in bridging the divide between theoretical inquiry and practical outputs in the political economy. There is no mandate to apply their insights *in praxis*—either because the EU is unwilling to cast its net for critique, or because it is structurally and functionally ill-equipped to make good on the insights that critiques on this crisis have to offer.

Institutional and descriptive narratives and, of course, political perspectives (read: agendas) all constitute an indispensable corpus of literature for existing and future policy learning, as well as for historical inquiry. However, even here, there is no workable consensus on the dimensions of reform—except that their final form will ultimately revert to the will of the Franco-German centre. To take one example, in 2017, two radically different blueprints for change were published: one which envisages no less than five different possible footpaths (including a return to a basic trading zone), while another makes inroads towards a more fully federalised EU.[7] These considerations are shaped by shifting electoral pressures regarding what is an acceptable trajectory to propel the EU forward. The lack of clarity or coherence in mapping a path forward is one example of the deeper existential crisis that the EU is currently confronted with. A core problem is that the capacity of the EU establishment to learn from this and aligned crises, and adopt an authentic route towards recovery and reform, is mediated through the 'Conventional Wisdom' rather than through a truly *responsive* critique.

Importantly, many analyses on the crisis have, understandably, grappled with this issue from a purely economic stance. But there is much more to these events than economics, and efforts to fully engage with it through a 'lone lens' critique may turn out to be inadequate—in particular with respect to conveying the profound *existential* significance it has had for people and nations. Indeed, each distinct dimension of the EU's architecture—whether they be economic, political, or social—throws cross hairs across the others and provides their own contributions to the character of the EU.[8] For example, the EU has been weighed down in

[7] These are, respectively, its 'White Paper on the Future of Europe: Reflections and scenarios for the EU27 by 2025' (European Commission 2017a) and its 'Reflection Paper on the Deepening of the Economic and Monetary Union' (European Commission 2017b).

[8] For a further discussion on the range of crises currently assailing the EU, see Schwab (2012).

certain countries by deep *social* pathologies exemplified in compromised health status, homelessness, and unemployment—which have proliferated in tandem with the unfolding consequences of austerity-based policy responses to the economic crisis.[9]

Thus, analysis may benefit from being filtered and refracted through another lens—one that is less willing to casually accept institutional 'givens' and, instead, emphasises the importance of rigorous and reflective critique. To take some examples, vague aspirations relating to 'unity', 'equality', and 'diversity' make little sense in an environment where these concepts are susceptible to distortion, denial, and the debilitating effects of political agendas. The reality is that the EU is fractured and unequal—Greece is demonstrably less 'equal' than Germany at every level. The givens that underpin the sociopolitical and economic legitimacy of the EU are in need of excavation, and the normative principles underpinning its responsibilities towards its members (for example, in the principles of solidarity and subsidiarity) are in need of reanimation.

With this in mind, we seek in this book to engage with a set of the fundamental issues besetting the EU today in a manner that integrates a *philosophical* dimension—reflecting on issues such as austerity, autonomy, and its broader 'existential crisis'. These issues are distilled through the concept of Troikanomics. The overriding aim is to imbue the more explicitly sociopolitical and economic arguments with greater conceptual and normative weight. One could hardly overstate the importance of this quest for Europe at this point in time. Europe's Debt Crisis remains unresolved, even as the EU seeks to move beyond 'the great recession'. The expectation that this would lead to the restoration of political stability across the EU has not materialised. Indeed, the Migration Crisis has exacerbated anti-EU sentiment contributing to tectonic political shifts in EU member nations, including Germany, France, and Italy. The EU's Brexit-related travails reflect the prevailing political dissonance. At the

---

[9]To take just one metric, as of Q4 2017, Greece had an unemployment rate (age 15–74) of 21.2% and Spain a rate of 16.6%. All of these are above the EU average of 7.3%, in particular Germany at 3.5% (Eurostat 2018a). What is even more telling is that in Greece, long-term unemployment (12 months or more) accounts for 71.8% of unemployment—again far above the EU average of 44.5% (Eurostat 2018b). For further insights on the relationship between austerity and health status, see Karanikolos et al. (2013).

same time, Europe is moving towards a change of leadership in the Commission, the ECB, and the European Parliament: the core institutions that were, in effect, the transmission belt shaping Troikanomics and the Debt Crisis. It is not clear what, if any, lessons have been learnt, the extent to which they have been critiqued, or how far they will be reflected in post-2019 Europe. These are themes which we critique in this book.

## Constructing an Economic–Philosophical Critique

While initially they may appear to be disjunctive, economic and philosophical critiques can in fact be mutually reinforcing. Economic principles are laden with ethical norms concerning issues such as justice (e.g. allocation of resources), rights (e.g. the provision of social welfare), and duties (e.g. the payment of taxes). Alongside this, economic policies and practices have real and measurable consequences on people's welfare—depending on the form that they take and the function that they aim to perform within society. Philosophical critique can, in this instance, contribute to our understanding of the methodological, conceptual, and theoretical foundations of economic principles and practices—and our ability to discern their strengths and weaknesses.[10] Such critique demands conceptual clarity—a return to 'first principles', enabling economic matters to be problematised in a new and novel way.

This form of inquiry is inherently interdisciplinary in its attempt to identify, examine, and resolve social pathologies, such as the Troika's austerity measures. For example, in the context of our present analysis, it can provide insights that inform policy makers on precisely why they should understand the concept of autonomy as integrally bound up in the sustainability of the European Project, and how they may ensure

[10] It should, of course, be highlighted that there are mainstream economists whose analysis is permeated by a strong ethical perspective. Joseph Stiglitz is a notable example who has written eloquently of the nihilistic underbelly of austerity—and with the authority of someone who has designed and participated in missions for the World Bank. He is, however, a rare exception that proves the rule.

that the EU is equipped to uphold these principles. In this regard, philosophical critique can help to bring about *actionable* responses to sociopolitical and economic concerns.[11]

What we are speaking of here is a reflective evidence-based model for correcting imbalances—in this instance between 'core' and 'peripheral' economies—informed by a robust political economy which reanimates Social Europe and philosophical critique of 'Europe'. This interdisciplinary approach enables existing empirical analysis—all of those petabytes of data—to be supported by interpretive insights that can inform our understanding of the flawed nature of the Troika's principles, policies, and practices.[12] Philosophical argumentation places itself at this juncture in its attempts to elevate our appreciation for the ethical significance of the economy. Specifically, our approach uses the framework of existential philosophy (and, as a corollary, existential psychology) through which to reflect on the chronology of events, the nature and modes of interventions in the lives of countries and people, and the *not-yet-fully-realised* outcomes of these events.

How has the EU descended so far down its current path? One perspective relates to a neo-liberal ideology that permeated the EU and its institutions from the mid-late 1980s, paving the way for an emerging supranationalism and subjugating national autonomy as obsolete in an era of globalisation. J. K. Galbraith's (1958) deconstruction and application on the concept of the 'Conventional Wisdom' offers a prophetic response to such questions. He criticises the various 'Conventional Wisdoms' that permeate social thought across the economy and society (such as within large firms), and how this leads to economic analysis that possesses no substantive social utility. This concept conveys how there are sets of beliefs that are 'owned' by particular groups/societies/cultures that are 'beyond reproach' (a convention that is an obstacle to the acceptance of new modes of thought). This can breed intellectual inertia—an unwillingness/inability to provide new perspectives, instead fueling an obdurate adherence to convention.

---

[11] For a further discussion on this point, see Christman (2009a, 2009b).

[12] Economists such as Amartya Sen attest to the mutually beneficial nature of aligning philosophical and economic critique.

There is a strong sense that the cultural shift at the heart of Troikanomics was symptomatic of a prevailing orthodoxy that froze out new, challenging modes of thinking—fearful of any opposition to its dominance and actively shunning reflective critique. The Conventional Wisdom is a strategic ally of political orthodoxies that are intent on perpetuating established power dynamics: zealously reiterating conventions, which become 'normalised' regardless of whether or not they hold merit. Galbraith (1973) has argued that the emancipation of belief is required in order to challenge hegemony of accepted beliefs which prevent a full appreciation for how the economy works.[13] His objective was therefore to increase openness to alternative ideas about practical economics and the policy agendas required once people have an understanding of the economy's true nature and purpose. The current model is long past the point of needing systematic deconstruction—an imperative that has been conspicuously absent from most official critiques. It is here that the experience of existential crisis can have a vital role to play—impelling, as it does, discourse beyond intellectual stasis.

Troikanomics is a perfect example: the establishment, fixated on defending their own agenda (the Eurozone above everything else), had the political power to enforce it. The Bailout countries had little or no countervailing power to resist the Conventional Wisdom being imposed on them. However, it is notable that the larger Bailout countries, including Spain, did have significantly more clout in their negotiations with the Troika than did smaller member countries—notably Greece and Ireland. The EU had become transfixed by the idea that if concessions were made in the name of, for example, 'social justice' to one country, they would necessarily be demanded by all countries, regardless of circumstance. This prevented reflection on and rethinking of issues such as accession and exit. This is a mind-set that obsesses over preventing sovereign countries exiting, while at the same time refusing to engage in the question as to *why* members might feel impelled to exit in the first place.

The Conventional Wisdom on austerity led the EU into an intellectual and ethical quagmire where, we believe, the only discernible road

---

[13] For a detailed analysis on the economic contributions of Galbraith, see Dunn and Pressman (2005).

forward is (paradoxically) through a revisiting of the foundational values that catalysed the European Project in the first place. The nomenclature of the ECB and the EC simply do not engage with this process. To take an example, when the Troika require a 'resolution' of non-performing mortgage assets, it means encouraging banks and other institutions to repossess homes—with no engagement with the question of the social costs that this visits on families. This, of course, is not normatively defensible—private sector institutions get their legitimacy from the community, whose interests are sacrificed by prioritising 'the resolution of balance sheets' at the expense of sequestering homes. An economic orthodoxy that seeks to vindicate Troikanomics, not just as an abstract construct but as a policy template which is imposed on the welfare and governance of countries, should be willing to engage with the ethical repercussions that are inferred from its convictions.

Five years after Ireland 'exited' the Troika's austerity programme, and notwithstanding strong economic growth in recent years, there are issues that are yet to be resolved, such as the scarring imposed by debt repayments whose legitimacy is problematic and by related casualties in the social economy, notably in housing and homelessness. The same issue arises to an even more marked extent in Greece. Two generations will never be free of such debt—almost €250 billion—and may never own their own homes. Those who manage and profit—exceedingly—from all of this, including 'Vulture Funds', will have acquired and sold on these homes. The economic austerity visited upon Greece—the epicentre of Western philosophy—is a metaphor for the failure of mainstream analysis in understanding the complementarity of economic and philosophical models. Austerity has been driven by philosophically anaemic and ad hoc responses that have convulsed the EU and traumatised the lives of millions of its inhabitants. Philosophy broadly, and ethical enquiry specifically, has much to say on these issues. But its practitioners are seldom on the same plane, or stay in the same hotels, as those who are in a position to instigate change. Those who are vested with the power to implement change simply operate in a different world, one removed from deeper normative and social consequences of their policies.

## Above the Parapet: The Necessity of Critique

Ongoing events within the EU and across the broader geopolitical landscape have cast a long and deeply troubling shadow over its status as an institution that is still connected to, and capable of making good on, its foundational commitments. Alongside the Banking and Debt Crisis, other such events have included Europe's biggest Migration Crisis since World War II, Brexit, military adventurism, a rise in 'Populism', and increasingly asymmetric relationships. While each of these constitutes a crisis in their own right, *collectively* they illustrate the deeper existential malaise that is exacerbating the EU's loss of identity and direction. Whether or not the EU is capable of providing answers to the questions that these events are posing depends largely on whether the 'reforms' it endeavours to implement offer decisive change, or perpetuate the fallacy that a little more of what has not worked will resolve all of the contradictions.

The EU is conflicted, with a trajectory of 'reform' revolving around the Franco-German duopoly. Troikanomics has been a catalyst in calling into question the mind-set underpinning the *modus operandi* of the EU elite. What is clear is that something far more reflective is required, such as a form of governance that respects and values—rather than grudgingly tolerates—the autonomy of its member nations. Something more substantial than a few more institutions and a few more vice presidents—a critique of ethics as well as economics that moves beyond the 'convergence criteria' mentality.

Egalitarian intra-community relations are found within an environment that makes room within its Public Square for dissenting voices. The EU, however, does not easily accommodate to 'dissenting voices'. It does not countenance the integrity of propositions that are willing to ask difficult questions, operate counter to the status quo, and propose reflective solutions. While simply asking a question is not *automatically* advocating a particular course of action, it does raise core problems which a thousand official reports evade: casting into sharp relief the deeper philosophy espoused by the EU. The Eurozone will continue as a suboptimal set of arrangements for as long as it suits the purpose of Germany, France, and the smaller 'core' countries. The externalities will continue to be imposed on the 'the others', including those countries that exist on the margins.

This is also why we advocate for a critique that takes account of economic's normative dimension and also sets a place at the table for ethicists where these issues are debated. Prior to the emergence of the Banking and Debt Crisis, criticism of the Eurozone was regarded as largely unwarranted. It was deemed to be unsubstantiated naysaying that failed to appreciate the communal ethic at the heart of the EU. This ignored the reality that there were earlier misgivings on the part of some economists about the feasibility of a common currency in Europe—sound and grounded economic critique that questioned the nature of convergence criteria and its disassociation from the intricacy of the European Project; such perspectives have since come to be acknowledged as a form of reasoned responsiveness.[14] Troikanomics brought them into the open—and they still remain unresolved, as is clearly reflected in the 2018 stand-off between the anti-Austerity Italian government and the EU Commission.

The dearth in rigorous, uncompromising critique has not only stymied the EU's efforts to resolve its existential crisis, but prevents it from taking the necessary steps in mitigating against the crisis' continued development. The nature of the EU, encompassing its identity and purpose, is an ongoing construction, navigated amidst the constraints and opportunities that 'community' offers. Precisely because it is a process, it requires continuing critical reflection, that is, a willingness to contextualise the present in light of past experiences and future aspirations.[15] The irony is that questions are often only granted their legitimacy within the sociopolitical consciousness *once their concerns have come to pass*—at which point the mission becomes battling the flames rather than preventing the initial spark. This is, in part, the tragedy of the EU—notwithstanding its extraordinary achievements.

The events that continue to unfold within the EU have, however, given critique a *raison d'être*. It is on this platform that we reflect on some of the

[14] For example, prominent economists have argued that the Eurozone failed to meet 'Optimum Currency Area' requirements—see Krugman (2012), Pisani-Ferry (2013), and Gibson et al. (2014). Dow (2016) also discusses issues centering on design flaws within the EMU—including its *presumption* of convergence.

[15] See Lapavitsas' *Preface* to Lapavitsas et al. (2012) for a similar perspective.

central problems at the heart of this book, such as 'How has the autonomy of participant members of the EU been undermined?' and 'How may it be subsequently restored?'. It was the tensions arising from conceptual and institutional flaws in the design of the Eurozone that transmitted contagion from the US financial markets. It was this dynamic that magnified the 'shock' across EU economies and in particular those of the peripheral indebted countries. It was to save, at all costs, the Eurozone that Troikanomics was visited on these economies—deflecting all the while from the root causes of issues such as the Migration Crisis and the madness of militarisation.

The collateral damage to Project Europe, with all of its achievements, has been enormous. Current proposals for resolving the crisis in the Eurozone advocate what are essentially pan-EU policies, such as an EU Minister for Finance. These are institutional responses to something that goes much deeper. If you begin your reforms with inadequate critique, and within a flawed and contradictory Eurozone that remains in crisis (notably in Italy and the periphery), there is a very real risk that the 'solutions' are likely to perpetuate the ongoing questions about legitimacy and hegemony—and a continuation of existential crisis is the inevitable corollary.

## References


Berschens, R. (2017). *EU Official: Troika Role Is Over*. [Online]. Retrieved from https://global.handelsblatt.com/finance/eu-official-troika-role-is-over-796952

Christman, J. (2009a). *The Politics of Persons: Individual Autonomy and Socio-Historic Selves*. Cambridge: Cambridge University Press.

Christman, J. (2009b). Autonomy, Recognition, and Social Dislocation. *Analyse and Kritik, 31*(2), 275–290.

Dow, S. (2016). Ontology and Theory for a Redesign of European Monetary Union. *World Economic Review, 6*, 1–11.

Dunn, S. P., & Pressman, S. (2005). The Economic Contributions of John Kenneth Galbraith. *Review of Political Economy, 17*(2), 161–209.

European Commission. (2017a). *White Paper on the Future of Europe: Reflections and Scenarios for the EU27 by 2025*. Brussels: European Commission.

European Commission. (2017b). *Reflection Paper on the Deepening of the Economic and Monetary Union*. Brussels: European Commission.

European Parliament. (2014). *Role and Operations of the Troika with Regard to the Euro Area Programme*. Brussels: The European Parliament.

Eurostat. (2018a). *Unemployment Rates by Sex, Age and Citizenship (%) [lfsq_urgan]*. [Online]. Retrieved June 5, 2018, from http://appsso.eurostat.ec.europa.eu/nui/show.do?dataset=lfsq_urgan&lang=en

Eurostat. (2018b). *Long-term Unemployment (12 Months or More) as a Percentage of the Total Unemployment, by Sex and Age (%)*. [Online]. Retrieved June 5, 2018, from http://appsso.eurostat.ec.europa.eu/nui/show.do?dataset=lfsq_upgal&lang=en

Galbraith, J. K. (1958). *The Affluent Society*. New York: Houghton Mifflin.

Galbraith, J. K. (1973). *Economics and the Public Purpose*. Boston: Houghton Mifflin.

Gibson, H. D., Palivos, T., & Tavlas, G. S. (2014). The Crisis in the Euro Area: An Analytic Overview. *Journal of Macroeconomics, 39*, 233–239.

Hall, P. A. (2012). The Economics and Politics of the Euro Crisis. *German Politics, 21*(4), 355–371.

Karanikolos, M., Mladovsky, P., Cylus, J., Thomson, S., Basu, S., Stuckler, D., Mackenbach, J. P., & McKee, M. (2013). Financial Crisis, Austerity, and Health in Europe. *The Lancet, 381*(9874), 1323–1331.

Kinsella, R. (2012). *EMU's Biggest Threat Is Political Contagion*. [Online]. Retrieved from https://www.omfif.org/analysis/commentary/2012/june/emus-biggest-threat-is-political-contagion/

Krugman, P. (2012). Revenge of the Optimum Currency Area. *NBER Macroeconomics Annual, 27*(1), 439–448.

Lapavitsas, C. (2012). *Crisis in the Eurozone*. London: Verso.

Pisani-Ferry, J. (2013). The Known Unknowns and Unknown Unknowns of European Monetary Union. *Journal of International Money and Finance, 34*(C), 6–14.

Schwab, K. (2012). *The Re-emergence of Europe*. s.l.: World Economic Forum.

# Part I

## Crisis and Catharsis in the Heartland of the European Union

# 2

# A Critical Inflection Point for the EU

## Introduction

The decade from 2008 to 2018 is scarred by the most destructive narrative in modern European history. The epicentre was a financial crisis that enveloped the EU's wider economic landscape and then developed into a political moment of catharsis that called into question the sustainability of the Eurozone (as well as the wider 'European Project').

The lead-up to the crisis was characterised by persistent disavowal—particularly on the part of politicians—even as it was evolving. This included a deference to the dysfunctional behaviours of both banks and sovereigns (which were thoroughly intertwined in their respective states of turmoil (Schwab 2012)). The interesting point here is that the basic models of political engagement and also of banking have remained essentially unchanged, even in the aftermath of Troikanomics. Consequently, even as the Banking and Debt Crisis revealed itself, the EU was lacking in the institutional mechanisms necessary to provide an adequate response.[1] Its primary response vehicle, Troikanomics,

[1] There are arguments that, aside from the numerous practical inadequacies in implementing the Euro, it was *in principle* an unsustainable undertaking—given the latent heterogeneous nature of



R. Kinsella, M. Kinsella, *Troikanomics*, https://doi.org/10.1007/978-3-319-97070-7_2

took the cult of austerity to a whole new level: a tool for repressive economic intervention and coercive political intrusiveness. It marked a decisive shift *away* from the fostering of countries' autonomous capacities, and instead a move *towards* the imposition of centrist hegemony (in particular, under Germany).[2] To that extent, greater recognition of national autonomy on the part of the EU, and aligned efforts to create an environment within which it is fostered, will be a measure of what the establishment has learnt from this experience.

The oft-invoked metaphor of the EU finding itself at a 'crossroads' has become jaded, bordering on a truism; nevertheless, the image it invokes has never rung more true. It succinctly conveys three fundamental truths of where the European Project—after over 60 years of triumphs and tribulations—now finds itself. Firstly, there is a pressing need to decisively move beyond reactive sociopolitical and economic responses. Secondly, there are a number of potential paths from which it can choose to move forward, as is borne out by the European Commission's (2017) White Paper which outlines five such directions (which vary in their feasibility). Thirdly, the EU has—in spite of its options—become frozen by an ambivalence that has stymied its capacity to reanimate what Project Europe was originally about. In particular, this will involve acknowledging the legitimacy of the concerns that impelled the rise in Populism and disenchantment with the content and direction of European policies, particularly in the economic sphere.

Moving beyond this crossroads involves more than simply leaving behind *past mistakes*. It entails *building towards* a future on the foundational community-orientated values that at one time inspired the *telos* of the European Project, and have since largely been extinguished. The original success of this Project was not fortuitous; nor could it have been

---

the countries it was composed of; e.g. Feldstein (2012), Moravcsik (2012) and Lane (2012). This issue is discussed in greater detail in Chap. 5, in particular within reference to the EU's status as an 'Optimum Currency Area'.

[2] Crawford (2010) also makes reference to the hegemony exercised by Germany within Europe. Hillebrand (2014) provides a discussion on Germany's place within the Eurozone and the Eurozone Crisis.

taken for granted—it was an outcome of the character, beliefs, and integrity of purpose to which Europe was directed. In this context, the 'character' of Europe was the antithesis of what we observe in Troikanomics and raises serious questions regarding the erosion of this culture—and therefore its identity. Post-2019, as the EU faces into the headwinds of change, could such an initiative be born (or reborn) in the EU's present culture—one that leverages, for example, the intrinsic values of Christian Democracy, which was the platform upon which Europe was founded. Whatever the 'right' direction forward may be, it will remain hidden for as long as the Conventional Wisdom rooted in what Europe has become is the only source of critical insight with which the EU establishment are willing to engage.[3]

## Uncovering the EU's Existential Crisis

The concept of an 'existential crisis' expresses the distinctiveness and the gravity of the inflection point that the EU currently finds itself in. It is no small thing for Germany—the political and economic powerhouse of the EU—to find itself in a catharsis that threatens its long-established political consensus, for the United Kingdom to be on the point of departing the EU, or for Greece to be condemned to remaining under 'close surveillance' for the foreseeable future, still burdened with enormous debt. The concept of existential crisis is also intrinsically antagonistic. It serves more than just a descriptive function. The term conveys that we are speaking of something that is fundamentally *critical*—calling into question the very architecture of the EU (and the Eurozone), as well as its deepest aspirations.

As a 'crisis', it evokes a period of intense difficulty precipitated and perpetuated by a diverse set of events—both within and beyond the EU's borders. The EU's crisis is 'existential' not simply because of the scale and scope of the events underpinning it, but because these events raise

[3] We discuss the concept of 'Conventional Wisdom' in greater detail in Chap. 1.

concerns that strike at the heart of the EU's place in the world, its identity, its sense of purpose, and its longer-term viability.[4] This crisis is, therefore, more than just a matter of needing to shift the *status quo*—it calls into question the survival of the vision for Europe that is currently being pursued. This is expressed, amongst other ways, in overpowered bureaucrats, political communique-speak, increased dependency leading to the marginalisation of smaller countries (including those Eastern European countries with a culture that is at variance with the orthodoxy of the centre), and the emasculation of its constitutive values. Amidst these factors, the EU is caught in a stasis of its own making.

'Crisis' is not *necessarily* an inherently negative experience, and should not be dismissed as an undesirable aberration. When attentively internalised, it can provoke catharsis, whereby an opportunity and impetus to change can present itself. Before this can occur, the EU must first believe that such change is both necessary and attainable. In spite of being inherently challenging, the *lived experience* of existential crisis *can* produce considerable positive consequences and can certainly be more constructive than existential apathy. Indifference breeds stagnation, a disassociation from the necessity for reflective critique, and a lack of concern for change (and the possibilities it can bring, such as (re)discovering a sense of identity and direction). Conversely, crisis—whose most profound symptom lies in the question 'Who am I?'—pulls us towards a questioning stance, a first step in moving beyond a perpetual 'crossroads'.

The achievements of the EU are extraordinary. From its inception in the European Coal and Steel Community, it introduced a platform for transnational democratic dialogue that helped to redeem Europe from the atrocities of World War II and to reinvent its identity. A key issue here relates to the direction of change in contemporary EU and whether this direction was embedded in the genesis of the European Project. What is increasingly evident is a clash between the assured and consensual

[4] Sen (2012) also acknowledges how failed economic policies influence more than individual social metrics such as unemployment and poverty; within the context of the current crisis they place our sense of European Unity itself at risk.

values of 'old Europe' and a new and very problematic paradigm of a 'false Europe' (Bénéton et al. 2017)—reflected not least in Troikanomics and, more recently, in a nihilistic drive towards European militarisation. Since its foundation, it has continued to evolve into a unique geopolitical entity whose ultimate goals, and how they will be accomplished, are an enigma. The welfare enhancement of its members has at least in part been sequestered by the preservation and enhancement of its own institutions. Increasingly, the EU resembles a multinational corporation, whose mission statement has become tarnished by a self-interest which has become its overarching goal—its architects far removed from the lives of those over whom their policies hold sway. Seen from this perspective, the EU seeks to evoke any activity—however contrary to its foundational values—that vindicates its continued existence. Here, for example, the militarisation of the EU raises notable concerns.

Events such as these are not some random tragedy that have been visited upon Europe, they have not been created *ex nihilo*; rather, they have gestated within an increasingly ambitious but, as we will see, flawed and incomplete system—one that suggests a need for a fundamental shift in the EU's culture and psyche. Once such issues become embedded, they breed and mutate, and can exacerbate the pre-existing conditions that brought about their initial creation—generating a negative feedback loop. They are, at least in part, a consequence of an EU elite who have neither the humility to accept some culpability nor the clarity of thought to forge an effective and principled response. This is bleeding the credibility of all that 'Europe' stands for.

The 1980s were marked by a number of milestones that point to the genesis of a crisis which triggered the anti-democratic response embodied within Troikanomics. EU financial markets were impacted by the liberalisation of financial markets in the United States—deregulation and the commoditisation of risk. At the same time, the so-called Washington Consensus prescribed an economic/political orthodoxy that took little cognisance of the potentialities and capabilities of individuals who, as events transpired, bore the costs of institutional failures. To identify the DNA of Troikanomics, look no further.

Parallel to this there was a determined effort by the EU establishment to introduce a secular Constitution for Europe, referencing pretty well every aspiration while simultaneously excluding God, much less Europe's Christian roots and the social responsibilities that flowed directly from these. This led to disagreements between, on the one hand, the emerging secular movement led by France and, on the other hand, Germany, Italy, and a number of other countries. The proposed European Constitution produced by the 'Convention on the Future of Europe' under Giscard d'Estaing was rejected by France and the Netherlands, and it foundered. This goes to the heart of a political and cultural fracturing, which in 2018 divided Germany and further undermined the stability of the EU. It has marked a decisive shift away from a system of moral and normative thought that has shaped its identity since its inception. The extent of this problem became clear following massive migration—a clash of cultures emerged. A difficulty here arises from the dilution of foundational values and their substitution by an expanding set of contractual rights imposed from the centre which go against the sense of identity and norms, notably in some of the Eastern European countries.

The question 'Where is Europe going and what will it look like when we get there?' has been coloured by crises within Europe and within the wider global geopolitical environment marked, in particular, by the Trumpian imperialism. It is sometimes argued that these questions cannot be answered and that attempting to do so is counterproductive: the important thing is the journey itself. This is both seductive and facile. What has become the EU had a starting point and a mission. To leave the destination clouded in ambiguity is disingenuous and offensive to its foundational principles, including solidarity and subsidiarity. There has, of course, always been an undercurrent of contrived obscurity: a fear lest in some countries too honest a position might 'frighten the children' (aka voters)—better play to these sensibilities while the adults in the room get on with the business of destination, roadmap, and timetable. This perspective is grounded in a *faux realpolitik*, and it has imposed very significant costs. In the face of the widespread asymmetries in power and disenchantment among voters across Europe, the EU has yet to acknowledge that what assails it is more than just an unresolved economic crisis: it has to do with a sense of identity that also encompasses the legitimacy of national autonomy. Looking into the future, a challenge the EU faces is its capacity to reanimate its substantive mission in the face of competing ideological pressures.

This crisis is not just about the EU's *international* relationships; it is primarily about its relationship with those in its community whose peace and prosperity it ultimately holds accountability for. It was precisely these lives that were traumatised by Troikanomics, notwithstanding the collective expertise of the multiple institutions which constitute 'official' Europe and, as we shall see, there remains a dissonance between the two. And here, we ask: Where is this existential crisis to be found? In the cabinet rooms of ministers and government representatives? In the boardrooms and balance sheets of bankers and market analysts? In the homes of those left disenfranchised and despondent? Across the EU, over 500 million individuals get on with their lives and the meeting rooms of the Commission and the ECB continue to hum, driven by the 'busy schedules' of the elite. The connectivity between both is not evident to the voters in many EU countries. It is no longer clear what it is all for, other than to perpetuate the existence of these same institutions. In these circumstances, the *reasoned* recourse for Europe is a radical critique leading to a recovery of its vocational compass—which inspired its origins and empowered its development. The extent to which the EU accomplishes this will act either as a vindication for, or as an indictment of, its current trajectory.

## Manifestations of the Crisis

Amidst the wider issues that are currently affecting the EU, our analysis focuses most explicitly on the Banking and Debt Crisis—encompassing both the range of its antecedents and the responses that the EU has adopted towards it. At the heart of ongoing sociopolitical and economic developments within the EU is what we define as 'Troikanomics'. For millions of people in the EU's peripheral economies it will stand as an existential reality from which there is little reprieve; for historians it will remain as a defining manifestation of the anti-democratic orthodoxy now typifying the Union's power relations.

The name derives from the 'Troika'—a type of 'special purpose vehicle' drawn from the capabilities of three institutions: the EC, the ECB, and the IMF. It was charged with developing, overseeing, and enforcing a programme of austerity to be imposed on five peripheral member countries—one that was completely unprecedented in terms of its severity and magnitude.[5] Non-negotiable acceptance of a mandated austerity programme was required of these debtor nations in exchange for conditional finance—a 'Bailout'—to prevent sovereign default. Had these defaults transpired, it would have precipitated the implosion of the Eurozone.

Austerity is a template for fiscal correction in countries that have been impacted by public finance imbalances—often arising from deficiencies in domestic practices and/or external 'shocks'. It signifies an unapologetically rigorous and demanding means of rerouting a country back to 'living within its means', of adjusting sovereign income/expenditure ratios to ensure sustainable debt levels. This is particularly vital when countries are enmeshed in a highly interconnected and multivariate economy such as the Eurozone, where financial market indicators of instability in one member country 'spill over' into the wider markets.

Austerity is not the only, and seldom the most appropriate, template for rebalancing an economy. Nevertheless, there are occasions when a realignment of either public or private consumption, alongside saving, is necessary; for example, it can be implemented to avoid balance of payments difficulties, including a build-up of an external debt burden which cannot be satisfactorily met from export earnings. Difficulties such as this can engender oppressive debt repayments, discourage foreign and private investment, incentivise additional (potentially unsustainable) borrowing, and leave an economy hostage to external pressures and credit downgrading.

But the cult of austerity—both in principle and in practice—is in general acutely flawed: often counterproductive and deeply damaging to nations' medium-term macroeconomic stability. The irony here is that it is the 'dominant' countries that benefit most from these vulnerabilities since it is they who have most to gain from an undervalued exchange rate and from the outflow of wealth, income (including interest payments), and a disenfranchised labour force.

[5] These countries were Greece, Ireland, Portugal, Spain, and Cyprus.

Alongside this, other events of the last decade continue to test the resilience of the EU. The Debt Crisis, and the cult of Troikanomics that followed, is symptomatic of a more pervasive shift in the culture and ethos of the EU—of which there are other coexisting manifestations.[6] Included among these crises are the sequestering of member nations' decisional and volitional capacities, the Migration Crisis, Brexit, and the EU's increased militarisation. These developments are emerging within the context of the EU's accelerated efforts to push for further EU 'integration', which have resulted in larger outflows of member nations' autonomous capacities. Power differentials have become more acute by granting non-national decision-makers *preferential* status over those of national authorities. This process has, paradoxically, been buttressed by an air of 'constitutional tolerance' from members.[7] An EU divided—from the clique of the core to the shadows of the 'peripherals'—cannot heal where defence mechanisms are employed to shield it from facing 'facticity' and from the reflective critique that this would produce.

Brexit stands as a manifestation of Europe's existential crisis. The scheduled date for the formal exit of the United Kingdom (UK) from the EU is 29 March 2019: a process that began on 23 June 2016 when the citizens of the UK voted by way of Referendum to become the first member nation to voluntarily exit the EU. This decision was as divisive as it was historically decisive. There was a singular irony in the fact that it coincided with the 60th anniversary of the Treaty of Rome. For the UK it is, in all of its ramifications, the single biggest constitutional catharsis in centuries. Brexit might have been seen in retrospect as *the* event that was capable of compelling the EU to address the need for more inclusive intra-communal relations. It might have been the catalyst for reform and renewal; self-evidently this has not been the case. Not least because of its size, the UK was spared the 'unthinkable', that is, an intervention into its sovereign affairs by a Troika of unelected and unaccountable institutions. It remained free to implement its own policies to mitigate the impact of the crisis which decimated other parts of the EU. Proponents of Brexit

[6] Raines et al. (2017) provide an analysis of these factors.

[7] The concept of 'constitutional tolerance' is discussed in greater detail by Lindseth (1999).

highlight the importance of control over borders, a repatriation of sovereign responsibilities, as well as an end to the jurisdiction of the European Court of Justice (ECJ). This leaves open this question: it was clear to those who favoured Brexit what they wished to walk away from; what is less clear is the kind of society which they now wish to develop and build, in an environment where 'Brussels' is no longer perceived as telling them what to do. The irony is that both Brussels and the UK are engaged in a search for redemption and a new sense of identity.

The tide of Euroscepticism has been running strongly across the EU for some years—and not alone in countries impacted by Troikanomics. It has not been addressed. In the UK, Brexit has led to an ongoing agonised debate between those who wished to remain and those who unequivocally wished to exit. Inevitably, there are those in the middle—seeking to remain in some form or another, to vote again, to allow Parliament to make the final decision—and everything in between. It is changing every domain of life within the UK and, importantly, within its engagement with its nearest neighbour, the Republic of Ireland, with whom it shares a land border.

In all of the arguments and counterarguments about Brexit, it is clear that for the *albeit* smallish majority of the voting population, the UK is not so much leaving the EU as leaving what the EU *has become*: centralised, hegemonistic, and progressively suffocating the identity of the UK and its capacity to exercise its national autonomy. Both the UK and the EU establishment were emphatic that Brexit was to be no mere façade; the departure was to be real—a rather naïve form of which has been expressed in the form 'Brexit means Brexit'. As the process continued to unfold through the different phases of the negotiations, this proved to be a formidable challenge for both. The task of setting out a trajectory for their future relationship has been fraught, as this process is very much uncharted territory. Ultimately, its success or failure will be primarily determined by how the EU *chooses to respond to it*. Germany and France can afford to ignore the concerns of smaller countries and, as we have seen, have continued to do so. Brexit is different. It has laid bare the anomalies and inequalities that are now endemic in the EU.

It's important to recognise that the Article 50 process is clear, straightforward, and non-adversarial. Nonetheless, the 'temerity' of the UK's decision presented itself to the EU establishment in the form of implicit threats to 'make the UK pay' for its rejection of the European Project—and to ensure that no other member could consider choosing such an option. This was, for example, reflected in the September 2018 Salzburg Summit. This tells its own story. More generally, the very idea of consulting voters on the future of Europe has been castigated by the same orthodoxy that very evidently *do not* know best nor who have to endure the consequences of their policies. Will the EU position, for example, become obdurately defensive in their new trading relationship and seek to freeze the UK out, therefore setting a precedent for other countries who have now learnt that the question of departure is no longer an unspeakable transgression? This decision will have political and should, we believe, have philosophical repercussions. The EU, who since its inception has orientated itself towards the accession and integration of new members, now finds itself in the position where it must decisively respond to the exit of one of its members in a manner that both respects the autonomy of their decision while simultaneously understanding that the integrity of the Union is best served by tolerance and by the overriding importance of a cooperative and accommodating future relationship.

The vote for Brexit, while dramatic, is by no means inexplicable. It illustrates an increasingly endemic defiance towards the EU, as is evidenced in the rise of 'Populist' parties across the continent in recent years. While Emmanuel Macron's significant victory over Marine Le Pen and the National Front in 2017's French Elections may have signalled a reprieve from this trajectory, subsequent elections across the continent belie this presumption. Across Germany, the Czech Republic, Austria, Italy, and Sweden a wave of parties with an agenda that is actively opposed to the wider dictates of the EU establishment have been gaining ground.[8] The rise of the so-called Populist parties was, and remains, rooted within their own national circumstances and cultural values. Nonetheless, collectively they express the discord between the 'political elite' and the

[8] For example, in September 2017, the Alternative for Germany (AfD) won 12.6% of the German vote, attaining 94 seats in the Bundestag. Alongside this, in March 2018, the Italian anti-establishment Five Star Movement led by Luigi Di Maio became the party with the largest number of votes.

wider set of voters impacted by their policies. To bridge this divide requires a greater emphasis on 'representativeness' within the national demos, which should be acknowledged and respected by the EU elite.

Populism has been challenged as capitalising on a prevailing zeitgeist of disenfranchisement with the EU—in other words a reactionary movement that seeks to politicise the more exclusionary aspects of nationalism. A more balanced perspective is that, in general, Populism is largely a consequence of policy failure and the associated strains on social solidarity: it's not 'capitalising' on disenchantment with the EU—it's an expression of that disenchantment, for example, from policies that are perceived to be the consequence, direct or indirect, of their dependency on the EU establishment. Concerns about the legitimacy of its motivations and manifestations are important and warrant further reflection, but such reflection cannot be achieved if it is pejoratively dismissed *out of hand*; in particular, when it has increasingly come to embody not just economic disenfranchisement, but wider issues such as understanding the cultural sensitivities and fears behind national opposition to mass migration, the emasculation of national autonomy, and the perceived lack of democratic representativeness within the European community.

In his 2016 State of the Union address, the then European Commission president Jean-Claude Juncker (2016) highlighted the main theme of this book. He said: 'Our European Union is, at least in part, in an existential crisis'. In the realm of international relations, there is nothing more existential than the reality of war. Defence, security, and foreign policy are central to the political governance of the sovereign nation. The EU has continued, notwithstanding the questions raised by the Banking and Debt Crisis, towards full political union and, ultimately, a supranational identity. Since it is precisely in defence, security, and foreign policy that many of the prerequisites of autonomy subsist, this would, inevitably, contribute to further centralisation of the EU 'core' and the continued diminution of the autonomy of smaller member nations. This merits further reflection.

One of the most striking differences in the pre- and post-crisis era relates to the much greater and still accelerating increase in the militarisation of the EU—in late 2018, President Emmanuel Macron and Chancellor Angela Merkel reinforced this in their call for a 'real' European Army, in its own way a further and alarming milestone in this process. To be specific, the last decade has seen the greatest ramping-up in EU military deployment, across the board, since World War II.[9] This, broadly, reflects three factors.

The first and most obvious is the illegal annexation of Crimea by Russia—or, from a Russian perspective, its reintegration of Crimea into the national territory defined in terms of history and culture, and the 'righting' of an injustice perpetrated during the Soviet period. Whatever the interpretation and wherever the balance lies, what is clear is the enormous impetus that this has given towards militarisation. What is much more opaque, however, are the different subtexts, in terms of causes and impacts, of this development: they include the perceived threat to US hegemony arising from Russia's economic stabilisation and recovery in the wake of the collapse of the Soviet Union. There are also enormous commercial interests, as well as geopolitical issues, including the future role of NATO and trade—from weapons to natural gas—that are caught up in EU militarisation.

The second factor is the assertion in 2017 by the then newly elected president Donald Trump that the United States has borne a disproportionate and unfair financial burden for the defence of Europe, and his insistence on increased levels of defence spending by European countries. These developments, between them, have given an enormous impetus to the EU militarisation process. They have taken a wide range of institutional forms and initiatives in a process that is akin to the 'colonisation' of the European Project.

Notwithstanding all of this, there is a deeper agenda. There has been a long-standing overt policy intent geared towards developing a military capability as a political expression of Europe's nascent identity. The Lisbon Treaty, to take just one example, provided for the development of Permanent Structured Cooperation (PESCO).[10] More recently, there has

---

[9] The scale—and the rapidity—of the build-up is chronicled by The International Institute for Strategic Studies (www.iiss.org) and Chatham House (www.chathamhouse.org). For an insightful graphic of the extent of NATO's 'encirclement' of Russia, see, for example, Batchelor (2017). O'Hanlon (2017) provides a rigorous account of the institutional dimensions, and limitations, of NATO's strategy.

[10] The Permanent Structured Cooperation (PESCO) Agreement, signed by 23 EU member countries in November 2017, represents a further step forward in the militaristic colonisation of the EU. It is an EU agreement on greater cooperation on global military missions—including defence

been a wide range of initiatives including the establishment of an EU Common Defence Fund. Here, EU members must live up to the commitment to allocate a minimum of 2% of the gross domestic product (GDP) to the EU Common Defence Fund (of which 20% is allotted to research and development (R&D) and new European defence industry) (Camporini et al. 2017; Council of the European Union 2017).

The net effect of these developments is an existential phenomenon that could hardly have been envisaged by Europe's founding fathers, namely, a return of the spectre of the preparation for war across the European sub-continent, and a process of 'cooperation' driven, not by peace-building but by militarisation. Returning to our point at the beginning of this section, the identification by the then President Juncker of European 'Defence' as an element of its existential crisis reinforces the arguments made elsewhere in this book, namely, that the EU's existential 'crisis' is a multi-dimensional phenomenon and invariably involves sometimes startling dichotomies. For example, the enormous costs visited on individual countries by Troikanomics might have been expected to lead Europe to a much greater emphasis on capacity building and the development of a 'Social Europe'. To observe, instead, such an enormous emphasis on the business of war points to a serious inability on the part of the European elite to grasp and reanimate what once motivated Europe.

Thirdly, at another level, recent years have been marked by the trauma of a massive migration crisis caused, in part, by the EU's military adventurism. Financially, there is a seeming paradox in Europe's positioning of itself as a force for peace at the international level while, at the same time, failing to engage with peace-building and trade development in its relationship with Russia—a point not lost on some political leaders in Europe. The EU has discerned in the recent 'world view' a self-serving and essentially adversarial dimension to US foreign policy, including using defence and foreign policy for commercial leverage.

---

projects, services, programmes, and procurement. Operating in close coordination with NATO in all of its military-related activities, the crucial issue is not so much about what this agreement *is*, as what it will *allow for*; that is, providing major momentum towards a common defence policy—and, more specifically, what President Macron called in 2018 a 'real' European Army. In the wake of the enactment of the PESCO Agreement, an EU army is a reality that current policies and practices are not simply setting a precedent for, but establishing an *expectation* for.

What Troikanomics should have taught Europe is that the unreflective and adversarial use of power is intrinsically oppressive and destructive. What is quite certain is that Europeans will not necessarily sleep easier because, at the insistence of the United States, they are spending significantly greater amounts on armaments and military. It may be that the 'new unilateralism' of US foreign policy towards Europe will serve, instead, to encourage the EU to seek a closer rapprochement, both in security and in trade, with Russia with whom it shares the sub-continent.

Throughout all of this, migrants continue to drown in desperate attempts to reach the EU mainland, there to confront a kaleidoscope of responses, from walls and barbed wire to a divisive administrative 'processing'. In the nature of these events there is always a single event that captures the essence of the crisis.[11] On 2 September 2015 a three-year-old boy Alan Kurdi from Syria was found face down in a red T-shirt on a Turkish beach. He and his mother had died trying to reach Greece. In his death, his photograph joined the ranks of those iconic images of others—'Tank Man' in Tiananmen Square in June 1989 and the children fleeing the My Lai massacre in Vietnam in March 1968—who became metaphors for truly nihilistic events. This highlights the importance of upholding the dignity of each individual, whatever their circumstance—a truth that is embedded in Christian Democracy. It is, of course, speculative but reasonable to assume that Chancellor Merkel's decision to open Germany's doors to migrants reflected the Christian Democracy that shaped her own personal upbringing. That being so, it highlights the reality that such principles are part of a culture, a conversation where all of society is speaking the same language. But in contemporary Europe they are not—in schools and universities and cabinet rooms they are speaking a language bleached of such values.

And so the EU has been divided on exactly how to handle this crisis, varying between policies of unrestricted access to no access. While some EU members, including Germany, Italy, Sweden, and Austria among others, initially welcomed remarkably high numbers of refugees, the

[11] According to the *Independent*, in June (2018), '[a]t least 660 people have died crossing the Mediterranean Sea so far this year'.

political reaction by voters has forced a significant reversal. Some Central and East European states, from the outset, rejected quotas imposed by Brussels and focused instead on security arrangements and border controls. The crisis has been assuaged by a tenuous agreement between the EU and Turkey over how to best handle ongoing flows of migrants. The scale, and age composition, of migration resonated with concerns about integration and 'cultural colonisation' as a key issue in national elections in Europe. Public anxiety about the Migration Crisis was rooted not alone in humanitarian and financial implications, but also in relation to perceived security threats. The issue of migration impacted the outcome of the 2018 Italian election and, more dramatically, the decision by Chancellor Merkel to stand down as Chair of the CDU following significant loses in German regional elections.

The response by the establishment to the Anti-Austerity movement across the EU was to dismiss them as anti-EU 'Populists'. The response to concerns about migration on the scale of recent years has been to dismiss them as 'xenophobic'. Neither responses were intellectually grounded—both reflected an inability to listen to concerns and fears related to the scale and form of inward migration. Germany's 2015 'open-borders' decision, however well intentioned, also reflected a 'unilateralist' mind-set—much the same as in Troikanomics. There had been little consultation on Germany's decision; policy was largely based on ad hoc responses as well as authoritarian proposals, including the imposition of mandatory quotas—the same mind-set that drove the establishment's approach to the EU economic crisis.

It is beyond the scope of this book to review the wide range of suggested responses to the Migration Crisis—within individual EU countries, across the wider EU, and importantly in the countries from which the migrants continue to arrive. However, in all of this it is important to note the efforts by the EC for financial support towards the member countries most affected. Over €1 billion had been provided up to 2018 to Italy, Greece, Bulgaria, Croatia, Germany, Sweden, and Spain. At the margin, such funding is important. But it does not begin to address the longer-term issues and recurrent costs of the crisis. Nor, and it is no facile comparison, does it align with the prospective financial costs of the militarisation of Europe—but, of course, as the political cliché has it weapons create jobs. That is part of the calculus of politics and, in its own way, it highlights the profound moral confusion that pervades what 'Europe' has become—and the photograph of little Alan to which we referred earlier evokes, as substance and metaphor, a gaping wound in the EU's psyche.

## References

Batchelor, T. (2017). *The Map That Shows How Many Nato Troops Are Deployed Along Russia's Border.* [Online]. Retrieved from https://www.independent.co.uk/news/world/europe/russia-nato-border-forces-map-where-are-they-positioned-a7562391.html

Bénéton, P., Brague, R., Delsol, C., Joch, R., András, L., Legutko, R., Manent, P., Matlary, J. H., Pavón, D. N., Scruton, R., Spaemann, R., & Jan Spruyt, B. (2017). *The Paris Statement: A Europe We Can Believe in.* [Online]. Retrieved from https://thetrueeurope.eu/a-europe-we-can-believe-in/

Camporini, V., Hartley, K., Maulny, J.-P., & Zandee, D. (2017). *European Preference, Strategic Autonomy and the European Defence Fund.* s.l.: Armament Industry European Research Group.

Council of the European Union. (2017). *Council Decision Establishing Permanent Structured Cooperation (PESCO) and Determining the List of Participating Member States.* [Online]. Retrieved May 12, 2018, from http://www.consilium.europa.eu/media/32000/st14866en17.pdf

Crawford, B. (2010). The Normative Power of a Normal State: Power and Revolutionary Vision in Germany's Post-Wall Foreign Policy. *German Politics and Society, 28*(2), 165–182.

European Commission. (2017). *White Paper on the Future of Europe: Reflections and Scenarios for the EU27 by 2025.* Brussels: European Commission.

Feldstein, M. (2012). The Failure of the Euro. The Little Currency That Couldn't. *Foreign Affairs, 91*(January/February), 105–116.

Hillebrand, R. (2014). Germany and the Eurozone Crisis: Evidence for the Country's 'Normalisation'? *Fulda University of Applied Sciences: Discussion Papers in Business and Economics, 10.*

Independent. (2018). *At Least 46 Migrants Drown off Tunisia After Boat Sinks in Mediterranean.* s.l.: s.n.

Juncker, J. C. (2016). *State of the Union Address 2016: Towards a Better Europe – A Europe That Protects, Empowers and Defends.* [Online]. Retrieved from https://europa.eu/rapid/press-release_SPEECH-16-3043_en.htm

Lane, P. R. (2012). The European Sovereign Debt Crisis. *Journal of Economic Perspectives, 26*(3), 49–68.
Lindseth, P. (1999). Democratic Legitimacy and the Administrative Character of Supranationalism: The Example of the European Community. *Columbia Law Review, 99*(3), 628–738.
Moravcsik, A. (2012). Europe After the Crisis: How to Sustain a Common Currency. *Foreign Affairs, 91*(3), 54–68.
O'Hanlon, M. (2017). NATO's Limits: A New Security Architecture for Eastern Europe. *Survival – Global Politics and Strategy, 59*(5), 7–24.
Raines, T., Goodwin, M., & Cutts, D. (2017). *The Future of Europe: Comparing Public and Elite Attitudes*. s.l.: The Royal Institute of International Affairs.
Schwab, K. (2012). *The Re-emergence of Europe*. s.l.: World Economic Forum.
Sen, A. (2012). *What Happened to Europe?* [Online]. Retrieved from https://newrepublic.com/article/105657/sen-europe-democracy-keynes-social-justice

# 3

# The EU Experience: Confronting the Existential Realities of the Crisis

## Introduction

Every person, at some point in their life, will be confronted by inescapable existential realities; identity, meaning, finiteness—each, in their own way, acts as a catalyst for crisis, catharsis, and change. In constructing our analysis, we are mindful that the concept of an 'existential crisis' most fully pertains to the psychological and philosophical critique of individual *persons*, as opposed to geopolitical communities such as the EU.[1] Nevertheless, this field of inquiry—and the broader themes and concepts that are derived from it—provides a very insightful reflective device through which to identify and articulate a cohort of the pathologies at the heart of the EU's current malaise.[2]

Much has been made of the EU's 'recovery' in the wake of the winding down of the Troika's Bailout Programmes and the move towards alterna-

[1] Psychological critiques on the 'existential crisis' are highly influenced by Erikson's (1970) concept of 'identity crisis'—seen as, broadly, a time of intensive analysis and exploration of different ways of looking at oneself.

[2] The emphasis that the philosophical school of existentialism places on themes pertaining to the nature of personhood and personal experience makes it a fertile ground from which psychological discourse can emerge.



R. Kinsella, M. Kinsella, *Troikanomics*, https://doi.org/10.1007/978-3-319-97070-7_3

tive responses to issues such as asymmetric 'shocks'. The process of recovery reflects a complex set of forces impacting on political economy, rather than reflecting the putative benefits of austerity. Macroeconomic stabilisation and a continued accommodative monetary stance by the ECB is part of a more dynamic process. What is missing is a growth dynamic that is inextricably bound up with national autonomy. Refracting our analysis through an existential lens enables us to explain more fully why a shift in the EU's *mind-set* can create real, substantive, and sustainable changes—the kinds that are redemptive. This has yet to truly materialise, and without it the EU will remain trapped in the regressive intra-community relations that have increasingly come to typify the experiences of its members. For the EU to take ownership of this crisis and its still-unfolding consequences, it is required to acknowledge—even to a limited degree—its antecedents, accepting, where appropriate, any culpability. While this process is challenging, it is a prerequisite to ensuring that this crisis has not been in vain, and can in fact be used as a springboard for positive developments within the EU.

## Navigating the Mind-Set of the EU

In the years leading up to the European Banking and Debt Crisis, the word 'vulnerability' was not an active part of the vocabulary used to describe the Economic and Monetary Union (EMU). Was there a deliberate attempt to diminish apprehensions related to the EMU's inadequate infrastructure or the unsustainable behaviours of banks/sovereigns? Was there a facile oversight by those (in both public and private domains) caught up in the opportunities that the EMU now afforded them? In either case, the irony of this attitude was that it bred an unwarranted sense of security in the EMU's strengths—not the kind of security that emboldens optimism about the future, but the kind that eschews any critique that would help in preparing it for future challenges. In the wake of the crisis, the EU establishment has been forced to accept the reality that this vulnerability remains a very real and present threat. To think otherwise would be to perpetuate the very same outlook that contributed to this crisis in the first place.

It is unrealistic to assume that the EU's various structural and functional inadequacies (including those of its child, the Eurozone) will ever be overcome *in toto*. It is, after all, an ever-evolving entity composed of countries that are *themselves* in a state of constant political, economic, and social flux. A commitment to existential critique, however, offers a means through which to proactively recognise and engage with the distinct 'vulnerabilities' that the EU is being faced with. This process of critique is not so much about indicting the EU for its failings; it is in fact inherently *redemptive*. It is underpinned by the belief that critique can offer the EU a roadmap away from political discourse that is weighed down in internal dissonance and dependent on defence mechanisms, and instead provide guidance towards optimal functioning. The point here is that existential crisis should not stultify the EU into submission; rather, it can be used as a catalyst for rediscovering and reaffirming its identity, values, and mission; but all of this depends on how it is *responded* to.

Currently, a combination of hegemony, political expediency, and an increasing lack of internal cohesion means that the EU continues to operate at a *sub*optimal level. A defining hallmark of suboptimal functioning was the imposition of Troikanomics on weaker peripheral countries. This was a signal that the EU elite were prepared to socialise the costs of maintaining a dysfunctional set of assumptions, arrangements, and institutions rather than initiating any sustainable reforms. Consequently, a disproportionate amount of energy has been ploughed into maintaining an infrastructure in the vain hope that, à la Mr. Wilkins Micawber, 'something will turn up'. Sometimes, however, it does not. Decisions on the future of the EU that remain oblivious to the existential rootedness of this crisis are ultimately doomed to repeat its mistakes. Electoral arithmetic in 'centre' countries, in tandem with the coercion of ideologies, is not an adequate foundation upon which to make workable decisions about the future of Europe. They cannot be optimal because they refuse to question the very attitudes and behaviours that sustain and propagate dysfunctionality.

Existential crisis is often accompanied by a sense of inner discord—a manifestation of one's attempt to decipher the seemingly disjunctive elements of one's identity and reinstate harmony amongst them. The existential mandate is therefore a call to shoulder the burden of progressing towards a greater feeling of inner clarity and coherence. This irrepressible 'self-critique'—the impulse to understand oneself better—is experienced as an instinct that cannot be suppressed, an imperative that cannot be delayed and a responsibility that cannot be shirked. As Soren Kierkegaard (1835) notes, '[t]he thing is to understand myself: the thing is to find a truth which is true for me, to find the idea for which I can live and die. That is what I now recognize as the most important thing'. The EU has become disconnected from the 'truth' that once inspired it and, with this, is losing its sense of inner accord.

Paradoxically, opening the door to self-critique often welcomes in more questions than answers—and, with it, elevated anxiety levels. The previously held 'givens' that were used to justify and perpetuate earlier attitudes and behaviours (e.g. the EU's belief that it had established adequate defences against asymmetric 'shocks') can suddenly become problematised. What was once predictable suddenly feels all too contingent, exposed to the ebb-and-flow circumstance and chance. The resolution of crisis is instigated by this calling to overcome philosophical complacency and, in so doing, actively carve out a more authentic existence. While it may at times *feel* like a negative experience, self-critique is developmentally necessary.

Identifying a 'good' or 'healthy' decision can be very difficult, as it is often accompanied by an expensive price tag that requires compromise and sacrifice. Their reward may also take time to manifest itself, testing one's patience and resolve. This sentiment, while true, has been used by the establishment to justify the implementation of the Troika—a short, sharp pain that will ultimately lead to healing. The scale of the shock in Ireland, measured across the fiscal consolidation and its consequences, was unprecedented—and yet we now know that the ECB, as one of the triumvirate, pressed hard for a more intensive front-loaded budgetary consolidation *aka* a ratcheting up of austerity. It is certainly the case that, for economies in crisis, rebalancing and adjustment necessitate some form of austerity—and that this catharsis can open a country to changes that, however painful in the short term, are beneficial from a longer-term perspective. That does not hold true in this instance. Troikanomics wasn't the 'hard option' imposed by a far-seeing and wise elite. It was an *easier* option, a consequence of inadequate mechanisms through which to cope with or implement economic adjustments in a more systematic or sustainable manner. Expediency all too often trumps effectiveness and, more importantly, ethics.

Troikanomics was imposed on countries that were already at their most vulnerable, with no option to devalue and no compensatory mechanism to mitigate the impact on their labour market. Shut out of the sovereign market, they had nowhere else to go. The establishment deemed it more efficient to 'work over' countries rather than work *with* them. This is borne out in the way the Greek government, with a democratic mandate to resist yet more austerity, was treated by its 'European Partners'. An account of the final talks in June/July 2015 between Greece and the Troika, and of the final cave-in by Greece to the brutal power play by Germany, demonstrates this reality.[3] Ireland is also a case in point. At a crucial stage in the implementation of the programme, when the government sought to impose burden sharing on senior bond holders, the ECB threatened that if Ireland attempted to do so and didn't fall in line, 'a bomb will go off in Dublin'. It should be said that the reference was undoubtedly a metaphor for the impact of cutting off access to temporary liquidity support—although, it should also be added, the Minister for Finance at the time was very clear in his submission to a subsequent Parliamentary analysis that there was no caveat to that effect in his conversation with the ECB.

Generally speaking, the negative repercussions of an action that runs counter to one's authentic nature are self-evident, and may be experienced as a sense of inner discord or disharmony. This perspective transposes straight from the personal to the political, that is, to the current narrative being played out within the EU. The question is whether or not the present orthodoxy sits well with how the EU sees itself and the values and commitments it believes itself to hold. Further to this, we can ask whether it provides members with sufficient opportunity to iteratively recognise and realise their autonomous capacities within this community and successfully work towards '*becoming oneself amongst others*'.[4] Our analysis now turns to prominent existential themes that offer insights into distinct facets of this point. Taken together, they aim to provide a more holistic appreciation for key tenants of this crisis and how it reveals itself within the EU.

[3] See Traynor (2015).

[4] We discuss the concept of autonomy in further detail in Chap. 6.

## Confronting Facticity and Countering Defence Mechanisms

'Facticity' is the experience of being confronted with the realities bearing down on one's life circumstances. If these are displeasing or disagreeable, then it is common to attempt to dismiss or disavow them (e.g. a person who is suffering from an addiction may practise denial, rather than attempt the demanding process of rehabilitation; a person who is in an abusive relationship may seek to rationalise their partner's behaviours, rather than risk the potential trauma of a breakup). This is because acceptance of a reality often entails an implicit commitment to then navigate oneself beyond it. Not to accept such realities is to live in a state of incongruence, of disconnect between one's actual situation and one's *perception* of this situation. If the EU is to overcome the challenging realities that are confronting it (among which are included the asymmetry in the burden of adjustment within the Eurozone, divisions and inequalities between the core and the periphery in the EU, Brexit, and, more generally, divisiveness in terms of institutional reforms) then this first necessitates accepting them (including their own culpability for such issues).

The political establishment's response to the Banking and Debt Crisis, for example, failed to adequately accept or engage with the existential facts confronting them, such as the ethical shortcomings of the shareholder-driven business model of banks, and the enormity of the impact of their decisions on the lives of people. Instead, their reaction was characterised by the ongoing application of defence mechanisms—in this context denial, rationalisation, and projection. In the immediate aftermath of this crisis, the EU was plunged into a state of shock for which its institutions were wholly ill-equipped. Central Banks and large retail banks, under the auspices of the Bank for International Settlements (BIS), had spent almost a decade updating the Basel Capital Accord. The EU Capital Adequacy Directive (later replaced by the Capital Requirements Directive in 2006) was supposed to mitigate risks; it was swamped. The BIS (2006) Advisory Paper on 'Core Principles for Effective Banking Supervision'—had they been monitored and enforced by the authorities—would have greatly lessened the scale of the crisis; it was a dead letter.

It was widely argued that much of the responsibility for the crisis should be placed on the shoulders of sovereigns, who had recklessly failed to act within the remit of the Stability and Growth Pact (1997) as well as respect the ancillary 'good faith' that was expected from participation in the EMU. There is something to be said for this perspective. What it doesn't take in to account, however, is the fallacy of conflating the meltdown in ethical sensibilities of global financial markets, with fiscal delinquency on the part of some sovereigns. In Greece, for example, an unsustainable level of public debt was amassed with shocking rapidity—compounded by a lack of transparency to the Eurozone authorities about the true status of public finances. Moreover, political establishments—or more specifically the behaviours of individuals and households—should not be expected to shoulder the full weight of responsibility when financial institutions and banks acted in a manner that was inherently 'delinquent'.[5]

However short-sighted and irrational member nations' actions were, the vector of the crisis travelled in parallel to the malign culture and behaviour of banks. This can be ascribed, in large part, to an obsession with maximising short-term shareholder value and corporate remuneration—an idolatry of money. In this light, as Michael Lewis (2010) so graphically explains, delinquent banks and flawed regulation are the proper responsibility of the EU—directly as well as indirectly through the whole pan-EU network of governments and Central Banks. Again, while we are careful not to completely dismiss the contribution that sovereigns made to the genesis and perpetuation of the crisis, the characterisation of 'delinquent states' is inherently misleading—a form of deflection by an establishment traumatised by crisis and unwilling to comprehend its own culpability.

The realities with which the EU establishment were confronted with included a systemic banking collapse (reflecting a flawed and unethical business model), regulatory and supervisory failures (which should have been anticipated by the European authorities), and an unprecedented meltdown in European economies, especially those on the periphery. The EU establishment had been given an answer to a question they had been too afraid to ask, namely 'Is the EU robust to shocks?' Its inadequacies

[5] See, for example, Busch et al. (2013).

and vulnerabilities had been laid bare. The instinctive response of the collective leadership was to cast their gaze as far away as possible from their responsibilities towards these economies—not just the banks, but the private sector as well (including households and businesses).

These developments, and their ongoing repercussions, *should* have instigated a catharsis in the EU. They did not. Instead, the EU cobbled together, more or less overnight, a new mechanism through which to mitigate contagion in the peripheral sovereign debt market and to placate very real fears regarding the sustainability of the Eurozone. The Troika's overriding objective was, in the short-term, 'to avoid a disorderly default and stop speculation on sovereign debt' (European Parliament 2014); mitigating against the social fallout from the crisis (or aligned adjustment methods) in these countries was secondary to these objectives. The form of collaboration between three very different institutions (the ECB, the EC, and the IMF), with very different mandates, had not been thought through—as became plainly evident. And, a point seldom considered in innumerable reports, the enabling legislation was rushed through parliaments with no scrutiny whatsoever, undermining any pretence to democratic legitimacy.

The Troika operated as a defence mechanism, shielding EU institutions from the fundamental truths regarding the causes of the crisis, the scale and scope of its consequences, and how it could (and, more specifically, *should*) be *sustainably* resolved. While these mechanisms differ in how they function, they all serve the same broad purpose—namely, to protect from the experience of excessive anxiety or to cope with anxiety-arousing situations. In other words, these are coping mechanisms initiated by efforts to mitigate against possible trauma in the individual person—and they apply too to the 'body politic'. These operate just beyond the grasp of conscious apprehension—which can often allow them to go undetected until one is impelled towards introspection. While they can aid in adapting to a challenging situation, they can turn pathological when they become habitual—when their persistent usage systematically undermines the capacity to engage with *reality*, and therefore to most constructively respond to the challenges that are being faced. There are, as noted earlier, several defence mechanisms at multiple levels which are reflected in this context: denial, projection, and rationalisation.

Denial is the act of rejecting the reality of a situation that is being or has been experienced, in an effort to hamper its perceived negative effects. This is accomplished by attaching a negative marker to perceptions or thoughts, preventing them from infiltrating one's consciousness. This rejection process may reduce one's initial anxiety but also reduces the capacity to most fully and authentically engage with reality, with resources instead being used to maintain a psychological façade. The denial by the EU occurred both prior to and during this crisis, experienced at both banking and sovereign levels—the unfolding situation was an expression of an unwillingness/inability to hold particular entities accountable for their behaviour and to take ownership in motivating and regulating for change. With so many different institutions and organisations operating, all with their own interests at heart, accountability for the crisis became increasingly difficult to decipher.

In Ireland, even days before the Troika arrived, Cabinet Ministers were in denial over the scale of the crisis about to engulf the country's governance. At a European level, it encompassed a denial of the *consequences* of policies; a denial of what common sense, let alone Economics 101, should have been telling the Troika. To take just one example, more loans to 'help' Greece repay previous loans that themselves could not be repaid was itself a form of denial. Writing-off debt was imperative. The IMF knew that and said so both within its own organisation and publicly. But the ECB—and Germany in particular—would not countenance the idea. In this context, denial sought to negate the severe impact these measures would, and did, have on the welfare of millions of people. This was evident right through the covering up of the true extent of fiscal deficit in the aftermath of Greece's accession to the Eurozone, in the actions of Western financial institutions that facilitated this, and in the actions of financial markets that ravaged the Greek sovereign when the new 2009 government acknowledged the true state of affairs and attempted to address it systematically. The endless crisis meetings by one group or another, followed by the obligatory 'family photo' of smiling European leaders, were successful in denying (or at least distracting from) the issues—but for only so long.

Projection is the act of misattributing undesired thoughts, feelings, or impulses onto someone who may not themselves have those thoughts, feelings, or impulses. It is used when one is ill at ease with possessing these and seeks to 'off-load' them. Projection is itself a more complex version of denial, for this reason: it is not the reality of a situation itself which is denied, but one's relationship *with*, or responsibility *for*, that situation. This requires the ability to differentiate between one's own internal functioning and that of external bodies, and the development of internal standards by which certain thoughts and feelings are judged. The EU/Troika chose to attribute responsibility to reckless and irresponsible national governments. In spite of there being some merit to this argument, it deflected from the larger truth that European institutions failed to anticipate what had been unfolding since years previously and also failed to construct the mechanisms to mitigate against their ascendency or consequences. There was a hurricane blowing on a half-finished house and it was the tenants, not the builder, who were exposed to the elements.

Banks were also unwilling to countenance the responsibility they played in the crash.[6] Instead, blame was placed on the people who were perceived as complicit in this process of over-leveraging (e.g. families who took out mortgages they could not realistically afford on houses whose prices were astronomically inflated). There was a perverse duality. On the one hand, by seeking public funding, banks tacitly acknowledged accountability for their failures. At least, most of them did—in the United States, Goldman Sachs received funding in 2008 but they denied that they needed assistance in the first place. On the other hand, by having taken such funding they were both disowning accountability and choosing to ignore the fact that by having recourse to government at a time of enormous stress, they were contaminating the sovereign and its capacity to deliver services to its citizens. This process contributed towards changing what was initially a banking crisis to a sovereign debt crisis.

Rationalisation is the act of placing an event that has unfolded in a different light—attempting to reduce anxiety by creating excuses to justify decisions or behaviours that may feel to be unsatisfactory and regrettable, or may have been originally arrived at for different reasons/motivations. It is a first cousin to the kind of revisionism which the EU has exhibited in revisiting Troikanomics. So, for example, in engaging

[6] Famously, in a statement to the *Financial Times* (2007) the Citigroup—a leading lender to private equity buy-outs—Chief Executive Chuck Prince said in 2007 that while none of what was happening made sense, '[w]hen the music stops, in terms of liquidity, things will be complicated. But as long as the music is playing, you've got to get up and dance. We are still dancing'.

with success, or failure, people may attribute achievement to their own qualities while failures are blamed on other people/external forces. The Troika attempted to rationalise the imposition of their austerity measures by stating firstly that their harshness was unavoidable, and secondly that they were ultimately successful.

This is, however, problematic. It presents a very narrow metric for what constitutes 'success'. It ignores the collateral damage in the form of emigration, failed businesses, scarring associated with long-term unemployment, and the impact of indebtedness. It also ignores the hidden political agenda which can be inferred from the sharp divergence in the analysis and recommendations of, on the one hand, the IMF and, on the other hand, the European Institutions. While they may have served the immediate needs of the Troika's mandate, the needs of member nations and their citizens were wholly absent from their decisional processes. Ultimately the Troika served the purpose of inoculating against contagion, at the expense of the welfare of the more vulnerable countries. For the countries that effectively controlled the Troika, this was the chosen means through which contagion could be arrested, and no other route was given its due regard. It rationalised this process by asserting that it had secured the short- to medium-term survival of the Eurozone through enacting measures which, through their own lack of good sense and short-sightedness, 'debtor' nations had in fact brought upon themselves.

## Articulating a European Identity: Unity Amidst Discord

People are most fully functional and psychologically healthy when they possess a distinct sense of their identity; this enables their different (potentially disparate) personal characteristics to coexist more effectively, as well as facilitates greater internal consensus in their decisions.[7] Understanding

[7] To provide some insight into the dynamic nature of 'identity', it is useful to note Sherman and Cohen's (2006) definition of the 'self-system', derived from their analysis on 'Self-Affirmation Theory'. Here, 'the self-system' is understood as being composed of distinct yet interrelated 'domains', which include a person's roles, values, social identities, and belief systems. A crucial point, in this instance, relates to the need to possess a fully rounded sense of self, wherein one has actively sought to understand and develop

'who I am' (even to a minimal degree) is therefore a vital component in addressing the question 'what life shall I lead?' and in taking ownership over its unfolding direction.[8] Identity crisis can present itself in an inability or unwillingness to systematically explore or make commitments to one's identity, and can be a precipitating factor in an existential crisis—leading to a sense of internal dissonance and dysphoria. The EU is currently confronted by a form of identity crisis that is apparent at two distinct yet related levels. Firstly, the institution of the EU has become increasingly opaque and diffuse with respect to its motivating values, underlining mission, and the remit of its mandates. Secondly, vast swaths of EU citizens do not possess any great sense of 'European identity'—instead, they feel disconnected from and resentful towards the EU, more especially in the wake of the Migration Crisis. These issues are in need of resolution; the EU cannot begin to exercise control over its sociopolitical and economic trajectory unless it possesses some sense of 'unity' through which to find the resolve to move past internal discord.

Extending the remit of the concept of 'identity' beyond the individual person and transposing it onto political entities is challenging—even more so the case when we consider a transnational entity such as the EU, given the diverse histories, cultures, governments (and so on) that it is comprised of. More specifically, it is difficult to critique issues relating to the form and substance of the EU's identity, beyond its institutional and legal constructs, in the way one can critique distinctive national identities. Where, indeed, is its identity to be found? In seeking to address this question, one useful approach is to distinguish between three established understandings of the EU's identity: firstly, as a 'cultural identity' comprised of shared history, language, values and aspirations (mediated through, for example, literature and art); secondly, as a 'political identity' comprised of shared democratic institutions and practices; and, thirdly, as an 'economic identity' comprised of multilateral arrangements centred on issues such as the free movement of labour, capital and goods.[9]

---

the different components constituting their identity. When a person feels threatened in one 'domain' of their life, they can draw strength and stability from contemplating and acting on another domain, helping to maintain their overall sense of self-integrity.

[8] For further psychological insights on the dialogical basis on identity formation, see Schwartz et al. (2012), Layder (2004), Wenger (1998), and Shahar et al. (2003).

[9] For a further discussion on this, see Prutsch (2017).

In each domain, their realisation necessitates democratic inclusiveness at both civic and national levels. Through its architecture, the EU has attempted to serve these 'polarities'—for example, through providing means through which citizens can ostensibly participate both in their own countries' and the wider EU's democratic processes. A coherent and cohesive sense of 'identity' is a vital means through which to come together in the discussion and resolution of the pressing issues facing the EU today. In this context, the EU has long sought to nest itself in the hearts and minds of its inhabitants and affirm its democratic legitimacy through a sense of cultural identification.

Identification is an 'in relation to' phenomenon, in which one orientates a particular facet of one's identity towards an entity that at once both exists external to oneself and resides internally. It is experienced as both evaluative and emotional, and can be a useful tool in inculcating a sense of belonging. Identification is multivariate and complex, wherein a person can have a number of identifications coexisting within their own personal identity—such as nationality, culture, and religion. It helps ensure that members of a community find ways to create shared understandings and experiences—even amidst different backgrounds. From this experience of identification flows an array of social necessities (not just 'goods', but goods without which a community would find it very difficult to function effectively) such as coherence, shared objectives, and solidarity; where there is none, there is generally division and an inability to build common ground.

Here, it can be argued that there is a very large imbalance between the sense of identification that the EU's inhabitants possess towards the EU (or 'Europe' for that matter) and that which they possess towards their own nationality. This disconnect raises concerns about how best to approach the task of European cooperation. It conveys a basic sentiment at the heart of difficulties in the European Project that—in spite of its best efforts—'Europe' is still an ethereal entity whose characteristics are difficult to articulate, let alone grasp in any deeper sense of shared *zeitgeist*. A *country*'s national identity, however, is visceral, real, and lived.

The concept of being 'European', while having a primary allegiance to one's country of origin, is well-established. At the same time, the increasingly complex set of institutions and decision-making procedures of the

EU has manifested itself in a political status quo that feels inaccessible to many. The European citizenship has progressively felt a sense of disenfranchisement with the political/legal infrastructure of the EU. It is important to acknowledge the wide set of protections that have been generated by European Institutions which do not immediately impact themselves on the consciousness of people in their daily lives. Nonetheless, many simply do not understand its form, its function, or what relevance it has to their lives.[10] This goes deeper than a communications gap. One of their most direct interactions with it in recent years has been through austerity measures, which have compounded their lack of identification with the EU. This has resulted in a form of 'democratic deficit'—where national governments are viewed as expressing the democratic ideal to an extent and in a manner that the EU (as essentially administrative and anomalous) cannot. This is reflected, for example, in the increasingly low voter turnout for European Elections, standing at 42.54% for all European voters in 2014. This is the lowest of any national election in the 28 countries of the EU, where turnout at national elections averages 68%.[11]

This deficit is symptomatic of a deeper malaise and sense of disconnect between the individual countries and the EU, wherein even if the administrative components of the relationship are formalised, they will still have to contend with a dearth of transnational cultural identification. Administrative authority is an important means of aligning potentially disparate perspectives, but it can never take the place of a sense of co-belonging. Within the context of the Troika, aside from the actual *content* of their interventions, it was the very *principle* behind their imposition—undercutting national autonomy as they did—that was so egregious to many.

A key question in this regard is whether there is, in fact, a role for the nation state in the development of a European identity? Here, 'The Five President's Report' (2015) envisaged a spectrum of possibilities which

[10] This point is acknowledged by the European Commission, noting that 'many Europeans consider the Union as either too distant or too interfering in their day-to-day lives. Others question its added-value and ask how Europe improves their standard of living. And for too many, the EU fell short of their expectations as it struggled with its worst financial, economic and social crisis in post-war history' (European Commission 2017).

[11] For further information, see The European Parliament – Public Opinion Monitoring Unit (2014).

goes to the heart of the concept of identity, from a stripping back of the status quo to a full political union. This development is nothing new; from its beginnings, the EU has faced the dichotomy between fostering sovereign states or being *a* sovereign state itself. Here, it can be argued that what had initially been conceived as a 'straightforward' system of intergovernmental relations has, over time, developed into a more complex (and contentious) form of federalist statehood. More recently, the EU establishment has been zealously pursuing a more extensive form of 'union', which is contrived as the most efficacious means of attaining a coherent and cohesive sense of the identity and dampening endemic discord. Alongside this, it is argued that there are many potential benefits that can be reaped from a more immersive form of political integration, including economies of scale in the provision of federal public goods and the ability to internalise shocks over larger areas.[12]

This goal of integration has presented itself in a number of different ways. The most explicit example is, of course, the establishment of a monetary union. EMU embedded in the Maastricht Treaty was designed with the objective of bringing about a sense of economic cohesiveness. With the asymmetries and deficiencies embedded in its underlying mechanisms, coupled with pre-existing economic imbalances, this goal has largely not been achieved.[13] Paradoxically, its shortcomings have set a precedent for even greater fiscal oversight moving forward. There have also been other attempts to capture a distinctly European zeitgeist in a 'symbolic' manner, such as the EU flag, anthem, and motto (*In Varietate Concordia*, 'United in Diversity'). These symbols are more generally applied (and, arguably, more appropriate) within a national context, and have garnered limited results. There was also a concerted attempt at introducing a European Constitution in 2004, but it ultimately did not succeed in being ratified due to a veto by France and the Netherlands, although it was to later present itself in the Treaty of Lisbon (2007)—which attempted to implement a number of the reforms that would have been encompassed in the Constitution.

---

[12] See, for example, Spolaore's (2013) analysis.

[13] This perspective is discussed in greater detail in Chap. 4.

To date, many countries have been unwilling to countenance the federalist impulse, citing that while distinctive cultural identities and norms can coexist in a collaborative and complementary manner, there will always remain a level of sociopolitical incommensurability that will make an 'EU statehood' a logistical impossibility. There is a real dichotomy here. The EU's efforts presuppose a level of democratic legitimacy which is at odds with the resistance to this same orthodoxy: perhaps a different kind of EU or one of the five different types of associations which the European Commission (2017) was impelled to set out could be fruitfully worked at. This resistance waxes and wanes—in the wake of the austerity it has become tidal. But the establishment has never conceded legitimacy to this view, hence the virulent resistance to Brexit.

The EU has grown and diversified exponentially over recent decades. As a consequence, its 'communal' heritage—in principle and in practice—has undergone a radical upheaval. Such divergences have led to the following fundamental question: Which country represents a typical member state of the Eurozone?[14] The EU is not expanding into a vacuum; under its mantle are countries that possess their own hard-fought cultural heritage that is engrained in its citizens—a *demos* that resides firmly within their national borders.[15] In this regard, the aspiration that a diversity of national cultures can help create a more dynamic and richer union is important, and should be acknowledged and embraced by the 'old establishment' of EU governance.[16]

The *underlying* view of the EU establishment, whatever its protestations of openness, transparency, and accountability, is that ultimately a form of transnational 'EU' identity will take hold, perhaps even superseding *national* identification. It is a strange reading of European history that has

[14] See Tovias (2017).

[15] We can, provisionally, understand the demos as a group of people, through whose shared experience and collective will a legitimate democracy can be formed. For further information on 'demos', see Cederman (2001), Weiler (1999), and Innerarity (2014).

[16] A recent expression of this inner discord is apparent in the contentious disputes over Brexit. Bogdanor (2018) has noted that the epochal constitutional importance of its outcome is precisely that the primacy of the people prevailed over the preferences of the political establishment.

yet to bear fruit. The Conventional Wisdom has never comprehended that there is more to fostering autonomy than administrative efficiency and economies of scale. This sentiment has been met with various challenges confronting the EU in terms of possessing a coherent sense of 'self'. The ongoing addition of sociopolitically and economically diverse members, the iterative refinement of its legal, administrative, and political mandates, polarised elections across the EU, and the lurch towards militarisation are all developments which run the risk of distancing it from a coherent and cohesive sense of 'identity'.

From the outset the EU was premised on the possibility of constructing a European identity that does not *replace* the one already possessed by citizens at national level, but complements it. The European Project needs to be reengineered to take account of the multidimensional nature of personal identity, where one's status as 'European' can meaningfully coexist with the identification people feel towards their particular nation state—*distinct*, but not diametrically opposed. At this critical juncture, it is a pressing requirement that the EU reach out to the people under its umbrella, and work with them in finding a way in which they can *make space* for the EU as a component of their personal identity.

Ultimately, the EU will continually be confronted with the same reality: it possesses over 500 million inhabitants dispersed across a diverse and (at times) contrasting continent. While people will continue to contribute to the sustainment of the European Project, for example, through voting and participating in the labour market, it is, nevertheless, still largely opaque and distant to a majority of them. National borders continue to retain their indispensability. For the vast majority of the EU's inhabitants, they will continue to be—first and foremost—citizens of their home nations. The EU, notwithstanding its rich history, does not have a *people* to take ownership over it—to claim it as their own. For this reason it is likely to continue to rely for its legitimacy primarily as an organisational construct, as opposed to a democratically representative and accountable polity that seeks to displace the primacy of national autonomy.

## Struggling for Survival: Justifying a Suboptimal Existence

History teaches that every ascendant empire (and the EU is increasingly taking the form of an empire) is faced with an unalterable existential truth: it will, in time, meet its demise. The fire that burned brightly in the shared hearts and minds of its demos—fuelling common identity and conquest—will one day be extinguished. 'Finiteness' is, therefore, not a condemnation shouldered by the few, but an inalienable sentence shared by all—a fact that can be deeply fear-inducing. This truth is not something that can be unlearned; knowledge of it shapes one's disposition towards life itself—an unalterable bookend in its unfolding narrative. Paradoxically, while this awareness is troubling, it is also necessary for one's self-preservation—acting as it does as the prism through which the consequences (both positive and negative) of decisions are weighed. This also brings with it a plethora of *un*knowns. In moments of existential uncertainty, questions are constant and all-consuming. In what way will death finally arrive? What legacy will we leave behind? What of ceasing to be, as we know ourselves to be, at a point in time? A core tension is found in being confronted by the reality of death, while deeply desiring to somehow transcend its limitations.

In this context, inasmuch as all empires pass away, so too will the EU. The anxiety which currently grips tightly at it is so debilitating because it is not simply a question of what form its future will take, but whether it will even come to possess a future. The anxiety that arose during the time of the Banking and Debt Crisis provoked a series of responses from the establishment that sought to quell this anxiety rather than courageously engage with the causes of it. The EU is infected by inequalities and asymmetries in power; it is held together less by shared convictions than by a real, and a latent, knowledge that it is no longer tethered to foundational communal values. What *was* a community has become a bureaucratic superstructure that is no longer optimal. Project Europe has become at least in part a self-serving institution that speaks to its own agenda, to political expediency, and to the survival of the elite. This is in part rooted in a fear that its paradigm is being challenged, while it would prefer to subsidise it, rather than to engage in an existential critique.

How might its death manifest itself? What possible circumstances could precipitate such an event? The iterative exit of countries from the Eurozone? The drum beat of war? The corrosive societal consequences of an aggressively secular quasi-Marxist culture? The institutionalisation of the mind-set embedded in Troikanomics? In all of this, the issue of exit by a participating state should have been confronted and articulated—not least because it was already provided for in Article 50. It is easier, as we argued earlier, to have defence mechanisms attend to these uncomfortable realities. It is this disposition that feeds into its insistence of maintaining the current suboptimal status quo, rather than risking in acquiescing to the calls for change. Crippled by a fear of such a 'death', the EU is afraid to embrace the opportunities that reform and reanimation can bring, and that can truly provide it with a new lease of life.[17]

The thought of a collapse of the Eurozone conjures images of complete and irreversible annihilation of the European Project, as opposed to a (yet unforeseen) opportunity for a new paradigm in inter-European relations to emerge. More generally, attempts to rigidly hold on to the EU as is, and not to internalise the need for change, may ironically be the catalyst for its demise. It is this fear that drives the EU to deflect from fundamental reforms that are as challenging in this generation as its founding vision was in its time. Such changes can present the opportunity to embrace a new mode of relationship within which, importantly, the autonomy of its members would be empowered rather than continually diluted. Why this resistance? Because in doing so, in the development of more autonomous economic relations, the EU would have to compromise on what has become its *idée fixe*—centralised power in a hegemonistic Europe.

## References

Basel Committee on Banking Supervision. (2006). *Core Principles for Effective Banking Supervision*. Basel: Bank for International Settlements.

[17] In one of his most influential books, existential psychiatrist Yalom (1980) presents his four 'ultimate concerns': death, freedom, isolation, and meaninglessness. He argues that a tension is created between one's awareness of the inevitability of death and one's wish to continue to be, and that this tension presents a core existential conflict.

Bogdanor, V. (2018). *Brexit and Our Unprotected Constitution*. London: The Constitution Society.

Busch, K., Hermann, C., Hinrichs, K., & Schulten, T. (2013). *Euro Crisis, Austerity Policy and the European Model: How Crisis Policies in Southern Europe Threaten the EU's Social Dimension*. Berlin: International Policy Analysis.

Cederman, L. E. (2001). Nationalism and Bounded Integration: What It Would Take to Construct a European Demos. *European Journal of International Relations, 7*(2), 139–174.

Erikson, E. (1970). Autobiographic Notes on the Identity Crisis. *Daedalus, 99*(4), 730–759.

European Commission. (2017). *White Paper on the Future of Europe: Reflections and Scenarios for the EU27 by 2025*. Brussels: European Commission. Retrieved March 12, 2018, from https://ec.europa.eu/commission/sites/beta-political/files/white_paper_on_the_future_of_europe_en.pdf

European Parliament. (2014). *Role and Operations of the Troika with Regard to the Euro Area Programme*. Brussels: The European Parliament.

European Parliament – Public Opinion Monitoring Unit. (2014, October). *European Election 2014: Analytical Overview*. Retrieved from http://www.europarl.europa.eu/pdf/eurobarometre/2014/post/post_2014_survey_analitical_overview_en.pdf

European Union, C. o. (2007, December 13). *Treaty of Lisbon Amending the Treaty on European Union and the Treaty Establishing the European Community. 2007/C 306/01*. Retrieved May 29, 2018, from http://www.refworld.org/docid/476258d32.html

Financial Times. (2007). *Citigroup Chief Stays Bullish on Buy-Outs*. Retrieved May 15, 2018, from https://www.ft.com/content/80e2987a-2e50-11dc-821c-0000779fd2ac

Innerarity, D. (2014). Does Europe Need a Demos to Be Truly Democratic? *LSE 'Europe in Question' Discussion Paper Series, 77*.

Kierkegaard, S. (1835 [2000]). Early Journal Entries. In H. V. Hong & E. H. Hong (Eds.), *The Essential Kierkegaard*. Princeton: Princeton University Press.

Layder, D. (2004). *Social and Personal Identity: Understanding Yourself*. London: Sage.

Lewis, M. (2010). *The Big Short: Inside the Doomsday Machine* (1st ed.). New York: W. W. Norton & Company.

Prutsch, M. J. (2017). *Research for CULT Committee – European Identity*. Brussels: European Parliament, Policy Department for Structural and Cohesion Policies.

Schwartz, S. J., Donnellan, B. M., Ravert, R. D., Luyckx, K., & Zamboanga, B. L. (2012). Identity Development, Personality, and Well-Being in Adolescence and Emerging Adulthood: Theory, Research, and Recent Advances. In I. B. Weiner, R. M. Lerner, M. A. Easterbrooks, & J. Mistry (Eds.), *Handbook of Psychology* (Vol. 6). Wiley.

Shahar, G., Henrich, C. C., Blatt, S. J., Ryan, R., & Little, T. D. (2003). Interpersonal Relatedness, Self-Definition, and Their Motivational Orientation During Adolescence: A Theoretical and Empirical Integration. *Developmental Psychology, 39*(3), 470–488.

Sherman, D. K., & Cohen, L. G. (2006). The Psychology of Self-Defense: Self-Affirmation Theory. *Advances in Experimental Social Psychology, 38*, 183–242.

Spolaore, E. (2013). What Is European Integration Really About? A Political Guide for Economists. *Journal of Economic Perspectives, American Economic Association, 27*(3), 125–144.

Tovias, A. (2017). Solidarity in the Eurozone: Spontaneous, Organized or Inexistent? In A. Giannakopoulos (Ed.), *Solidarity in the European Union: Challenges and Perspectives* (pp. 20–30). The S. Daniel Abraham Center.

Traynor, I. (2015, October 22). *Three Days That Saved the Euro*. Retrieved from https://www.theguardian.com/world/2015/oct/22/three-days-to-save-the-euro-greece

Weiler, J. (1999). *The Constitution of Europe*. Cambridge: Cambridge University Press.

Wenger, E. (1998). *Communities of Practice: Learning, Meaning, and Identity*. Cambridge: Cambridge University Press.

Yalom, I. D. (1980). *Existential Psychotherapy*. New York: Basic Books.

# Part II

## Development of the Crisis: Architecture, Agendas and Austerity

# 4

# European Monetary Union and the Challenge of Economic Integration

## Introduction

In this chapter we address the process of Economic and Monetary Union (EMU)—its origins and architecture—and its vulnerabilities which put Project Europe at risk during the European Banking and Debt Crisis. From the outset, the implementation of EMU was an extraordinarily ambitious undertaking—albeit, one based on a flawed model. Moreover, it was one which necessarily involved its members ceding their monetary sovereignty in the form of their Central Bank and, in time, by extension, their fiscal sovereignty. In any event, the absence of fiscal federalism meant that some countries were intrinsically vulnerable, that is, the model was lacking in prior mechanisms that could off-set 'shocks' of the magnitude of the Global Banking Crisis. When 'external' factors came into play, such as market 'spill-over' from the US Subprime Crisis, an *already* precarious intra-European economic template became deeply exposed. The impact has since generated extensive reforms, particularly in the fields of banking regulation and supervision, which are focused primarily on enhancing a European dimension to banking supervision.

A small subset of Eurozone members were involved in the Bailout Programmes (or their equivalents, such as conditional balance of payments assistance from the IMF). For those countries that were impelled into such



R. Kinsella, M. Kinsella, *Troikanomics*, https://doi.org/10.1007/978-3-319-97070-7_4

programmes, it is now clear that deficiencies in the infrastructure and environment of the Eurozone were at least a contributory factor exacerbating the impact of their own national debt crises. Its consequences resonated in numerous ways throughout the wider European landscape—reflected in negative social consequences as well as in the diminution of their national autonomy.[1] In 2017, the European Commission (2017b) published its roadmap to full EMU, with the intention of implementing measures before the 2019 European Elections.[2] These measures, if implemented, envisage amplified fiscal consolidation and will be transformational in their impact on the political status of Eurozone members. In this context, they do, however, raise the question as to whether the 'deepening' of the Eurozone will see the further extinguishing of national autonomy as a central principle in sustaining transnational EU relations.

## Crisis in the EMU: Architecture and Aspirations

The European Debt Crisis did not emerge *ex nihilo*. It reflected serious weaknesses in fiscal policy as well as irresponsible banking practices, including excessive credit creation. At the same time, it was also an outcome of the Eurozone's ontological peculiarity, where heteronomous economies and fiscal regimes assembled under a largely homogeneous monetary union. More specifically, these peculiarities were observable in the *infrastructure* of the Eurozone (such as deficiencies in financial regulation and governance) and in the *environment* of the Eurozone (such as the ethic of short-sighted and socially destructive business models).

The creation of a monetary union was rooted in the conviction that it was a necessary means through which to attain greater European integration and an aligned, more robust, sense of European identity. For prospective participants, incentives to join came in the form of two assurances:

---

[1] In this context, Shambaugh (2012) discusses how the Eurozone was confronted by three distinct yet connected crises: a banking crisis, a sovereign debt crisis, and a growth crisis.

[2] Addressing the proposal, President Jean-Claude Juncker stated that '[a]fter years of crises, it is now time to take Europe's future into our own hands. Today's robust economic growth encourages us to move ahead to ensure that our Economic and Monetary Union is more united, efficient and democratic, and that it works for all of our citizens. There is no better time to fix the roof than when the sun is shining' (*cited by* the European Commission 2017a).

greater economic prosperity and increased political solidarity.[3] It would deliver on: reducing transaction costs, increasing pricing transparency, and facilitating trade and labour force movement—all of which would strengthen competitiveness and deepen the EU's financial markets. This would, it was argued, culminate in *equitable* economic prosperity, aligned towards positive social outcomes.[4] The opportunity to not simply *join* Europe in progressing towards becoming a global economic powerhouse, but *to be that Europe*—one and the same—would be a huge coup for potential entrants.[5]

Politically, Europe's future had been increasingly problematised in the preceding years. Global tensions between East and West had ebbed and flowed, all the while Europe appeared to be largely incapable of weighing in on global events as a unified political voice. EMU would help to bolster the credibility and influence of Europe on the international stage by reinforcing its capacity to speak *as one*.[6]

For decades, the EU's economic and political trajectory had been headed towards the establishment of some form of monetary union. It was argued that the full realisation of the European Project which had begun decades earlier made economic integration not simply desirable, but *necessary*—a vital mechanism in ensuring that its needs (such as trade and labour mobility) within a rapidly developing marketplace were most fully attended to.[7] In spite of the first iteration of the Werner Report (1970) foundering, it set down a marker of future intent.

---

[3] Here, Feldstein (2012) has argued that *political* considerations and interests were a more central determinant of the EMU's design and function than issues concerned with its *economic* merit. A similar point is also noted by Hall (2012), who discusses how the Euro is the outcome of a *political will*.

[4] For a further discussion, please see Krugman (2013), Gibson et al. (2014), and Fagan and Gaspar (2007).

[5] A further testament to accession being a political endeavour is the requirement that new members must adhere to more than just economic criteria. Here, Article 49 of the EU Treaty (2007) states that 'any European State which respects the principles set out in Article 6(1) may apply to become a member of the Union'. The principles of Article 6(1) are 'liberty, democracy, respect for human rights and fundamental freedoms, and the rule of law'.

[6] Here, Feldstein (2012) notes the centrality that bolstering Europe's role in world affairs has as a *political* motivator.

[7] Economic integration is the process wherein countries design and develop a set of market conditions most conducive to cultivating successful trade relationships with other countries—often rooted in their desire to capitalise on preexisting trade incentives, for example, geographical proximity. The goal is that the determinants of cross-border trade will be stimulated, and in doing so productivity, competitiveness, and socioeconomic parity will be achieved. This process is demarcated by specific phases. In brief, these encompass the following:

The genesis of the Eurozone was embedded within the Exchange Rate Mechanism (ERM)—a Franco-German response to mitigate against the impact of global exchange rate instability witnessed in the EU during the 1970s. The ERM was the necessary precursor of a single currency, and provided a platform for convergence towards a fixed exchange rate system. The Delors Commission was the inflection point in the process: having negotiated the Single Market, Delors headed the Report which provided the blueprint for the Maastricht Treaty and the impetus towards creating an institutional infrastructure within which the Eurozone could take shape.

From a distance, this process appears to be inevitable and seamless. It was neither. It was an enormous logistical accomplishment whose successful outcome seemed problematic given the scale of the 'buy-in' that was necessary from the markets and from nations. Goldman Sachs, for example, had a metric measuring the probability of completing the project which, at times, suggested serious reservations. Moreover, the single currency was not the only option on the table. In addition, there were proposals for a 'common currency', a 'parallel currency', and other variations which allowed for the retention of an autonomous *national currency* while underpinning the economics of the single market. The single market *itself* had, after all, been a definitive achievement.[8]

Directly prior to the Debt Crisis emerging in the balance sheets of banks and across financial markets in late 2008, confidence in the Euro was high, in particular across the political establishment. A superficial assessment of the internal market conditions it had helped to instigate was (seemingly) sufficient evidence to confirm that EMU was now an essential cornerstone of intra-European peace and prosperity. The EU's

1. Establishing favourable trade conditions (from preferential trading through to free trading), which reduces the costs incurred on the movement of goods and services between member countries—for example, customs tariffs, thereby incentivizing trade partnerships.
2. Establishing a customs union, which sets up exclusivity arrangements between countries by implanting external trade barriers and further incentivises mutual trade relations.
3. Instituting a common market, which adds the free movement of labour and capital to the customs union.
4. Implementing a common currency within the common market (which may or may not implement fiscal conditions), for example, European Union after Maastricht Treaty.

[8] A reversion to a trade association was, for example, one of the Five Options set out in the European Commission's (2017c) White Paper on the Future of the EU.

attempt to economically integrate sovereign states in the pursuit of efficiency gains had proved to be as politically seductive as it was audacious.[9] Among its successes, it contributed to low inflation and low interest rates, more developed transnational trade relations, positive flows in labour/commodity markets, and a steady rise in real income per capita. The Euro was strong and in addition to the 16 participating members which had joined by 2009 there were other countries in the process of seeking membership.

This construct was corroded by strains across banking markets which subsequently undermined the sovereign debt markets. The regulatory structure buckled under the pressures and both politicians and regulators found themselves in unfamiliar territory, with wholly inadequate instruments and a seriously deficient infrastructure for intervening. The circumstances had been neither anticipated nor provided for in the design of EMU. 'Proof of concept' had been too easily attained. In stepping outside of the laboratory conditions in which convergence metrics were first designed, it wasn't long before a 'black swan' had flown in to confound any earlier hypotheses. As the escalating Banking and Debt Crisis manifested itself in late 2008, there was a pervasive sense of shock across the politics of EMU. Quite simply, the system had not been stress-tested.

The harbinger of the crisis was the implosion of the banking system: balance sheets upended by bad loans, difficulties in accessing funding from the markets, and a concomitant downturn in the real economy. Large European banks had taken bad lending decisions and needed support from their governments, necessitating new forms of intervention by the ECB. The problem here was that the governments (the 'sovereign') were themselves under pressure as the contagion spread. The Banking and Debt Crisis first appeared when peripheral Eurozone countries were unable to repay or to refinance their sovereign debt, or to provide bailout assistance to their commercial banks without external recourse. Many of the positive metrics had been significantly fuelled by an overly favourable

[9] For a further discussion on prevailing economic and political sentiments in the years after the instigation of the EMU, see Gibson et al. (2014) and Wihlborg et al. (2010). The European Commission (2008) was highly optimistic in its Report on the Euro, going so far as to note that the EMU had in fact improved the Eurozone's resilience against adverse external developments—thanks to measures such as 'renewed budgetary discipline'.

credit climate that was semi-detached from reality (e.g. not distinguishing between the creditworthiness of centre and peripheral countries) and by capital inflows/outflows that were compounding peripheral economies' current account deficits (i.e. creating a 'bubble'). The abrupt halting of these capital flows, reflected in the 'Credit Crunch' across the markets laid bare the unsustainable levels of sovereign and private debt that had been accumulated over the preceding years, as well as the yawning competitiveness gap that had opened up between the centre and the periphery.[10]

The financial interconnectedness which the EMU had created (as is displayed, for example, in the level of debt that German and French banks held with Greece) meant it was simply a matter of time before the crisis was to bleed into the wider EU via economic, political, and social contagion—and insolvency became endemic. The existential threat that this posed was immediately apparent, and discussions on the Euro's inadequacies soon shifted from being abstract academic exercises to being very real political emergencies. Here, it is important to differentiate between the *principle* of monetary union and the extent to which—in the context of the EMU—it could be successful *in practice*.

Monetary union, as a means through which to foster communal integration across the EU is *in itself* justifiable within an 'optimum currency area', and generally builds on already successful economic integration (which acts as a 'proof of concept'). The question arises as to whether the institutional and operational characteristics of EMU meant that it was able to cope with an unprecedented and asymmetric 'shock'. Here, our argument is that the crisis emerged as a largely predictable upshot of actions by the architects who had shaped the project—and was by inference *preventable*. The consequences that emerged were, as we see in the case of Ireland and Greece, visited on anaemic governments and socialised across deeply burdened societies. In the following two sections we discuss these conditions in more detail, namely, deficiencies in the infrastructure and environment of EMU.

---

[10] The nature and extent of these competitiveness gaps is discussed in greater detail by the European Commission (2017b). The World Economic Forum's 'Global Competitiveness Reports' (2017) defines competitiveness as 'the set of institutions, policies and factors that determine the level of productivity of a country'. This determines the returns obtained from investments in an economy and influences the country's broader level of economic prosperity.

## Infrastructural Antecedents of the Crisis: Convergence and Divergence

In reflecting on the antecedents to the crisis, we are, in effect, looking at why it was that Troikanomics came to be the mode of intervention for dealing with an event which had not been provided for in the architecture of EMU. The irony here, of course, is that the Franco-German axis, around whose agenda EMU was fashioned, was the same dominant duopoly who dictated that Troikanomics should be the chosen mechanism to respond to the deficiencies that it failed to anticipate.

Aside from issues of autonomy and sovereignty, the management of the Eurozone was charged with the heavy burden of having to operate as a monetary union—and all the economic prerequisites that this necessitates—without the bulwark of a fiscal union to consolidate and stabilise the system. With the 1986 Single European Act (and subsequent Treaty of Maastricht) laying out the foundations for how the Euro would take shape in practice, no progress had been made towards fiscal integration. The important point was that monetary union was *itself* considered a step too far—because it would entail the surrender of core elements of national autonomy, as Prime Minister Margaret Thatcher was not slow to remind the EC. Instead, fiscal policy remained decentralised, with member nations enjoying freedom over their own macroeconomic policies and practices, such as taxation and public spending.

In the logic of EMU, the coordination of national fiscal policies was an essential dimension reinforcing monetary discipline across the Eurozone. At the same time, national fiscal policies could, in principle, help to mitigate against the risk of contagion by allowing individual countries to manage domestic imbalances through, for example, monetary policy and exchange rate adjustments. What is of central importance in this regard is that in the design of EMU, no consideration had been given to compensating national economies for the loss of policy independence involved in fiscal and monetary coordination. Accordingly, when the crisis impacted at a national level, they were constrained in responding while the EU, for its part, lacked the EU-wide support systems and crisis management capability that might have compensated for these shocks.[11]

[11] See De Grauwe (2011) for a further discussion on this design aspect to the Eurozone. Fischer (2011) notes that the outcome of this has been the creation of an (unworkable) dual identity of a

The EU had previously set out provisions aimed at reducing (while never, however, envisaging having to offset) potentially negative externalities from unsustainable intra-community borrowing and/or lending practices, as well as mitigating against the threat of sovereign default. In 1992, with the signing of the Maastricht Treaty (and later with the Stability and Growth Pact (1997)), members pledged to maintain control over their deficit spending and debt levels—specifically, with the size of annual budget deficits being capped at 3% of GDP and the stock of public debt of 60% of GDP.[12] The success of this approach would be rooted in the degree to which participants sustained their fiscal discipline. To bolster incentives to maintain this discipline, a 'no bailout' clause (which was subsequently suspended by the ECB in its 'whatever it takes' QE initiative) was implemented, with the implication that should a member fail to meet its debt obligations, then a sovereign default would ensue.[13] It should be noted that, in spite of these efforts, the Stability and Growth Pact's capacity to intervene was stymied from the beginning in that the implementation of sanctions was to be decided by the political body The Economic and Financial Affairs Council (ECOFIN). As events were to bear witness, this provided a 'buffer' from the consequences of dysfunctional behaviours that enabled countries to contravene such rules.[14]

As a prerequisite to EMU accession, countries needed to fulfil a set of economic 'convergence criteria'.[15] This was to help ensure that they were

confederation that is at once adamant to uphold both the wider monetary union and their own fiscal sovereignty.

[12] Set out by the European Council in (1997), the Stability and Growth Pact is an agreement to facilitate and maintain the stability of the EMU. It draws its legal legitimacy from Articles 121 and 126 of the Treaty on the Functioning of the European Union. Members commit to being monitored by the European Commission and the Council of Ministers, and to abide by annual recommendations for policy actions. However, there was a lack of rigour to the metrics and mandates laid down in this Treaty which, as Busch et al. (2013) argue, were brought to the fore by the crisis.

[13] For a further discussion on this point, see Lane (2012).

[14] This issue is discussed by Tovias (2017).

[15] From this, there were a set of so-called 'Convergence Criteria' (see European Central Bank 2018), among which are included the following:

1. Price stability: A country's inflation rate could not exceed more than 1.5% above the rate of the three best-performing member states.
2. Sustainable fiscal policy: Government deficit could not be higher than 3% of GDP.
3. Debt sustainability: Government debt could not reach any higher than 60% of GDP.
4. Exchange rate stability: The candidate had to participate in the exchange rate mechanism (ERM II) for at least two years without strong deviations from its central rate and without devaluing its currency's bilateral central rate against the Euro in the same period.

in a position to most fully economically integrate and contribute to the sustainability of the economic community. There are compelling reasons for arguing that a major locus of the European Debt Crisis—and its counterpart Troikanomics—was rooted in the inflexible imposition of these criteria. This is apparent from two perspectives. The first argument is that convergence criteria were developed in and for 'standard' circumstances: they reflected the common-sense realities of sustaining a monetary union in normal times. But the events that were transpiring were wholly abnormal—the morphing of financial delinquency on an epochal scale into an unprecedented economic crisis; the rapidity of the contagion, and the complete unpreparedness of the EU as well as of national authorities, had never occurred before in modern European history. In these circumstances, the rigid insistence on the retention of convergence in what amounted to a different environment to the one it started out in was the height of folly: peripheral economies were impaled on these criteria—Greece still is. And as recently as late 2018, Italy's new anti-EU government railed against these same criteria.

The second argument is that the criteria that were put in place paid scant regard to the macroeconomic distinctiveness of each country, or to their wider market influencers. Convergence benchmarks were at best an indicative means of attempting to establish fleeting economic equity, and at worst a cynical attempt at knowingly creating the façade of such equilibrium. The very fact that some countries found it necessary to effectively *scramble* to adhere to these metrics raises serious questions as to their relevance in an entirely different monetary and economic environment.

While the Maastricht Treaty was justified in insisting that a degree of convergence was essential to legitimising a country's participation in the Euro, it underappreciated the structural complexities of intra-community economic relations. Amidst all of these promises, policies, and pursuit of the European ideal, a fundamental question was consciously side-lined, namely: was the EU an appropriate environment within which to establish a single monetary union? The central conceit was that between the dual forces of the introduction of a secure and sustainable monetary

5. Long-term interest rates: The long-term interest rate should not be higher than 2% above the rate of the three best-performing member states in terms of price stability.

union and the implementation of convergence criteria, that integration would iteratively reveal itself.

This ethic of 'if you build it they will come' placed a heavy task on the Eurozone of being a catalyst *in and of itself* for legitimising the single currency.[16] As we now know, because of embedded inequalities between member nations, the journey towards economic harmonisation was deeply fraught. A single one-size-fits-all monetary policy is hazardous when it operates within the constraints of economic incommensurability. The latent inefficiencies in peripheral nations were exacerbated by the far greater economic capabilities and clout of centre countries such as Germany, and their higher levels of productivity. Their ability to operate on an even keel was undermined from the very get go.

The crisis exposed the reality that a young adult growing up in Spain was by orders of magnitude more likely to be unemployed than his or her peer in Germany, while a pensioner in Greece would not benefit from the same levels of welfare entitlements as someone in the Netherlands. As it transpired, the nations that were most vulnerable to the emergent crisis (e.g. those whose debt/GDP ratios were unsustainable)—compounded by their participation in the Eurozone—lacked the economic infrastructure or political mandate that would equip them to decisively and authoritatively tackle it.[17] This includes issues such as adapting interest and

---

[16] The concept of 'Optimal Currency Area' made its stake in the sphere of economic debate in the 1960s, thanks to influential works by Mundell (1961), McKinnon (1963), and Kenen (1969). The largely theoretical debate concerning the criteria underpinning areas for which economic integration is deemed strongly viable came to the fore as the EU continued with its ongoing expansion into countries that appeared to be economically disparate. Prominent economists have argued that the Eurozone did not meet OCA conditions—see, for example, Krugman (2013), Pisani-Ferry (2013), and Gibson et al. (2014). Further to this, not only does the Eurozone not meet sufficient criteria for a currency union, but it has become increasingly dependent on political will as a means through which to compensate for a latent lack of economic strength. For a further discussion on this point, see Moravcsik (2012) (who notes that the inherent disequilibrium within the EMU makes the range of policy responses to date, e.g. budgetary austerity, the micromanagement of national budgets, fiscal federalism, and bailouts, insufficient to solve this problem alone) and Wihlborg et al. (2010). Dow (2016) also discusses the need for real convergence as a prerequisite for the success of the single currency.

[17] The Treaty of Lisbon (13 December 2007) Article 125 states that '1. The Union shall not be liable for or assume the commitments of central governments, regional, local or other public authorities, other bodies governed by public law, or public undertakings of any Member State, without prejudice to mutual financial guarantees for the joint execution of a specific project. A Member State shall not be liable for or assume the commitments of central governments, regional, local or other public authorities, other bodies governed by public law, or public undertakings of another Member

exchange rates (Feldstein 1997) or competitively devaluing their currencies (Draper 2013).

This lack of adequately developed internal adjustment mechanisms to draw on in times of economic distress is considered to be a significant contributor towards the unsustainable debt levels at the heart of the crisis.[18] It has also been identified as a significant potential impediment to the sustainability of the EMU.[19] The capacity to introduce an initial exchange rate devaluation, or have the ECB act as a lender of last resort, might well have helped to kick-start the process of economic recovery and competitive reintegration. Without these mechanisms, member nations were no longer in a position to authoritatively assure bondholders that they would be in a position to repay issued bonds at maturity.[20] Markets' belief in their stability had been lost, trust had gone astray.

Imbued with the task of being a reserve currency, the economics of a single currency dictate that there must be a single interest rate prevailing across the Eurozone. By extension, there must also be a single monetary policy formulated and implemented by a single Central Bank—the ECB—to which the Central Banks of members are subservient. Policy is determined at the centre and is implemented by national central banks, the satellites of the ECB, lacking the autonomy to customise policy to the unique needs and capabilities of their country. For countries in difficulties, there are different dimensions to the issue: national Central Banks cede control over their interest rates/exchange rate. Crucially, devaluation is not an option in rebalancing the economy through, for example, improving competitiveness. This left countries dependent on the ECB's 'one size fits all' exchange rate. The country under pressure is therefore at risk when an

State, without prejudice to mutual financial guarantees for the joint execution of a specific project; 2. The Council, on a proposal from the Commission and after consulting the European Parliament, may, as required, specify definitions for the application of the prohibitions referred to in Articles 123 and 124 and in this Article'.

[18] This point is also noted by Wihlborg et al. (2010) and Krugman (2013).

[19] For further analysis, see, for example, Lane (2006), Feldstein (1997), Wyplosz (2006), Chryssogelos (2016), and Ash (2012).

[20] It is worth noting that the argument by the then German finance minister Wolfgang Schäuble was precisely that, by pushing Greece into Grexit it would mitigate instability in the Eurozone. At the same time, it was clear to some observers that this would also lead to a devaluation of a new Greek currency which would facilitate Greece's ultimate recovery.

external disturbance impacts on the system and the response is determined externally—and by an institution whose mandate was based solely on price stability and thereby lacking the flexibility of a dual mandate (such as that of the US Fed) which takes into account employment rates.

Robust institutions are central to the effective functioning of a country across multiple levels. The Central Bank of a country is one such irreplaceable institution. It can print a national currency backed, in the final resort, by the capabilities and capacities of the country's citizens. It can align monetary policies to mitigate inflationary policies through, for example, managing interest rates and the provision of liquidity to the financial sector. In principle, it can manage the external value of the currency—the exchange rate—in such a way as to enhance the competitiveness of its exports, and thereby strengthen its balance of payments. Depending on its mandate, the Central Bank can also act to ensure price stability and/or balanced growth of the economy. This is an institution that is focused unequivocally on the welfare of the country. It is therefore easy to see how it gives expression to a nation's autonomy—supporting and facilitating their present and prospective capabilities.

EMU generated important benefits for the Eurozone and the wider Single Market. The costs, however, also became all too evident during the crisis. Notwithstanding subsequent economic recovery in the Bailout countries (much more muted and problematic in Greece), these costs were very considerable and, in relation to indebtedness, resulted in intergenerational effects. This can be stylised as follows: countries join a monetary union with the aspiration of greater economic prosperity; the (short-lived) prosperity that they *do* enjoy catalyses a domestic economic backlash; their membership of that same union renders them incapable of responding to the crisis in ways that would prove to be necessary or mindful of their own country's particular needs. At the same time, the ECB exercised pre-emptive and coercive authority, directed towards the interests of the Eurozone, whose governance and modes of adjustment were weighted towards the interests of its centre.

While it is true, therefore, that the crisis did not originate *solely* within the confines of the EU, the Eurozone certainly acted as a conduit through which it was transmitted and magnified, while leaving indebted and marginalised countries doubly vulnerable: they now lacked the autonomy to default or devalue (which, importantly, is one of the adjustment mechanisms frequently advocated by the IMF), while being open to repressive measures from the institutionally bolstered dominant countries.

It is clear from the way the ECB engaged with Ireland prior to the imposition of Troikanomics that what was important for the orthodoxy was the protection of EMU and rogue and irresponsible banks, and that the Irish people were expected, under duress, to 'take one for the team'. The point was—and remains—that the ECB dictated the response in a way that need not have happened.

By contrast, for the core countries, adherence to the convergence criteria was never an issue: Germany enjoys a surplus while France attained the 3% deficit target (at 2.6%) for the first time in a decade in 2018 (RFI 2018). There were, of course, multiple reasons, some of them self-inflicted, why the peripheral indebted countries impelled, kicking and screaming, into the 'Troikanomics Trap'. The trap was this: the institutional failures of the Eurozone contributed significantly to the crisis, yet the 'core countries' were *largely* safeguarded from the strictures of the convergence criteria. This was because the burden of adjustment was primarily on debtor and not on surplus countries. To put this differently, the core countries had most to gain from EMU, while at the same time they were the ones who were more protected from the fallout of failures.

## Environmental Antecedents of the Crisis: When Banking Loses Its Way

The Eurozone was architecturally predisposed towards economic crisis for an additional reason. This relates to the *environment* within which it developed—where there was a high degree of interconnectivity between the banking system and the EU's wider economic structure. There has been significant progress towards mitigating the vulnerabilities embedded in this interconnectedness, notably through the development of the ECB's regulatory and supervisory powers. Nonetheless, this merits a more discursive treatment. These developments, their causes and their consequences, were worked out within a monetary union and sets of institutions that had given little regard to wider issues relating essentially to the public good.

A country's banking sector acts as its macroeconomic central nervous system, sending and receiving 'signals' (in the form of payment transfers, and credit/debit facilities) throughout the wider corpus of the country. It continuously innervates the various parts of its economy (such as corporates, small to medium-sized enterprises (SMEs), and households) to achieve optimum functioning. It responds to events both nationally and abroad—often in the form of automated responses that seek to protect the country from 'shocks'. So embedded are banks that it is impossible to fathom the successful operation of households, corporations, and government bodies without them facilitating and intermediating in the process.

This embeddedness comes at a price, however, when the nervous system lacks the structural or functional capacity to protect the body. This is even more so the case when banks are such a prominent force in the intermediation of corporate and sovereign credit/debt; to take one example, in 2012 total bank assets as a share of Eurozone GDP were 360%.[21] In this context, while the Debt Crisis certainly had a sovereign component, there was another principle catalyst in provoking it. Here, we must look to the behaviour of the *banking* sector in the lead-up to the crisis in order to fully appreciate how the environment was systematically inducing an implosion in financial stability.[22] It was the endemic failures of national commercial banks that led to negative feedback loops between thoroughly anaemic banking systems and the crucial issue of market confidence in the sovereigns.

Financial markets (encompassing both sovereign and banking) exploited the credit worthiness associated with their participation in the Single Currency. They were complicit in the illusion that their status as 'EMU-certified' provided a guarantee on the ongoing accumulation of

[21] For a more detailed discussion on how such interconnectivity is evident in a number of specific ways, see Shambaugh (2012) and Pisani-Ferry (2013). These factors provide a rationale behind differences in EU and US responsiveness to the crisis.

[22] Lapavitsas et al. (2012) also make this argument concerning the primacy of the *banking* crisis.

debts, in effect negating market risk derived from their status as debtor countries.[23] In less frenetic times, markets would have been far more responsive to the questionable outflow/inflow ratios of debt that were building between centre and peripheral countries, for example, by raising interest rates. Of course, their inaction was rooted in the flawed idea that sovereign bonds were necessarily secure, regardless of the member nation they were issued to.[24]

As we noted elsewhere, this myth melted under market pressures in the period immediately before intervention by the Troika. An environment comprised of a single monetary policy, deficiencies in the scope for intervention to mitigate pressures on national authorities, combined with the rigours of the convergence criteria, contributed to an inherently unstable policy regime that further pressurised the crisis. It may be helpful to take one example of this latent instability. In the wake of the more liberal market conditions that arose after the 1998 introduction of the Euro, a cohort of these countries were finding it increasingly difficult to operate within the constraints of the Maastricht Criteria and turned to securitising future government revenues to reduce their debt/deficit ratios. In the case of Ireland, for example, the loose credit conditions contributed to a 'construction bubble' which in turn greatly augmented government revenues and fiscal space—while also leaving the government's fiscal position highly vulnerable to the implosion in revenue that occurred as the economic crisis unfolded. There was an inability within the Eurozone to counter with any real clout or follow-through the unsustainable building of public (and private) debt. What followed was a series of fiscal policy choices related to government revenues and expenses that were in complete contravention of established best practice. The period from 2002 to 2008 was marked by negligent and short-sighted credit conditions that encouraged high-risk lending and borrowing practices. Once the crisis struck, repayment rates increased considerably for Eurozone countries that had accumulated debt, making it impossible to refinance their debts.

[23] Endowed with such a forgiving financial environment, both public and private entities responded by increasing their borrowing; in effect, they lost the run of themselves—as is noted by Ash (2012).
[24] See Schwab (2012).

While each country—Spain, for example, was quite different to Cyprus—had their own distinctive narrative through which they arrived at this juncture, a common precipitant was the chronic failure to adhere to regulatory and governance mandates underpinning established best practice. Regulatory and governance requirements are one area in which there have been subsequent transformational changes to counter the risky behaviours that enabled the crisis. Back then, sovereign markets remained complicit in such practices for extended periods of time. Common prudence would have dictated a much more risk-averse stance in relation to participation in systematic indebtedness.

It is an axiom of financial theory that markets are (perceived as) efficient and rational. But the operation of markets in the lead-up to the economic collapse was captured by a paradigm detached from an understanding of markets' true value and a recognition that ultimately all business gets its legitimacy from its community. It is the community that provides stable deposits, that generates the demand for productive loans. It is the community that provides the expertise that sustains banks.[25] Ultimately, it is the community that picks up the tab when something goes very, very wrong.

In the lead-up to and during the crisis, the public—and social solidarity—were held hostage to the mind-set and business models of banks and institutions, and the robustness of the regulatory systems and calibre of leadership by which they were directed. This is one of the factors that enabled the banking sector and credit market to operate as prime catalysts in instigating the crisis and as a means through which contagion was transmitted. And yet, in spite of the central role that they have played, they were largely insulated from the consequences of their actions at two different levels. Firstly, by shareholders (including pension funds—the irony!), whose investment in the banks had been diluted by capital-raising to mitigate disastrous strategic and operational decisions. Secondly, by governments and global central banks, who had bailed them out.

[25] As the Compendium of the Social Doctrine of the Church (2005) notes, '[a] financial economy that is an end in itself, is destined to contradict its goal, since it is no longer in touch with its roots … it has abandoned its original and essential role of contributing to the development of people and the human community'.

The prevailing business model of financial institutions, and particularly investment banks, moved towards a cult of selling what amounted to a culture of indebtedness to families. This model gave, *and still gives*, overriding priority to shareholders; it is configured to optimise short-term earnings, driven by perverse incentives, and motivates the taking of unacceptable risks. It eschews responsibility to the broader stakeholder community that includes customers, employees, and the national interest. Aligned with this permissive approach to regulation that actively accommodated dysfunctional behaviours, there was a radical shift in how risks were understood. A financial industry became premised on the goal of monetising risk through radicalising its commercialisation, rather than avoiding it. Financial institutions had made the destructive leap from ethical intermediation to wholly unethical speculation within a culture that esteems the next quarter's earnings as more important than long-term sustainability.

This vision had already been dissected and shown up for what it is: an insistent manipulation of the markets and businesses, sequestered by the elite through 'rent seeking' and objectively excessive remuneration. Banks, being incentivised to take on board excessive levels of risk on the assumption that the government protected them—and in so doing socialising the costs of their mistakes—thus underwent a radical transformation. In particular, their constitutive purpose became seriously distorted by self-serving speculation.[26]

It is worth reflecting on the paradox that underlines all of these developments. At one level, the banks (and also governments) were at least in part responsible for inducing a laxity in relation to the accumulation of indebtedness. This was one facet of a culture of consumerism and irresponsible marketing of debt. At another level, this was the catalyst for retribution in the form of austerity and the subsequent imposition of Troikanomics. Both of these behavioural and policy patterns of thought were equally malign in their mind-set and in their consequences. It would appear—and this in conjecture on our part—that the democratic systems in individual countries, and within EU institutions, had little understanding of the extent to which the abandonment of normative principles—drawing on the rich virtue-based philosophy of the Greeks

[26] See Menéndez (2014).

and mediated to modern Europe through Christian Democracy in post-war Europe—carries very definite risks that can both be painful and cast long shadows.

More generally, there was the absence of any form of principles-based economics within governments and institutions—least of all private institutions, which were driven by maximising short-term shareholder value and obscenely high remuneration. The level of expertise in major institutions on esoteric financial engineering products was extraordinarily specialised—but few, if any, could talk of or see the relevance of the Common Good. In this, one of the defining crises of the twentieth century, the overriding priority for governments and for the EC *should* have been as the advocate for the dignity of people and communities. After all, banks and financial markets get their legitimacy (and bailouts) from the community and not the other way round. Ultimately, a financial system is only as robust as the economy it *serves*. But that wasn't their priority. There was no substantive normative reference point for asserting that the welfare of individuals is central to the mandate of healthy institutions. To the extent that Troikanomics was a consequence of fiscal delinquency and a culture of consumerism across a number of the debtor countries, this offers no defence of the decision by the dominant countries to develop and impose such harsh remedial action.

When these values are forfeited, economies and the communities they underpin unravel—collapse comes from within. This collapse radiated outwards through contagion—the effects of which cannot be measured solely by their impact on the balance sheets of financial institutions, or even the functioning of credit markets—even though these are unprecedented. Contagion creates a virus-like pathology in the heart of households and in the social economy—impacting on the lives and living standards of individuals and families. This was unsustainable; the ratio of debt to disposable income, to take just one metric, rose to levels that took swathes of the population into a new form of dependence. It left many corporates overleveraged and vulnerable to shocks, with all of the attendant consequences for their workforce.

Lending by banks involves transforming short-term liquid deposits (including volatile short-term borrowings from the markets) into long-term assets: houses, hotels, and other assets that are not equally liquidated or only at a significant loss—even more so, when bank borrowers and the banks themselves come under pressure. Banks don't just (re)lend customers' deposits. They also borrow, mostly from the markets to supplement these funds they have on deposit. In the case of Ireland, the banking crisis originated not alone from irresponsible domestic lending by banks but also from excessive borrowing by those same banks to fund this lending: borrowing that was typically short-term in nature often in the form of 'rolling over' existing credits and, therefore, vulnerable to a loss of confidence. It can easily just melt away if markets get spooked. That means that the banks themselves cannot lend and may begin to call in loans, even from sound companies or customers, or perhaps begin to sell off the loans on their books—'deleverage'—to ensure it is balanced against lower levels of the capital it holds as a kind of 'safety net'.

Finally, consider an economy whose banks are in real difficulty for the reasons set out earlier. Banks are required to maintain sufficient capital to absorb 'shocks' and sufficient liquidity to meet all normal withdrawals of deposits: they must comply with terms and conditions—covenants—attached to their own liabilities in the form of borrowings in one form or another. When they can no longer comply with such requirements they come under regulatory scrutiny—as well as from markets and rating agencies. Their share price typically falls, eroding the confidence of domestic depositors and of foreign lenders and investors who hold their debt. Where banks are themselves unable to resolve those difficulties by repricing their loans, raising additional capital, and/or disposing of some of their assets for a fair price, they necessarily must turn to the Central Bank as 'lender of last resort'.[27] The importance of a Central Bank, managed with integrity and purpose, to the autonomy of a country cannot be overstated. *Conversely, the ceding of the capabilities and responsibilities of a Central Bank to other interests is a loss to the national interests for which a country cannot be compensated.*

So, where does all of that leave us? The mainstream model of Western banking cannot be trusted. Regardless of formal regulation and governance arrangements of one kind or another, the historical evidence and the experience forged in the recent crisis are simply overwhelming. The private incentives to subvert the model are too great. Mainstream politics

[27] For further insight, see De Grauwe (2011).

cannot be trusted either.[28] There are politicians, just as there are bankers, of great integrity. But the theoretical arguments, and history, attest to the fact that private incentives—primarily the urge to power and to the misuse of power—tend to corrode the integrity of politics. The social costs, which impact across the generations, are incalculable.

Some political systems are more robust than others. For example, certain provisions of the German 'Basic Law' vindicate the independence of politicians and their answerability to their conscience and not party political pressures, in carrying out their work. An attempt to introduce this provision into the Irish Constitution by the late, and far-seeing, Peter Mathews was summarily rejected by 'the system' which highlighted, once again, the depressingly familiar oppressive power of incentives. Politics played its part in the Irish banking crisis. It played a catastrophic role in the Greek Bailout and, as we point out later, failed the people. 'Promises' and ideological agendas are the currency traded in politics. The promises cannot be trusted and the political agendas are (very) unlikely to be aligned to the Public Good of the country.

National autonomy creates 'a space' for politics which citizens expect will vindicate and uphold their rights and freedoms. But Troikanomics demonstrates that sometimes this just does not happen—quite the opposite. The EU is predicated on the assumption that this national responsibility can be 'shared'. What that really means is 'outsourced'. We pointed out earlier the expectation, back in the day, on the part of smaller and vulnerable countries that the EU would take their part during the crisis and uphold their interests in the face of hegemonistic agendas. It did not. The Troika was the outcome. In the business of politics, 'trust' appears to be a marketable (but ultimately hollow) commodity. What the banks, and political parties, and the EU have in common is a purely contractual basis for relationships. The banks want your custom. Political parties want your vote. The EU wants your 'buy-in' to the agendas of the powerful. Where relationships are contractual, and where truth has been outsourced to the public relations/marketing departments, there can be no basis for trust.

[28] On this point, see, for example, Cliffe et al. (2000), alongside numerous others.

To put this differently, when political systems accommodate to a culture in which truth is subservient to expediency, then their responsibilities to the demos—which are not transferable—are betrayed by their politics. When banks engage with their customers on a purely contractual basis of what is in the best interests of large shareholders, society is always at risk. When the governance of the EU is controlled by the large and the powerful from the centre and the capitals of just a few countries, it has ceased to be a 'community' and there is no rational basis for ceding responsibilities for the welfare of citizens to such institutions. What this suggests is that the existential crisis that washed across the member nations of the EU and Project Europe reflected the abandonment of normative principles for a form of contractualism that has forfeited trust. That is why critique on the ethical legitimacy of the political and economic environment is so indispensible.

## References

Ash, T. G. (2012). *The Crisis of Europe: How the Union Came Together and Why It's Falling Apart*. [Online]. Retrieved from https://www.foreignaffairs.com/articles/europe/2012-08-16/crisis-europe?page=4

Busch, K., Hermann, C., Hinrichs, K., & Schulten, T. (2013). *Euro Crisis, Austerity Policy and the European Model: How Crisis Policies in Southern Europe Threaten the EU's Social Dimension*. Berlin: International Policy Analysis.

Chryssogelos, A. (2016). *The EU's Crisis of Governance and European Foreign Policy*. Great Britain: The Royal Institute of International Affairs.

Cliffe, L., Ramsay, M., & Bartlett, D. (Eds.). (2000). *The Politics of Lying: Implications for Democracy*. London: Macmillan Press.

De Grauwe, P. (2011). Managing a Fragile Eurozone. [Online]. Retrieved from https://voxeu.org/article/managing-fragile-eurozone

Dow, S. (2016). Ontology and Theory for a Redesign of European Monetary Union. *World Economic Review, 6*, 1–11.

Draper, T. (2013). An Analysis of the European Debt Crisis: Its Etiology, Current Status, and Possible Future Direction. *Cris Bulletin, 1*, 61–76.

European Central Bank. (2018). *Convergence Criteria*. [Online]. Retrieved from https://www.ecb.europa.eu/ecb/orga/escb/html/convergence-criteria.en.html

European Commission. (2008). *European Economy No. 2/2008 – EMU@Ten: Successes and Challenges After Ten Years of Economic and Monetary Union*. Luxembourg: European Commission.

European Commission. (2017a). *Deepening Europe's Economic and Monetary Union*. [Online]. Retrieved from https://ec.europa.eu/commission/news/deepening-europes-economic-and-monetary-union-2017-dec-06_en

European Commission. (2017b). *Reflection Paper on the Deepening of the Economic and Monetary Union*. Brussels: European Commission.

European Commission. (2017c). *White Paper on the Future of Europe: Reflections and Scenarios for the EU27 by 2025*. Brussels: European Commission.

European Council. (1997). *Resolution of the European Council on the Stability and Growth Pact Amsterdam*. [Online]. Retrieved from https://eur-lex.europa.eu/LexUriServ/LexUriServ.do?uri=CELEX:31997Y0802(01):EN:HTML

European Union, C. o. t. R. o. t. G. o. t. M. S. (2007, December 13). *Treaty of Lisbon Amending the Treaty on European Union and the Treaty Establishing the European Community*. Volume 2007/C 306/01.

Fagan, G., & Gaspar, V. (2007). *Adjusting to the Euro*. Frankfurt: European Central Bank.

Feldstein, M. (1997). The Political Economy of the European Economic and Monetary Union: Political Sources of an Economic Liability. *Journal of Economic Perspectives, 11*(4), 23–42.

Feldstein, M. (2012). The Failure of the Euro. The Little Currency That Couldn't. *Foreign Affairs, 91*(January/February), 105–116.

Fischer, J. (2011). *Europe's Shaky Foundations*. [Online]. Retrieved from https://www.project-syndicate.org/commentary/europe-s-shaky-foundations?barrier=accesspaylog#B3YdyoV1boL7zRkc.99

Gibson, H. D., Palivos, T., & Tavlas, G. S. (2014). The Crisis in the Euro Area: An Analytic Overview. *Journal of Macroeconomics, 39*, 233–239.

Hall, P. A. (2012). The Economics and Politics of the Euro Crisis. *German Politics, 21*(4), 355–371.

Kenen, P. (1969). The Theory of Optimum Currency Areas: An Eclectic Review. In R. Mundell & A. Swoboda (Eds.), *Monetary Problems in the International Economy*. Chicago: University of Chicago Press.

Krugman, P. (2013). *Revenge of the Optimum Currency Area* (pp. 429–448). s.l.: University of Chicago Press.

Lane, P. R. (2006, January). *The Real Effects of EMU*. Institute for International Integration Studies (IIIS) Discussion Paper, No. 115.

Lane, P. R. (2012). The European Sovereign Debt Crisis. *Journal of Economic Perspectives, 26*(3), 49–68.

Lapavitsas, C. (2012). *Crisis in the Eurozone*. London: Verso.
McKinnon, R. (1963). Optimum Currency Areas. *American Economic Review, 53*, 717–725.
Menéndez, A. J. (2014). The European Crises and the Undoing of the Social and Democratic Rechtsstaat. In J. E. Fossum & A. J. Menéndez (Eds.), *The European Union in Crises or the European Union as Crises?* (pp. 387–489). ARENA Report No. 2/14.
Moravcsik, A. (2012). Europe After the Crisis: How to Sustain a Common Currency. *Foreign Affairs, 91*(3), 54–68.
Mundell, R. (1961). A Theory of Optimum Currency Areas. *American Economic Review, 51*, 657–675.
Pisani-Ferry, J. (2013). The Known Unknowns and Unknown Unknowns of European Monetary Union. *Journal of International Money and Finance, 34*, 6–14.
Pontifical Council for Justice and Peace. (2005). *Compendium of the Social Doctrine of the Church*. Vatican City: Libreria Editrice Vaticana.
RFI. (2018). *French Public Debt Under 3 Percent for First Time in 10 Years*. [Online]. Retrieved from http://en.rfi.fr/economy/20180326-french-public-debt-under-3-percent-first-time-10-years
Schwab, K. (2012). *The Re-emergence of Europe*. s.l.: World Economic Forum.
Shambaugh, J. C. (2012). The Euro's Three Crises. *Brookings Papers on Economic Activity, 43*(1), 212–219.
Tovias, A. (2017). Solidarity in the Eurozone: Spontaneous, Organized or Inexistent? In A. Giannakopoulos (Ed.), *Solidarity in the European Union: Challenges and Perspectives* (pp. 20–30). s.l.: The S. Daniel Abraham Center.
Wihlborg, C., Willett, T. D., & Zhang, N. (2010). The Euro Debt Crisis: It Isn't Just Fiscal. *World Economics, 11*(4), 51–77.
World Economic Forum. (2017). *The Global Competitiveness Report: 2017–2018*. Geneva: World Economic Forum.
Wyplosz, C. (2006). European Monetary Union: The Dark Sides of a Major Success. *Economic Policy, 21*(46), 207–261.

# 5

# The Troika and Austerity: A Destructive Dyad

## Introduction

The Troika is now a historical artefact. Detailed analysis by the European Parliament (2014a) highlights serious criticisms of its engagement with vulnerable countries. The proposed Juncker Reforms (2017) envisage its replacement by a European Monetary Fund (EMF), which would be built on the European Stability Mechanism (ESM) and constituted from the EC and the ECB. In light of its antecedents and consequences (as well as its subsequent independent critics), this initiative is hardly surprising. Troikanomics was, in part, the outcome of a process that was subversive of foundational EU principles such as subsidiarity and solidarity. Initially, it damaged the credibility of the IMF, until that institution took a principles-based and data-driven approach to participation, which subsequently caused it to step away from the model used by 'the European institutions'. And it highlighted the fact that the European institutions and individual countries—notably Germany—were prepared to reject the best international advice on offer in pursuit of their own agendas: in other words, it was not the welfare of the individual country with which they were engaging that was their priority—it was the enforcement of their own



R. Kinsella, M. Kinsella, *Troikanomics*, https://doi.org/10.1007/978-3-319-97070-7_5

political calculus. The scale of the design flaws and the costs of its repressive and often incoherent short-term policies were enormous. They raise fundamental concerns that need to be critiqued and debated in the lead-up to, and aftermath of, the 2019 European Elections.[1] To put the matter tersely: what are people voting for—what are the agendas and the possible implications of the reforms?

When the Troika pushed rafts of legislation—literally hot from the printers—through national parliaments, with no scope for scrutiny, a grave disservice was being done to democracy.[2] It raises the question of whether it is prudent for any country to trust an EU orthodoxy which, when push came to shove during the crisis, resorted to brute political power to impose a form of intervention that went against every pretension of 'community' to which it had ostensibly aspired.

## The Troika: Nature, Aims, and Agenda

The circumstances precipitating the Troika's creation were exceptional—the EU had been plunged into an economic crisis characterised by a catharsis in banking and financial markets, macroeconomic instability, and unsustainable sovereign debt levels. It was all those things, but at its heart, it was also a systemic ethical crisis within the West, including the EU, a crisis which corroded trust at every level.[3] It is hardly surprising that political and policy responses should have been similarly infected. In the post mortems since the crisis, much has been made—and very rightly so—of the failures of financial institutions and of the architecture of the Eurozone: but very little of the business models within which banks operated (and still operate) or of the ethics of *political* governance.

The latter is central to our analysis since it highlights the confusion of what politics is about and the sometimes-arbitrary forms of power it

[1] Consider, for example, the burden imposed on Greece following what was supposed to be its 'exit': 'enhanced surveillance' for the next 40 years.

[2] The authors recall Irish legislators making this very point.

[3] The authors have made this point previously, such as Kinsella and Kinsella (2009).

inhabits. In recent years the massive concentration of wealth that has accompanied globalisation has received much attention. The concentration of power, including within the Eurozone, has received less attention. The 'forums' within which power is mediated implemented numerous banking 'reforms' without ever questioning the basic premises: in other words, how did the behaviours of banks reveal themselves during the crisis—and what should the *constitutive purpose* of banks and financial institutions be about? Nor have such forums questioned the functioning of democracy itself within the EU, including the extent to which it has been diminished in smaller countries.

Even as the Banking and Debt Crisis spread, the EU undertook policy responses intended to curtail contagion and to mitigate against a similar crisis arising again. Central to this process was the need to address a set of weaknesses within their policy toolbox, as well as shortcomings in the institutional architecture of the EMU that the crisis had both exposed and exploited. Steps were thus taken towards imposing greater fiscal oversight and surveillance across the EU, and within the Eurozone. These included the adoption of the 'six-pack' and 'two-pack' components of EU legislations, as well as the adoption of a new Fiscal Compact as part of the Treaty on the Stability, Coordination, and Governance in the Economic and Monetary Union (European Commission 2017). However, amongst the EU's efforts to 'firewall' the crisis, the Troika stands out as the most consequential and contentious.

The Troika—a small, centralised group of unelected officials—was an institutional construct hastily designed and imposed on debt-burdened peripheral countries so as to provide finance in return for an acceptance of rigorous austerity, accompanied by continual intrusive oversight. It drew on the capabilities of the EC, the ECB, and the IMF and operated as the EU's de facto 'fiscal enforcer'.[4] It was empowered to impose radical changes to countries' fiscal (and, therefore, sociopolitical) infrastructure, according to the will of creditors. The primary *modus operandi* of the

[4] 'Austerity' generally refers to the implementation of economic policies with the aim of correcting a country's public finances, which have arisen as a consequence of external 'shocks' and/or domestically generated imbalances. The process of reducing budget deficits can occur either through a reduction in government spending and/or an increase in government revenue (primarily through taxation).

Troika was liaising with the authorities and officials of member nations and providing conditional funding to those who had no access to the capital markets, were mired in a funding and/or balance of payments crisis, and were in need of support to facilitate the transition to a sustainable budgetary and balance of payments position. The provision of loans was predicated on debtor countries accepting the imposition of stringent fiscal and structural reforms, which were ostensibly designed to support adjustment and the repayment terms of their bailout loans.[5] These reforms were benchmarked against preexisting 'convergence criteria'—metrics originally conceived to hold the EU together under much more benign circumstances.

The Troika exercised a range of responsibilities. They took control of the debtor countries' sovereign budgetary responsibilities, set the terms (or, more appropriately, 'conditions') underpinning the delivery of financial assistance programmes, carried out regular assessments on countries' adherence to the Bailout Programme, and decided on the periodical release of funding tranches. These measures were accompanied by extraordinarily intrusive political oversight.

'Austerity', a child of the Troika, is more than a macroeconomic policy intervention. It is a mechanism that shapes the wider social fabric of the countries in which it is implemented and deeply influences the lives of their inhabitants. The *explanation* behind austerity was that national debts needed to be reengineered so as to ensure and expedite the payment of foreign debts.[6] This thought process does not, however, produce a satisfactory *justification* for the slew of interventions that followed its implementation. It does not answer why risks that should have been borne by the private sector were effectively borne by the public sector, or

---

[5] Financial assistance was provided by temporary special-purpose vehicles created by Eurozone countries, including the European Financial Stability Facility, the European Financial Stabilisation Mechanism, and also by the International Monetary Fund.

[6] In the IMF's Report (2013) on Greece's First Programme, it commented that 'the crisis and the recession that followed have had terrible consequences for Greece in terms of unemployment and have caused severe stress in society with extreme parties now gaining power'. Either the European Institutions did not see what was happening or they chose to effectively ignore what was so clear to the IMF. The various 'stresses' that austerity imbues can manifest themselves in negative health status outcomes, a perspective that is explored by Karanikolos et al. (2013). Kentikelenis et al. (2011, 2014) also examine this issue, with particular emphasis on the Greek experience.

why the social fabric was mortgaged to protect large countries' banking systems. While the need for reform and change in the aftermath of the crisis was patently evident, what is really at issue is the content of adjustment, the timescale it was to adhere to, and questions as to in whose interests the reforms were being carried out.

The arrival of the Troika in countries' national capitals caused trepidation among the politicians and civil servants whose job it was to 'negotiate' with a team who were already very clear on their instructions and were steadfast in seeing them through. En passant, it should be noted that a degree of cordiality did develop between elected officials and the non-elected. For a community supposedly underpinned by solidarity and subsidiarity, it was remarkable for the dominant surplus countries and institutions to even consider imposing on countries with no recourse. The debt-burdened countries, deprived of the option to devalue, were trapped in a crisis that the EU had not anticipated—and, all the while, being held hostage to the failure of the Eurozone to enforce a symmetrical adjustment process on surplus as well as deficit countries, or a compensatory mechanism to buffer asymmetric shocks.[7] The dominant EU countries and institutions were engaged in intensive learning on crisis management, while the weaker members had to mortgage their sovereignty to pay the tuition fees. Both during and after the Crisis, peripheral countries were caught between a rock and a hard place: on one side lay their own economic vulnerability and loss of autonomy, on the other side lay the hegemony exercised by the centre.

The consequence was dependency that undermined national autonomy and the integrity of supranational organisations. This was never in the script of Robert Shuman and the other Founding Fathers. And it is important to recall this, as Project Europe faces further radical reform in the form—one way or another—of the Juncker Proposals (2017). We point out elsewhere that these reforms address some of the design flaws that exacerbated the impact of the crisis on peripheral countries. But there is a lot more to it than that. Political amnesia is a terrible thing: the memories of causes and

[7] Krugman (2012) discusses the extent to which the risk of asymmetric shocks was not adequately countenanced by the EU. Aizenman (2016) also discusses the seriousness of the threat posed by asymmetric shocks to currency unions.

effects of Troikanomics—and the way power was exercised—continue to drain away. This is especially important as the strains of fragmentation in Project Europe—what President Macron has likened to a 'Civil War'—continue to loom large. The EU has become increasingly conflicted with respect to its identity and, as a corollary, is gradually walking away from its foundational values.

There is, of course, the question of how exactly Troikanomics could possibly be considered the best, or even remotely, the *fairest* mode of adjustment—all the more so in a highly integrated European-wide crisis. The priority of the EU was to prevent financial contagion and to protect the private sector banking system. The belief was that if a country within the EMU defaulted it would create a 'domino' effect, eviscerating market confidence, liquidity, and access to credit—both for the sovereign and for private sector banks. Beyond this, there was the existential concern that such a collapse might lead to the implosion—directly or indirectly—of Project Europe itself. Brian Quinn, the former Deputy Governor of the Bank of England, said at the time that his prayer before going to bed every evening was 'Please God, send me a small *orderly* collapse'. In the wake of the seemingly interminable crisis the issue was this: how far were the masters of the Troika willing to push the limits of oversight and conditionality in order to mitigate the risks that threatened their interests and, by extension, the stability of the European Project?[8] Contagion would have put all countries at risk, not just peripherals like Greece and Ireland, but large countries like Italy—whose financial system was simply too large to rescue and would not have been whipped into line by the Troika as easily as smaller countries.[9]

And so, the EU authorities defaulted back to technical 'solutions': ratios, resolutions, regulation, corporate governance, and, of course, recapitalisation. Bad loans and 'bad banks'. All of this encompassed in an ecosystem of acronyms where people spoke a different language and lived in a different world to the millions of Europeans impacted by their deci-

[8] See, for example, Kinsella (2012).

[9] Here, Munchaü (2018) makes the incisive point that 'Italy is the best example of why Eurozone reforms are existential. The Eurozone has no instruments to cope with an Italian sovereign debt crisis. Italy is too big to fail and too big to save'.

sions. Language matters. In an article on language and risk, the distinguished *Financial Times* journalist Gillian Tett (2018) pointed out that 'we are creatures of our own linguistic environment'. If in the middle of an unprecedented financial catharsis the EU talks the language of how 'convergence criteria' are being contravened, they won't be noticing the trauma of families suddenly hungry and out of work—or the Vulture Funds circling above their homes or national assets. In Cyprus, many depositors lost their life savings. In Ireland, Troikanomics impelled, inter alia, thousands of well-educated and experienced members of the labour force to emigrate—an enormous loss of capacity. Greece was similarly hit by extreme emigration—and many of those who remained have had to subdivide their homes to accommodate family members who had lost their jobs or had their pensions decimated. This is not just bad economics, it is anathema to the core principles of Christian Europe as reflected in Christian Democracy.

The nearest that the EU elite got to acknowledging any of this was in the facile clichés scripted for EU officials paying tribute to 'the sacrifices of the people of Greece/Ireland/Cyprus' for enduring such nihilistic rigours. That is precisely the rationale for our argument that adjustment to shocks needs philosophical critique, not alone in terms of causes and consequences but also because it provides a common language, a normative benchmark, and a moral template within which stakeholders can communicate and engage in constructive dialogue.[10] More generally, *genuine* collaboration—an expression of solidarity—was no longer considered by the 'top table' as the means through which to resolve the crisis or efficiently discharge the duties of the Troika. In Troikanomics, the courtesies of democracy were dispensed and displaced by a 'take charge' mentality.

But, in spite of this (or, perhaps in part, *because* of it) *political* contagion has not gone away—it is simply rebranded as 'Populism'. As the establishment impels the EU towards total political integration, it continues to raise the question: which is the *real* Europe? Is it the egalitarian

[10] Compare, for example, the language of the Eurogroup of Finance Ministers (2018) in their statement that 'congratulated' (!) the Greek people on completing the ESM programme and 'acknowledges the significant efforts made by the Greek citizens over the last years' with the language and sensibility of the IMF (2013).

and participatory community of 'we are all in this together' in the run up to the reforms? Or, alternatively, is it the EU *realpolitik* engaged where, in Yanis Varoufakis' evocative phrase, the 'adults in the room' i.e. Germany and France, explicitly call the shots. The most systematic critique of what underlies this process—'The Paris Statement: A Europe we Can Believe in' (2017)—draws a distinction between 'old Europe' and a 'false Europe', which captures the substance of our argument.

The economic rationale underpinning austerity is that bringing revenue levels into line with expenditure is a necessary condition for a country not alone to pay its way, but also to gain access, should this be necessary, to external credit. The counterpart of this external credit is official debt. The Irish experience was a singular—and cautionary—tale. The virtually unconstrained increase in private sector credit contributed to a property boom generating vast revenue for the government. But because it was unsustainable, it also contributed to the economic crisis and the subsequent collapse in revenue which then opened up a near chasm between revenue and expenditure which, in turn, led to the subsequent debt crisis in which government support for these same banks infected the sovereign and contributed to a full-fledged debt crisis. What it illustrates is a lack of fiscal discipline (a matter of domestic politics) and a rogue banking culture (which was observable internationally). What it *doesn't* show is this: In forcing Ireland to take on board costs that were more properly attributable to European banks—and preventing them from 'burning' some of the bond holders—the Troika cut the ground from underneath its capacity to manage domestically its necessary adjustments.[11]

Was there a punitive element to the mind-set and actions of the Troika? It can be argued, in this context, that the justifications on the part of the Troika to enact austerity measures included a normative dimension. Throughout the book we have highlighted the importance of critique and, by extension, the dangers that can arise when this is absent from policy approaches—in this instance Troikanomics. Accordingly, it will be helpful to look at two possible stances, coming from different places, in relation to the normative legitimisation of the Troika's course of action: Retributivist

[11] See the European Parliament Report (2014a) which critiqued the Troika Programme, noting, for example, that 'the programmes were not suited to comprehensively correcting macroeconomic imbalances which had accumulated, in some cases over decades'.

Justice and Utilitarianism. The retributivist perspective attempts to 'rebalance the scales' that have been left out of kilter by a particular wrongdoing. It does so by responding to an act in a manner that is punitive and in a way that is deemed to be *proportional* to the offence—focusing such punishment on *all* and *only* the guilty parties that were involved in perpetrating the wrongdoing. Here, the wider set of consequences that result from the retribution are not countenanced; alongside this (e.g. within a Criminal Justice context) the broader purposes of whatever 'sentence' is passed down—such as deterrence and rehabilitation—do not have a direct bearing on how it is decided that the offender should atone for their offence.

From the EU's perspective, 'delinquent' member nations had not only undermined the stability of their own national economies, but they had placed the community's economic infrastructure in jeopardy. Chronic macroeconomic mismanagement and fiscal short-sightedness were therefore deemed eligible for retribution. In receiving assistance (in part) from the very community whose economic health it had jeopardised, they would therefore have to also atone for their banking/sovereign wrongdoing—regardless of the potential consequences that oppressive oversight may bring. They did not, of course, say so explicitly but this line of argument runs through much (though not all) of the informal EU response to Brexit.

If Retributive Justice focuses on how to atone for past wrongs, then Utilitarianism seeks to endow positive *future* consequences from the response that is taken to a wrongdoing. In this context, we can think of Troikanomics as a Utilitarian exercise in 'social solidarity', that is, an unpleasant and uncompromising experience that may induce painful consequences for a minority of the populous of the EU, but one which ultimately would spare the Union from contagion. Each debtor country was called upon to shoulder the burden: to offer the EU a reprieve from the mounting threat of economic collapse and political instability.

It is not, of course, robust as a proposition—and far removed from the EU's original philosophy. The irony is that these means have come to undermine those very ends—creating a sense of despondency and disillusionment amongst those who have been left to carry the burden of these measures. In the same vein we can also say that a crisis that ultimately called forth intensive cooperation among the political elites of the member nations has ended up fostering hostility among the populous at large.

Drawing again on this theory of Criminal Justice, participation in the Troika programme has often been compared to a form of 'prison'—compounding peripheral countries' 'delinquent' status and holding them accountable for crimes against sound and sustainable economic behaviours. There is merit to this analogy, in particular when we observe a cohort of the aims that the Criminal Justice system seeks to achieve—among which, in this instance, its punitive dimension shines through. Alongside this, Troikanomics can be seen as a deterrent, seeking to prevent individual nations, as well as the wider community, from committing 'deviant' acts such as this again. This resonates the thinking of Germany in its engagement with the (then) newly elected Tsipras Government. The inference here is that in condemning countries (and their citizens) to toil under the heavy and restrictive burden of Troikanomics, it set a precedent for the future that such reckless behaviours would not be tolerated, and would come with extreme consequences. In this regard, the Troika's Programmes acted to incapacitate debtor countries from making inroads into immediate relapse by limiting their executive functioning, for example, by cutting them off from the international credit markets.

While each of the debtor countries, in their own way, was to some degree culpable for the events that transpired in the lead-up to the crisis, the call to 'atone' that was placed on their shoulders rests on three flawed assumptions. Firstly, there is the argument that the weight of guilt lay solely with debtor countries to which the financial assistance was directed. As we have seen, markets work through the reciprocal flow of capital. To receive investment they would have to have been *sent* investment. Foreign commercial banks (e.g. in Germany and France) were complicit in the short-sighted process of taking advantage of the conditions that the EMU had created, such as artificially low interest rates. Governments at the centre of the EU chose to take a moral high ground and extricate themselves as far as possible from any culpability in the events that transpired. Secondly, there is the argument that this crisis was caused mainly by the behaviours of *sovereigns*. However, this perspective discounts the significant role that the financial markets (*incentivised* to behave in a dysfunctional manner) played in causing the unsustainable creditor/debtor relations that led to the crisis, and in contaminating the balance sheets of the sovereigns to whom they then deferred when they needed rescuing.[12]

There is also the proposition that the debtor countries were the ones that gained from the Bailout/Austerity measures. It is something projected as an altruistic attempt to do whatever it takes to rebalance the EU. The reality is more prosaic. The banks of major European countries benefited enormously—and they socialised the costs through vulnerable countries. Greece received a very small proportion of the funds from the first two Bailouts—the rest went towards debt repayment to EU institutions and to rent-seekers of one kind or another. The Bundesbank and other EU Central Banks made very considerable profits from their engagement with the Greek sovereign. Arguably, this runs counter to any pretence of normative legitimacy.

## Contextualising the Troika: Less than the Sum of Its Parts

We now reflect on the institutions participating in the Troika and how, in practice, it became less than the sum of its parts. The narrative leading up to the Troika was something like this. By 2010, the Debt Crisis had reached a stage that warranted an exceptional intervention (as opposed to crisis resolution)—one that was unprecedented in terms of its size and which only the ECB had the capacity to provide. The subtext was that any such interventions should have an *a*political status and be unencumbered by affiliations with specific countries, enabling greater objectivity and mitigating against the 'moral hazard' which had mesmerised the Eurozone's establishment.

This was the purported justification for the Eurozone's Finance Ministers' decision in 2010 for the creation of an ad hoc crisis management group competent to provide advice on crisis resolution, structural adjustment, and financing. As we have previously pointed out, it is remarkable that

[12] For further insights on this point, see Fagan and Gaspar (2007), who discuss, for example, the sharp rise in household credit and debt levels. See also Blyth (2013), who provides a detailed critique on this issue.

such a capability did not already exist—it was a critical design fault. It is even more remarkable that, having *volunteered* the IMF into defending Project Eurozone, the EU establishment chose not to take its advice in key areas of policy; but that was the reality. The repayment of loans is of central importance, and few are more aware of this than the IMF. But, suppose a country is so stressed by the adjustments being imposed on it that loans cannot be repaid without destroying its productive capacity—both present and prospective. To reiterate once more the importance we attach to critique, the IMF asked this question; the European Institutions and countries (including Ireland, who had good reason to ask) did not particularly want to know. There can be no 'right' way to engage in the challenge of adjustment, including fiscal consolidation, without upholding an ethical dimension. The EU had lost that sensitivity—their 'right' to exercise adjustment failed to be balanced against any sense of 'duty' towards the particular countries undergoing such adjustments.

The Troika wasn't *a*political, it was hardly objective; nor did it prove itself capable of delivering the kind of economic and social literacy that was imperative. There were serious differences between the members of the Troika on issues from economic forecasts to Mission Drafts, and policy prescriptions in areas such as debt relief. More fundamentally, it politicised the IMF—until, notably in the case of Greece, the IMF took the principled decision to step back from a process which in its view was seriously flawed, namely a refusal by Europe to countenance debt relief. There was no precedent set for the creation of a body such as the Troika, and therefore no legislative or political directives by which it was to operate or be accountable—other than the political perspectives of the dominant countries.

The Troika, with its own self-appointed mandate, was a socioeconomic and political chimera—an omen to be feared, composed of disparate elements, and which, for the first time in Project Europe's 60+ years, explicitly intervened in the economic and political workings of member countries and subverted their autonomy. Much like a chimera, it also had no real objective basis in reality in terms of the philosophy underpinning its measures—a temporary solution to an endemic problem.[13] What the

[13] For further insights, see von Schwichow (2013).

Troika did was to desensitise smaller countries to the displacement of autonomy by coercive pressures that could not be gainsaid. It normalised the diminution of autonomy.

It's important to remember that the Troika was working against the background of a very specific mandate on the part of the ECB. Mandate is key to Central Banks. The mandate of the US Fed is to maximise employment, stabilise prices, and also moderate long-term interest rates. The mandate of the ECB is to maintain price stability—an overriding single objective which was transposed from the Bundesbank. The difference is of seismic importance to the stance taken by the ECB regarding the mission of the Troika and to the Troikanomics. The view of the ECB is that if they stick to price stability, then everything else—employment, living standards, and social solidarity—will fall into place. That is not necessarily so. What has been scarred into Germany's historical memory, and then transposed to the ECB, does not translate well across the wider EU. The dual mandate of the US Fed meant that it responded earlier and more proactively to the crisis, which was, as a result, of a much shorter duration than in the Eurozone.

The ECB, for its part, was focused on the monetary dimensions of banking in the EU. It had little competence in the domain of social policy or national governance—and yet its policies impacted profoundly on both. In its Quantitative Easing (QE) 'whatever it takes' strategy, it disregarded, according to the Bundesbank, its own rules. It was the fiscal enforcer of Troikanomics, and remains a prisoner of its own German-imposed mandate: at the outset of the crisis it had no mandate to look at how best to respond directly to the employment shock; nor did it have an organisational culture that was sensitive to the issue and to the wider political implications. It responded with a considerable lag compared with the United States—obliquely rather than in a targeted and nuanced manner.

The European Commission, for its part, might have been expected to advocate for the *demos* on whom the roof had collapsed. It did not, leading to much damage being done prior to the ECB wheeling its solution. Central to any learning outcomes is reform of the ECB's statutes to incorporate a dual mandate: not just price stability, but employment conditions, across the EU. It will not happen, of course: Germany would simply not permit such a move, notwithstanding the transformational impact it would have—not least as a witness to a Social Europe.

More generally, the provisions of the Treaty of Maastricht (such as Article 123 and the Article 125 'no bailout' clause) prohibited 'monetary financing', that is, direct funding by the ECB of countries' budgetary deficits. And yet this is what the ECB's QE programme *effectively* involved—a massive expansion of the ECB's balance sheet, swapping cash for government bonds.[14] It reflected the ECB's decision in 2012 to 'do whatever it takes' to oppose the meltdown of markets thoroughly spooked by the extent of EU sovereign debt markets and its failure to get ahead of the crisis. The view taken was that, laying its mandated responsibilities aside, what it did was contrary to its mission and its 'no bailout' clause in its Constitution—but was justified by the eventual outcome.

Its actions reinforced the extent of deficiencies in the Eurozone at two levels. Firstly, the prohibition on monetary financing reflected the brief that the Bundesbank insisted on for the ECB: price stability, encompassing Germany's own unique history of inflation. The US Fed, as we noted, is required to balance price stability against growth—which is why the United States was able to intervene massively and at an early stage in the crisis. The ECB, for its part, took those same powers on its own initiative, and went the long way about it. Secondly, it poses the question why an unelected and effectively unaccountable body felt empowered to take on such unmandated powers while, at the same time, resisting the obvious case for debt relief for Greece or, to take another example, to seek to insist on a degree of upfront austerity for Ireland that went well beyond what the IMF felt appropriate.

Turning to the IMF, it was established at the 1944 US/UK Bretton Woods New Hampshire Conference on institution-building for the post-war world. Its mandate was to provide conditional balance of payments funding to member nations. However, the scope of its policies has extended greatly over

---

[14] Here, as a means through which to justify their bailout, the EU would subsequently invoke Article 122 (2), which states that '[w]here a Member State is in difficulties or is seriously threatened with severe difficulties caused by natural disasters or exceptional occurrences beyond its control, the Council, on a proposal from the Commission, may grant, under certain conditions, Union financial assistance to the Member State concerned. The President of the Council shall inform the European Parliament of the decision taken'. Greece was therefore declared as being in the centre of a crisis that held the potential to envelop the entire Eurozone. This stands as a prime example of the 'second-best' improvisational approach that the EU was steered towards in its attempts to patch up its inadequate infrastructure.

the years. The IMF has long been engaged with the provision of policy advice, conditional financing, and technical expertise to individual European countries and agencies from within its own specialised domain. It is both highly adept at what it does and extremely professional in the manner of its engagements. It is impossible to envisage the kind of phone calls made by the ECB to Ireland (see our Case Study on Ireland) coming from the IMF.

The IMF was the only Troika participant that was well versed in the provision of conditional assistance, and knew the business of austerity and reform better than any government or agency in Europe. It has been criticised by authoritative economists, such as Joseph Stiglitz, for the economic orthodoxy on which its programmes are based, for the (Western) perspectives and interests embedded in its *modus operandi*, and for the harrowing outcomes of austerity in a number (though by no means all) of its client countries.[15]

Having said that, it is well used to taking the political heat for ineffectual governments. It has transparent internal review processes, from operational missions to board reviews. It also has a smooth-as-silk evaluation process and monitoring routine, and possesses a distinctive 'toolkit' through which it carries out its tasks—including devaluation, privatisation, and conditionality (including structural adjustment and tax reform). All of this was put at risk by its participation in the Troika. The IMF was essentially catapulted into a relationship with the ECB and the EC, and possessed a mandate and methodological approach to adjustment that was wholly out of sync with them. While it has always eschewed overt politicisation, its participation in the Troika corroded its independence and foundational mission—at no small cost. The collaboration could not have been thought through. From the start, the three institutions had different cultures and mandates, with different modes of operation, different technical assumptions, and different mind-sets. Paradoxical as it seems given the IMF's right-wing reputation, in both Ireland and Greece it was the European institutions which were the embodiment of Troikanomics—pushing for further austerity and political control.

[15] See, for example, Stiglitz (1992). See also Stiglitz (2016) for an insightful critique on the Euro and its consequences.

In the latter stages of the Troika's Greece mission, as we note elsewhere, the IMF withdrew from operational involvement having had its advice rejected by the EU—an anomaly that has received far too little attention. The IMF demonstrated its independence and credibility in its engagement with Ireland, where it advocated against the harshness of the ECB and also acknowledged that burning certain categories of bondholders might make a much less onerous burden for Ireland. And it did so in Greece where it refused to participate in the Third Bailout Programme, in the face of German and EU obduracy in refusing to engage with debt relief. Alongside this, in the lead-up to the Irish crisis it dropped informal hints to the Irish authorities that it was available for advice and to possibly fund a programme on 'stand-by' terms, available to those countries whom they believe are heading in the right direction.

Crucially, the IMF would normally have looked at external balance and the exchange rate. But devaluation aimed at increasing the competiveness of member nations' external position was, by definition, ruled out. What would have been a sensible option for a country in crisis was precluded for countries that ceded control over their Central Banks to the ECB but, in one of those paradoxes embedded in the Eurozone, simultaneously used it to threaten Greece with Grexit—*albeit* that Grexit would, in our view, have been the better option compared to what was ultimately imposed on Greece. Internal IMF protocols relating to the scope of lending were undermined, leading to some disenchantment among staff. Its preferred policies in relation to the pivotal issue of debt relief for Greece were ignored by the ECB/EC, with disastrous and ongoing consequences.

However, the EU and Troikanomics took the IMF outside of its own specialised domain and, for the first time, drew it into the realm of politics. It was an error of judgement—one over which the IMF had little control.[16] This raises issues for the EU, not alone of conditionality but also of morality. Indeed, when the IMF disapproves so strongly of the EU's economic policies for Greece that they went so far as to disengage

[16] Again, note the IMF's Report on Greece (2013), which states that '[w]ith regard to Fund involvement, it would have been better if the crisis could have been resolved within the EU/Eurozone, but neither the authorities nor the EC or ECB had the required programme experience. The Funds experience in crisis resolution made it a necessary part of the process'.

from any financial participation, it held up a mirror to the EU and its deployment of the Troika.

These issues are not, it must be pointed out, of recent origin. In 2013/2014, the European Parliament sent a delegation to peripheral countries that had received a Bailout in order to consider the impact of austerity on economies and social solidarity. In its Report (2014) the Committee noted that Greek Public Debt was 148% in 2010 and that 'austerity seems to have made the situation worse', with the ratio rising to 176% by 2013 and expected to decline to 170% by 2015. It did not—in 2018 it stands at approximately 180%. Alongside this, GDP had contracted for six years in a row and unemployment had soared. They went on to note that '[s]ince 2010 the Greek people have taken to the streets many times to protest cuts in pensions and salaries as well as the deterioration of health and other social services as a result of austerity'.

The comments of the President of the European Parliament, Martin Schulz, when he visited Greece in February 2012 are especially striking. He noted that '[a]s representatives of the peoples of Europe, we are convinced that budgetary consolidation must not imperil social justice', adding that the European Parliament had been consistent in advocating solidarity and a balanced mix of measures that included debt reduction as well as growth initiatives. Schulz's comments were three years *before* the Greek people finally voted for radical change. The European Parliament's commendable Report was two years prior to the most contentious EU summit meeting in recent history, full of anger and division at which still further austerity was imposed on Greece. Indeed, to avail of the final tranche of the third Bailout in June 2018, Greece was required to impose more austerity measures.

The point here is that the views of the European Parliament made no difference whatsoever to the Troika's treatment of Greece. It also, of course, cast a cold eye on respect for democracy within the EU itself, much less in its members. Notably, some 2–3 years after all of this there was no mention of 'social justice' or a 'balanced mix of policies'—much less debt relief—when Greece and the dominant powers of the EU sat across the table in Brussels in June 2015. In the Greek Government's 2018 post-bailout proposals there is still little or no scope for 'growth initiatives' that will make any appreciable difference to living standards.

The EC—the Civil Service that manages the EU—was the third participant of the Troika. The leadership of the EU is an institutional elite and manifestly politicised—and therefore focused on consolidating and projecting power. Mr Jean-Claude Juncker was President of the Commission for the majority of the crisis. For most of the latter period of his career Mr Juncker was immersed in the institutional minutiae of the European Project, committed to a Federal Europe, and latterly to the militarisation of Europe. Adviser and Head of the Commission, he exercises enormous influence. The appointment in 2019 of the next President of the Commission will mark a new phase of engaging with the multidimensional narrative that is Europe's existential crisis. The management of the Debt Crisis, encompassing the cult of Troikanomics, have generated an enormous extension of the Commission's powers of 'enforcement'. But they failed to advocate for the social dimension of the European Project during the crisis and in its aftermath.

When it mattered most—when the pressures on societies across Europe, arising from the crisis, were at their most acute—the EU prioritised defending the Conventional Wisdom over radically championing for rehabilitative social justice. It was the IMF—not the EC—that advocated against the impact of Troikanomics on the lives of people and for the welfare of the people of Ireland and Greece. From the EU's perspective, Social Economy is of course an established *national* competence. The EC subverted the capabilities of member nations to protect their own countries. It did so by eroding their autonomy and capacity to take responsibility for the welfare of their citizens while *simultaneously* garnering an enormous increase in power for itself from different interventions. It dismissed protests as right-wing (or left-wing) 'Populism'. In Greece, the EC missed entirely what was so obvious to the IMF as early as 2013: namely, that the impact of what we define as Troikanomics on society was causing enormous stress and pushing voters towards political extremes. It effectively ignored, as we have noted, the findings of the Report by the European Parliament (2014b) on the impact of the Troika on Greece.[17]

[17] In the words of the Prime Minister of Poland, Beata Szydlo, speaking at the EU Summit in Brussels in October 2017, '[t]he EU's principle of respect for the rights of its citizens will cease to be an empty one only when the debate about the future of the European Union takes place with the participation of all concerned, not in three or four capitals' (cited in Kelly and Sobczak 2017).

The EC, once considered to be an ally of smaller nations, lives in the rarefied atmosphere of high policy—of 'Semesters' and 'Six Packs'; of 'Initiatives' and 'Communications'. Participation in the Troika programme can, arguably, be seen as contravening the objectivity and independence of the EC.[18] What the people of Europe wanted was for the EC to have their back in their struggle into the headwinds of an enormous economic and social crisis. It did not—and it lost the support of the people who count. Disillusionment with 'Europe' is now widespread.[19] The terms on which Greece 'exited' its Bailout in June 2018 demonstrate that inequality only too well. It is a question that abides: how was it that in an existential crisis in peripheral, highly indebted countries, the establishment was still fixated by 'State Aid' and 'convergence criteria' rather than by what is now sinking in—that their role was to advocate for the people of Europe in a crisis generated by a flawed orthodoxy (both sovereign and banking)—and from which the 'rent seekers' within the economy profited. All of this resonates the deep divisions and tensions at the heart of the EU's crisis of 'identity' and the deepest questions of philosophy: *'Who am I? What is my purpose?'* It is, therefore, for the new post-2019 Commission to address this issue and for voters in the European Parliament to reflect on the candidates, and the groupings, that articulate these questions.

## The Troika in Action: Supremacy and Subversion

The Troika set a precedent in the extent to which vulnerable Eurozone members were expected to acquiesce to the demands of EU authorities out of desperation for a reprieve from the imminent risk of sovereign default. On paper, adherence to the 'Memorandum of Understanding'—the formal agreement between the Troika's participating institutions and

[18] Here, Soares (2015) points out that the Troika appeared to act in a 'subordinate position'.

[19] Fernandes and Rinaldi (2016) note that '[t]he economic and sovereign debt crisis—and the response to it, which largely consisted of fiscal consolidation—highlighted the imbalance between the economic and social dimensions of the European Project'.

the government of the state that was seeking assistance—was a collaborative process. In practice, the 'insights' provided by the Troika were not recommendations, they were strict *requirements*. The Memorandum was based on an audit of the available data—with each of the Troika's members having their own sources of information. The lens of critique was focused firmly on the macroeconomic infrastructure and practices of the *individual* countries (e.g. property and construction 'bubbles' in Ireland and Spain, dysfunctional tax practices in Greece).

The important point is this: the Troika's capacity to insist on the conditions for financial assistance far outweighed the bargaining powers of the countries that were bailed out—an asymmetry that reflected the preexisting imbalances in the burden of adjustment between surplus and deficit countries. The Troika's executive decision-making capacities and their unwillingness to consider any form of compromise was a key factor in the undermining of nations' autonomous capacities.[20] Peter A. Hall (2016) points to the paradoxical nature of the policies and practices of the EU at this time. The fact that Eurozone Heads of Government met so regularly over this period (54 times between January 2010 and August 2015) implied that perhaps the crisis had ushered in an era of renewed sovereign collaboration. The reality of these meetings was, however, a very different matter. In effect, the Troika occupied dual status as protagonist and antagonist, largely displacing member countries' own national parliament. The practical impact of Troikanomics was thus to impose on debtor countries the single greatest economic and social dislocation in the EU's history.

Every country locked into debt crisis must have regard to the 'fiscal gap'—that is, state expenditure relative to sustainable revenue—including social entitlements and structural rigidities impacting on productivity. The Bailout nations were impacted by a lack of access to liquidity as well as the costs of recapitalisation of their banking system. By ceding to the ECB the option to devalue, they were impelled, instead, into a repressive 'internal devaluation'. The Troika's strategy—like that of the major banks that had caused the crisis—was fixated on short-termism. Ireland was pressurised not to 'burn' bank bondholders who had made bad decisions for fear that the European banks might be impacted—leaving instead the costs to be absorbed by present and future Irish taxpayers. In

[20] See, for example, Antonio Goucha Soares (2015).

Cyprus, domestic customers found their deposits were effectively sequestered. In Greece, a swath of public assets were in essence seized by the Troika to act as collateral for loans by European financial institutions that should not have been made.

The targets for the Troika included indiscriminate 'cuts' to areas of a country's economic infrastructure that are bound up with social outputs: wages, working hours, healthcare, social expenditure, and so on. Countries' capacity to adjust to the ongoing wider crisis, while simultaneously having to service new debt/austerity repayments, was intensely onerous and oppressive. What seems clear, notably in the case of Greece, was that reforms were geared towards enhancing the repayment of bailout finances and 'rent-seeking'—only a small proportion of the first two Bailouts went to Greece to support the economy or to mitigate severe poverty. This created a one-dimensional metric through which to oversee the implementation of the Troika's measures. There was no critique of their impact. The requirement for countries to privatise and to dispose of national assets to overseas institutions, including 'vulture funds', was regressive and an affront to their autonomy and national interests.

Debt is not *in principle* a 'bad guy'. If complemented by a capacity to sustainably repay such debt and to use it as a catalyst to incentivise growth beyond iterative/organic levels, then it can be economically efficient and justifiable. Resentment towards the Troika was however still inevitable—a naturally occurring expression of each country's yearning to exercise their autonomous capacities and retain their national sovereignty. We highlight this point in our Case Study on Ireland. Such opposition does not, and should not—*in itself*—constitute legitimate grounds upon which to question the measures of the Troika. It depends on where the responsibility to order such measures remains and whether the aims are to protect the best interests of the public or, alternatively, external as well as domestic commercial institutions who took excessive risks and socialised them by transferring them to the citizens of broken-backed economies.

One of the defining characteristics of the Troika was its unaccountability to the people of the countries on whom it imposed its *fiat*—spanning the political, legal, and ethical mandates that should have underpinned its form and function within the EU. Authority and accountability go hand in hand. Democratic consensus grants those who are elected with the authority to (ideally) exercise the will of the people, and to be held accountable for their decisions. The Troika were unaccountable for the actual and prospective social and economic fallout from their decisions. Compounding this, the Commission attempted to discard accountability for the decisions taken during the financial assistance process.[21] This, of course, goes against the fact that the 'decisions' undertaken by the debtor countries were made under duress. If the Troika are to be recognised for positive outcomes of their programmes, then it should also assume responsibility for the 'scarring' of their actions on the wider populous. The Troika did not possess the status of a European Institution, exercised no formal legal mandate, and operated outside the pre-established provisions of the EU law. The irony of this is that the very purpose of the financial assistance measures was to shore up defence against the potential breakup of the monetary union. And yet the measures undertaken to accomplish this task were inherently undermining the status of those member countries that it ostensibly was charged to protect.

The legacy, direct and indirect, of Troikanomics has been to fragment the unity of what was initially conceived of as a 'community' (and later a 'union')—a concept which remains the core *raison d'être* of the European Project. This union has been pressurised by tensions between the core, the periphery, and the eastern blocks—with further enlargement set to exacerbate these further. More generally, the Eurozone has become locked into asymmetrical relationships whereby decision-making is effectively monopolised in favour of stronger, surplus countries (specifically Germany, and to a lesser extent France and the Netherlands), while marginalising the influence of debtor countries. Authority has been leached from members, not so much to a 'pooled sovereignty', but to a centralised union the governance of which they are, to a greater or lesser extent, excluded from. National politicians no longer possess the political clout to fight their corner—an issue which lies at the heart of the 2018 budgetary stand-off between the new Italian government and the EU establishment.[22]

---

[21] On this point, see Soares (2015).

[22] When the Greek people finally elected a government that was opposed to seemingly endless austerity, the new government was told in the most emphatic terms by creditor countries that the outcome of their election counted for nothing—and so it proved.

Alongside the anti-democratic manner in which it came into existence, Troikanomics encompassed several policies that entrench inequality.[23] Another way of looking at this is that the focus of the Troika was on extracting payment from vulnerable debtor countries with scant regard to the responsibility of the dominant countries whose banking institutions enabled the problems.[24] This is the power imbalance that Troikanomics exposes; the social consequences have been deeply negative and underlined the disparity in living standards across the union; meanwhile, the business model of the financial institutions have remained largely unchanged—albeit under heavier regulatory pressures.[25]

How far was Troikanomics a success? It imposed corrective measures that contributed to a restoration of internal and external balance—although, as we have suggested elsewhere, the imbalance in the case of Greece continues to persist. This rebalancing exacted an enormous price for the debtor countries and for the whole concept of democratic accountability. It marked a new departure for Europe in terms of the imposition of brute political force. It laid bare key deficiencies in the architecture of EMU, since it exposed fundamental weaknesses in the ability of Europe to support balanced and symmetrical adjustment in the face of unexpected shocks.

In any event, for Troikanomics, the metrics of 'success' are opaque. They are a trade-off between conflicting demands and inconsistent ideologies—between the national interests of individual debtor countries and the political agenda of the larger dominant countries. Success for debtor nations, for example, would be a return to internal and external balance without sacrificing their decisional and volitional autonomy. Success for the Troika, for example, involved the primacy of the survival of the EMU, with all of its deficiencies, and exacting repayment from debtor countries impacted, at least in part, by the disparities that existed between them and surplus countries

[23] Here, Tokarski (2014) notes that the most prominent message from the EU Parliament's Report on the Troika (2014) is that fiscal austerity *in and of itself* is not a sufficient mechanism for reform, and must be accompanied by *political* commitment.

[24] In the case of Ireland, see, for example, the blog of Diarmuid O'Flynn of the 'Ballyhea Says No' campaign—an insightful source which continues to highlight the ongoing costs imposed on Ireland, and documents the extent of these costs.

[25] See, for example, Cavero and Poinasamy (2013).

## References


Aizenman, J. (2016). *Optimal Currency Area: A 20th Century Idea for the 21st Century?* [Online]. Retrieved from http://www.nber.org/papers/w22097.pdf

Bénéton, P., Brague, R., Delsol, C., Joch, R., András, L., Legutko, R., Manent, P., Matlary, J. H., Pavón, D. N., Scruton, R., Spaemann, R., & Jan Spruyt, B. (2017). *The Paris Statement: A Europe We Can Believe in*. [Online]. Retrieved from https://thetrueeurope.eu/a-europe-we-can-believe-in/

Blyth, M. (2013). *Austerity: The History of a Dangerous Idea*. Oxford: Oxford University Press.

Cavero, T., & Poinasamy, K. (2013). *A Cautionary Tale: The True Cost of Austerity and Inequality in Europe*. Oxford: Oxfam GB.

Eurogroup. (2018). *Eurogroup Statement on Greece of 22 June 2018*. [Online]. Retrieved from http://www.consilium.europa.eu/en/press/press-releases/2018/06/22/eurogroup-statement-on-greece-22-june-2018/

European Commission. (2017). *Reflection Paper on the Deepening of the Economic and Monetary Union*. Brussels: European Commission.

European Parliament. (2014a). *Role and Operations of the Troika with Regard to the Euro Area Programme*. Brussels: The European Parliament.

European Parliament. (2014b). *Greece: Troika Success Story or a Warning Against too Much Austerity?* [Online]. Retrieved from http://www.europarl.europa.eu/news/en/headlines/eu-affairs/20140129STO34108/greece-troika-success-story-or-a-warning-against-too-much-austerity

Fagan, G., & Gaspar, V. (2007). *Adjusting to the Euro*. Frankfurt: European Central Bank.

Fernandes, S., & Rinaldi, D. (2016). *Is There Such a Thing as "Social Europe"?* s.l.: Jacque Delors Institute.

Hall, P. A. (2016). The Euro Crisis and the Future of European Integration. In BBVA (Ed.), *The Search for Europe: Contrasting Approaches* (pp. 46–67). Madrid: BBVA.

International Monetary Fund. (2013). *Greece: Ex Post Evaluation of Exceptional Access Under the 2010 Stand-By Arrangement*. Washington, DC: International Monetary Fund.

Juncker, J.-C. (2017). Authorised Version of the State of the Union Address 2017. In European Commission (Ed.), *State of the Union 2017* (pp. 5–22). Brussels: European Commission.

Karanikolos, M., et al. (2013). Financial Crisis, Austerity, and Health in Europe. *The Lancet, 381*(9874), 1323–1331.

Kelly, L., & Sobczak, P. (2017). *Polish PM Calls for an EU Where Christianity Is Not Censored.* [Online]. Retrieved from https://www.reuters.com/article/us-eu-poland-christianity/polish-pm-calls-for-an-eu-where-christianity-is-not-censored-idUSKBN1D92D3

Kentikelenis, A., et al. (2011). Health Effects of Financial Crisis: Omens of a Greek tragedy. *The Lancet, 378*(9801), 1457–1458.

Kentikelenis, A., et al. (2014). Greece's Health Crisis: From Austerity to Denialism. *The Lancet, 383*, 748–753.

Kinsella, R. (2012). *EMU's Biggest Threat Is Political Contagion.* [Online]. Retrieved from https://www.omfif.org/analysis/commentary/2012/june/emus-biggest-threat-is-political-contagion/

Kinsella, R., & Kinsella, M. (2009). Ethical Causes and Implications of the Global Financial Crisis in Ireland: Political Contagion and Political Transformation. *Studies: An Irish Quarterly Review, 98*(391), 285–308.

Krugman, P. (2012). Revenge of the Optimum Currency Area. *NBER Macroeconomics Annual, 27*(1), 439–448.

Munchaü, W. (2018). *Eurozone Downturn and Lack of Reform Presage Existential Crisis.* s.l.: The Financial Times.

Soares, A. G. (2015). EU Commission Participation in the Troika Mission: Is There a European Union Price to Pay? *Revista Brasileira de Política Internacional, 58*(1), 108–126.

Stiglitz, J. E. (1992). *Globalization and Its Discontents.* New York: W. W. Norton & Company.

Stiglitz, J. E. (2016). *The Euro: How a Common Currency Threatens the Future of Europe.* New York: W. W. Norton & Company.

Tett, G. (2018). *Risk? It's Probably That Thing You're Ignoring.* s.l.: The Financial Times.

Tokarski, P. (2014). *The European Parliament's Assessment of the Troika: Good Points, Bad Timing.* s.l.: The Polish Institute of International Affairs.

von Schwichow, L. (2013). *The EU's Existential Crisis.* [Online]. Retrieved February 18, 2018, from https://eu.boell.org/sites/default/files/uploads/2013/12/the_eu_s_existential_crisis.pdf

# Part III

## Autonomy and the EU Experience

# 6

# Autonomy Within the EU: A Relational Perspective

## Introduction

To what extent am I truly in control of the direction in which my life is heading? Is the path on which I am currently travelling the product of manipulative forces, of which I may not even be fully aware? How can I ensure, amidst such uncertainties, that I am exercising my decisional and volitional capacities to the fullest extent possible? Questions such as these are what orient contemporary philosophical perspectives on the concept of personal autonomy. In much the same way that our analysis on the EU's existential crisis draws on insights from the field of existential psychology and philosophy that pertain to *individual persons*, so too do the insights within our current discussion draw on philosophical perspectives on personal autonomy (in particular 'relational' models). Once again, we are careful not to conflate the 'personal' realm with the 'political' realm of nations and international communities. Nevertheless, as a reflective tool for critique, the insights offered by this field of philosophical inquiry hold much merit in terms of furthering our understanding of why autonomy is so existentially indispensable to the prospering of individual nations. This is the case, in particular, with respect to members of the EU, whose autonomy is so thoroughly intertwined with their larger community.



R. Kinsella, M. Kinsella, *Troikanomics*, https://doi.org/10.1007/978-3-319-97070-7_6

In this context, autonomy, as a form of self-law ('*auto-nomos*'), can be conceptually excavated in two distinct yet related ways. Firstly, from a *philosophical* perspective, it is a concept that contributes towards our understanding of the sociopolitical ontology of nations and their attendant sovereign status—out of which flows normative and legislative requirements. Secondly, from a *practical* perspective, it is the iteratively realised capacity that encompasses taking ownership not just over specific decisions and actions, but over a broader national narrative: to govern in accordance with justifications and motivations that are authentically the nation's own, rather than the product of coercive forces.[1] To address the question 'what path do we wish to carve out for ourselves as a nation?' therefore first necessitates answering, even to a limited degree, '*who are we* as a nation?' The goal of autonomy is, in this instance, to recognise and give expression to this insight—to progressively *become oneself amongst others* and, aligned with this, construct a national narrative that is both authentic and meaningful.

## Autonomy: A Relationally Fostered Capacity

Philosophy has a vital role to play in successfully navigating transnational relationships—demanding a *critical* approach towards the relational 'givens' that are so often perpetuated by the dominant and feared by the dependent. Accordingly, our analysis serves as both a *descriptive* and *prescriptive* device. From a descriptive perspective, our model frames national autonomy as an intrinsic, multidimensional, and relational capacity. Through clarifying autonomy's constitutive attributes and the role that it plays within the communal fabric of the EU, the goal is that we can more firmly ground the EU's attendant obligations towards its members' autonomy. Alongside this, it therefore provides *prescriptive* insights, informing the EU on how it may ensure, in practice, that members' autonomy is

[1] This definition is derived from Christman's (2015) introductory discussion on the constitutive components of personal autonomy—one in which he attempts to bring together, *in an introductory fashion*, general philosophical consensus on the concept. It is the inherent broadness of this definition (as distinct from the definition that he himself develops) that, for him, leaves it open to so much critical analysis and establishes it as such a fertile ground for philosophical debate.

fostered. In this context, it is essential that the EU retain its commitment to communally-rooted values—encompassed broadly in their relational stance, as well as in specific mandates such as solidarity and subsidiarity.

Expanding on our earlier summary, briefly, we hold autonomy to be the capacity for 'effective self-definition', that is, iteratively moving towards a sense of clarity and coherence in *who one is* as a nation and affirming this understanding within one's national pursuits—both domestic and foreign.[2] This expresses itself in the process of 'becoming oneself among others'. In our model, autonomy is exercised in degrees through the coming together of three autonomous capacities: self-governance, self-determination, and self-affirmation. *Self-governance* is a nation's capacity to critically engage with, and respond to, the range of characteristics that constitute its 'domestic identity'. *Self-determination* is a nation's capacity to critically engage with, and respond to, the range of characteristics comprising its transnational environment. *Self-affirmation* is a nation's capacity to trust in its own legitimacy as an autonomous entity—encompassing its right to affirm and be answerable for 'who they are' amidst a multitude of other nations.[3,4]

Relational' perspectives assert that autonomous agency can only be fully comprehended—and therefore successfully endeavoured towards—when 'embeddedness' is taken into account i.e. when autonomy is seen as a capacity that is nurtured (or indeed, as is so often the case, *impeded*)

[2] Our concept of 'self-definition' draws on Christman's (2014) work on the concept of 'self-narrative' and seeks to depict the experience of a historically cohesive security in 'who one is'.

[3] Here we make brief, provisional, reference to another concept of relevance for geopolitical communities, 'sovereignty'. We argue that autonomy is a necessary condition for national sovereignty, that is, before a nation can be regarded as ascending to the rank of a transnationally recognised sovereign—one that is both legally and normatively authorised to exercise ownership over their decisions—they must first be capable of autonomous functioning. Consistent with the relational model of autonomy, we therefore argue that sovereignty is also relational, born from recognising a nation's inherent autonomy. This perspective takes into consideration national interdependence—whereby sovereignty is drawn from both exercising autonomous capacities *alongside* its standing in relation to other sovereign nations. Sovereignty is therefore a product of the coexistence of, and engagement between, autonomous nations. For further insights, see de Benoist (1999) and Krasner (1999). Here also, Frigot and Bonadonna (2016) discuss the 'post-modern' view of sovereignty that highlights the cooperative nature to sovereignty within the community.

[4] This model draws on Kinsella (2015).

through the nature of ongoing relationships.[5] Consequently, it is a capacity that is progressively realised *amongst* others, as opposed to being in a state of radical extrication *from* others. This means that nations' geopolitical and economic interactions (as are apparent, in this context, in their membership of the EU) are not simply 'external' events to be navigated, but are internalised and imbue consequences that reverberate throughout the political, economic, and social fabric of the nation itself. Inasmuch as autonomy is an intrinsic capacity that each nation holds *in and of themselves* (i.e. prior to joining larger communities), the role of the EU is not to *instil* the capacity for autonomy itself, but to help create an environment in which members can more fully recognise and realise their autonomous capacities. This can be achieved in a number of ways, such as through the egalitarian and participatory dialogue that emerges when principles such as solidarity and subsidiarity are upheld.

Every country believes that they have a claim on autonomy—that their capacity to exercise ownership over their nation's trajectory is a *right* that should be legally upheld in the treaties, policies, and provisions that constitute their transnational relationships. Autonomy is central not just to taking ownership over the *specific* actions that they perform (their 'local' autonomy) but also to being a directive force in their own deeper unfolding narrative (their 'global' autonomy). This quest for autonomy thus serves as a motivational force. Countries are impelled towards it by nature, often stumbling; sacrifice, patience, resolve, all are called upon in this enduring journey. We find evidence of this quest in the manifestos of their politicians, in their democratic representativeness, in the economic niches they carve out for themselves, in the symbolism of flags and national anthems, in the companionship that comes after national tragedy, and in the pride that comes with national success. Each of these are, in their own way, expressions of this impetus towards not just taking ownership over one's national identity, but taking ownership over the *nation one wishes to become*.

[5] Dworkin's influential analysis (1988) plants the seeds concerning the extent to which we need to understand autonomy—and how it is fostered—as embedded in the interpersonal and temporally extended realities of social ontology.

A difficulty with journeying towards autonomy is that it is, at one and the same time, so valuable to the development and welfare of nations, and yet so deeply vulnerable to being undermined in a variety of ways. The complex communal tapestry within which members of the EU are interwoven can therefore both enable and impede them in reaching more optimal levels of functioning. Given that international communities, such as the EU, consistently struggle to stave off internal conflict (through means such as cooperation, compromise, and consolidation), national autonomy should not be seen as a realistic aspiration in any *'radical'* sense. Instead, it is achieved through negotiating the opportunities and constraints that communal participation brings with it—making the most of one's place in the community. While autonomy may be a worthy 'ideal' to strive towards, the *reality* of autonomy can therefore only be accomplished in a 'non-ideal' sense—always balanced between forces that nations are capable of maintaining control of and those that are beyond their grasp.[6] Therefore, while the full and unimpeded expression of nations' autonomy is not possible, the EU *should still* strive to create an environment within which their autonomous capacities can progressively be more fully recognised and realised.

In this context, it is important not to confuse autonomy with substantive independence, which would imply that participation in formal transnational relationships (be they bilateral or multilateral ) would necessitate the *sacrifice* of autonomy. This perspective could create an uneasy dialectic, namely that independence breeds autonomy and community breeds heteronomy. As discussed, the crux of the relational perspective is that a hard-line 'trade-off' between these two *seeming* polarities fails to do justice to the fact that dialogue is central to the fostering of autonomy. The oft-idealised goal of substantive independence is, in this reading, therefore rejected as being increasingly unworkable and counter to the growing interconnectivity between nations within communities such as the EU (as is apparent in trade relationships and labour mobility). Due to broader factors such as globalisation, communications technologies, and pervasive multinational corporates, the increased enmeshment of nations within their wider geopolitical tapestry is set to continue. The important point here is that *being-in-community* should not displace the inherent right that

[6] For further insights on this point, see Christman (2009a, 2009b).

nations have to exercise their autonomy, nor their capacity to do so. Rather, it places on their communities the responsibility to be attentive to the fostering of this ability and the upholding of this right.

Conventional Wisdom asserts that globalisation makes autonomy redundant—either as an achievement or an aspiration. This is, however, a clever piece of sophistry and fails to acknowledge the role that autonomy continues to play in mediating international relations, and their *very real* legal/normative underpinnings. It is a loaded argument that, for example, attempts to set a precedent upon which large transnational institutions, in *shadow* duopolistic relationships with multinational companies, are established. It is also pernicious to the relational view of autonomy because it leaches away the proper responsibilities of sovereign governments without safeguarding the scope for vindicating principles, such as subsidiarity, that draw on the internal capacities of nations. Troikanomics—in design and in its mode of enforcement—is a near perfect example of this leaching. This moves the conversation even further from national democratic authority and accountability, towards institutional oversight.

Autonomy does not call for 'external' political/economic relations to be necessarily rejected by a country, but rather that these countries express a degree of *ownership* when engaged in their relationships. Here, autonomy is very much distinguished from 'autarky', whereby external relations are not *in themselves* sufficient for a country's autonomous status to be compromised. If anything—as the very aspiration to partake in the EU attests to—relationships can be an essential means through which autonomy is fostered. In this context, participation in the EU—as a community that is constitutive of, but not reducible to, its sovereign members—can act as a catalyst for countries to express their autonomous capacities through the discovery and sharing of their capacities and strengths.[7] Participation in the EU is therefore not an autonomy-neutral endeavour; it can lead to both positive and negative consequences—dependent on the nature of the relationships that it fosters. For example, national policies may need

[7] The concept of 'catalysed' is used to distinguish the process through which autonomy is fostered from that by which it is 'created'. In this way, autonomy is an inherent capacity to be exercised through the utilisation of prior capacities, rather than something that is bestowed by one's external environment.

to be implemented with European cooperation, in compliance to European mandates, or in conjunction with established directives, for example, providing a percentage of national budget to the EU, adhering to energy regulations, or operating within monetary mandates.

In order to remain tethered to its foundational values and mission, the EU is required to be consistently mindful that the environment it helps to create will be internalised by their members—including the opportunities and constraints that emerge from it. This necessitates working towards a community that consists of a *shared democratic dialogue*—bringing to the fore the importance of re-patriating the decision-making powers that have been progressively syphoned off to Brussels back to national parliaments. In practice, the sensitivity of the EU orthodoxy to this understanding was negated by both the form and substance of Troikanomics and a denial of its real-world consequences in what is caricatured as 'Populism'.

Looking at the EU as a community necessitates a rethinking of how autonomy is upheld *in practice*. In this regard, democratic inclusiveness ensures that members' decisional and volitional resources are respected and valued rather than being jettisoned *in lieu* of oppressive forms of oversight and interventionism. An awareness of these considerations in the *realpolitik* of political engagement can enhance autonomy, while simultaneously animating interdependence.

If we look briefly at the foundational vision and values of the EU, two concepts have remained central to the ongoing construction of its narrative: solidarity and subsidiarity. These values can serve as *relational dispositions* (in keeping with the practice of democratic inclusiveness) through which the EU can provide nations with the opportunity to pursue their autonomous ambitions, secured within the European umbrella.[8] Autonomy's status as relationally rooted can be more fully attended to through solidarity that provides nations with transparent and supportive relationships to engage in. Autonomy's status as an inherent capacity can be more fully attended to through subsidiarity that provides nations with opportunities to exercise their various capacities.[9]

[8] For further insights, see Raspotnik et al. (2012).

[9] We discuss the concepts of solidarity and subsidiarity in greater detail in Chap. 8.

## Autonomy and the Quest for European Integration

Over the past 25 years, the EU has felt impelled to push forward with grand schemes, including EMU, as a means of consolidating integration. The radically increased scope and scale of intervention has brought with it ever greater risks towards member nations' autonomy. This process is central to what we define as the EU's existential crisis, for which Troikanomics is both a metaphor and substantive component. Part of the problem is this: the 'core' countries have retained an actual and presumptive control. They have not attempted to forge a form of integration that *explicitly* acknowledges national autonomy's intrinsic or relational status, or indeed the extent to which it enriches the wider Union. We have considered different forms of asymmetries; now consider this one: 'ever closer union' has impelled integration *as an inevitable end in itself*—not unlike riding a bicycle where simply turning the pedals is deemed to be more important than reflecting on what destination you are travelling towards.

So, for example, after the epic achievement of the single market—one whose internal logic and economic benefits constituted a positive sum game—the impulse was to keep the pedals turning and create a single currency. Its merit would be derived from not just whether it was viable *in principle*, but depended on how it was constituted *in practice*. Creating a single currency was a formidable technical and operational achievement. However, a single currency is not the same thing as a single market and entails the ceding by member nations of certain capacities, for example, setting interest rates or currency valuations. This means that it was not simply an operational matter of printing and distributing notes and coins; it was a profound *philosophical* matter—bearing directly on the identity of all participating countries and their capacity to discharge their own duties towards their citizens.

The form, mandate, and management of an ECB was shaped by France and Germany. Germany's 'red line' related to the mandate of the proposed Central Bank—that is, the Bundesbank's focus on price stability had to be transposed to the new institution. In reality, Germany's fears arising from the inflationary episode of its past—an existential experience if ever there was one—pre-empted what was needed for the future, not just of Germany but of a much wider set of countries. When the Banking and Debt Crisis struck Europe, the response was dictated by a mandate that prioritised price stability. By contrast, as we have previously argued, the dual mandate of the US Fed which embraces employment *and* price stability empowered the Fed to respond more quickly and flexibly. The ECB was left floundering, contriving a response that took longer and failed to go straight to the heart of the matter.

Importantly, the journey towards integration was kept going *as an end in itself*, rather than with a view to accomplishing normative social ends. Central Banks ceded control of their exchange rate and currencies to the ECB. They did not reflect on whether the single currency was engineered in such a way as to be 'fit for purpose' in *the event of a systemic crisis*. It wasn't—a deeply costly oversight to the architects' drawings. There was an implied assumption that it could be the next part of 'ever closer union'. This was the equivalent of saying 'that's okay, we will get the house insurance sorted later'. The consequence was a scramble across the Eurozone to do something—anything—to buy time to deal with structural and functional deficiencies which really should have been anticipated and provided for. In that respect, the mistake made by the architects of the EMU shares similarities with those that were made by Greece and Ireland, that is, an assumption that 'it will be alright on the night'. It was a catastrophic oversight; the autonomous capabilities of member nations (for example, in the form of national Central Banks) had been sequestered, without having ensured that adequate 'optimum currency area' mechanisms were built in.

These issues extend into the sociopolitical realm. The European Court's ongoing efforts to elaborate on autonomous supranational norms have been buttressed—paradoxically—by an air of 'constitutional tolerance'.[10] Here, legal norms—such as the doctrines of direct effect, implied powers, and increasingly opaque enabling legislation—are providing a legislative basis upon which to legitimise further political integration. Alongside this, as noted by Czaputowicz (2014), various treaties

[10] The concept of 'constitutional tolerance' is discussed in greater detail by Lindseth (1999).

have been iteratively chipping away at the sovereignty of members. The Treaty of Maastricht, for example, solidified the principle of qualified majority voting, while the Treaties of Amsterdam and of Lisbon expanded 'co-decision' procedures between the Council and the European Parliament.

In this context, the Treaty of Lisbon bears reflecting on, so as to more fully articulate the latent anti-democratic instincts and mind-set of the European Institutions and elite—which were central to Troikanomics' subversion of political governance. In the 2008 Referendum on the Lisbon Treaty, the Irish people voted decisively against ratification. The Treaty itself was, as we have discussed, essentially a repackaging of the measures contained in a proposed Constitution for Europe—rejected by referenda in France (May 2005) and the Netherlands (June 2005). The decision was then taken to enact the same measures via the Treaty. Consulting the people by way of referenda is fraught with risk. For the EU establishment, governments who are temporary trustees of democratic rights and freedoms are often more malleable and 'clubbable' than voters.

The outcome of the referendum was a tectonic shock to the political mainstream in Ireland, and also to Brussels. It undoubtedly expressed the democratic will of the Irish people; however, to Brussels and to the establishment, it was not the 'right' result. Tellingly, the vituperative response, with multiple accusations that should not be repeated in polite company (and which also alleged that the result would make Ireland a political 'pariah' in Europe), resonates with the outcome of the Brexit referendum in the UK. Democratic institutions, such as elections and referendums, are laudable. But they are also a catalyst for reproaches and recriminations when voters presume to take a different view to the Conventional Wisdom.

In fact, there were common-sense reasons why the referendum was rejected. These had to do with issues such as the (well-founded, as it has turned out) threat to Irish neutrality, perceived EU threats to Ireland's 12.5% Corporate Taxation regime (which is at the heart of its Business Model), and concerns about prospective intervention by the EU in Ireland's social legislation. There was also the small matter of understanding a Treaty which amounted to a series of amendments to previous Treaties. What is equally significant is the instinctual response by the political mainstream in both Dublin and Brussels to lay responsibility for the outcome at the feet of the voters and campaigners rather than those who had produced an opaque and almost indecipherable Treaty as well as its failure to engage with the profound concerns for the lack of democratic accountability.

There was also a deeper reason. This had to do with what one authoritative political analyst, Dr Bruce Arnold, called 'a deep-seated public suspicion about the European Union and what it stands for…[and] widespread doubts about the levels of democracy espoused by Brussels. It seemed that the Commission, the Council of Ministers and the Bureaucracy…had a cool view about the nature and interpretation of democratic answerability and transparency. They insisted on it for member states…but many of the elements in what was demanded from past and future EU members did not apply to the central Government of the EU itself' (Arnold 2009).

The core responsibility of a sovereign government is to uphold the national interest and the essential ethos which is at the heart of its sovereignty. The temptation, especially among smaller countries whose establishment is dependent on the grace and favour of the hegemony, impels them in a rather different direction. The Irish government, embarrassed by the temerity of its voters, pleaded its case to Brussels for 'concessions' in the form of 'undertakings' on certain issues, including neutrality. These were attached as Annexes to the Lisbon Treaty. A second referendum (Lisbon II) was therefore held in 2009. The extent to which this was effectively a rejection of the will of the people as expressed in the outcome of the first referendum is a moot point. In the event, the voters did deliver the 'right' result for the Irish and EU establishment, as they had done a decade earlier when the Nice Treaty was also rerun.

It is difficult to avoid the sense that the true loyalty of the national establishments in the smaller EU countries is to the EU establishment, rather than to its citizenry (which runs counter to the allegiances of the citizenry—whose national loyalties continue to supersede those they hold towards the EU). The experiences of both Greece and Ireland support such a hypothesis. It is the gravitational pull of dependency. There was perhaps more than a hint of hubris in the fact that Lisbon I and Lisbon II formed the backdrop to Ireland's emerging financial and economic crisis, when the country was to experience the full extent of its dependency and the lack of democratic accountability within the EU in the form of the Troika.

With regard to events under the Troika, developments such as these were not simply about the emerging pre-eminence of non-national decision-makers, but about the granting of *preferential* status towards them—dramatically altering the balance of powers within the EU and radically shifting the locus of nations' autonomy. The reasoning behind this is questionable at best, and at least in part derives from a belief that rationalising the management of nations by sequestering their political autonomy is the most effective means of bringing them into line and dissuading 'deviant' behaviour. This can take on many forms, including delegating matters such as trade, legislation, and administration to 'foreign' bodies. This process has succeeded in legitimising the question as to whether we are even justified in regarding the nation state's own political sphere as being their default locus of autonomy.

Has the concept of a politically autonomous nation become antiquated, semi-detached from the lived reality of contemporary geopolitical embeddedness? It would appear, certainly, that the dual forces of supranational federalism and globalisation have ushered in a paradigm shift in how we understand transnational interconnectedness. The EU's precursor, the European Economic Community (EEC), was described by its founder Robert Schuman as midway between *confederalism*, which recognises the complete independence of states in an association, and *federalism*, which seeks to fuse them into a super-state.[11] Attempts to sate both sides of this dichotomy have, ultimately, led to a limbo where the EU appears to be both a confederation of national states and a federalist state—and yet not satisfactorily at either level.

A democratic government is, in principle, an expression of citizens' deliberative consent to placing a particular administration in a position of authority *over* and accountability *towards* them and their country. The seat that governments occupy is therefore continually vulnerable to losing the collective resolve and commitment from the majority that placed

[11] As Spolaore (2013) discusses, Federalism is by no means a new endeavour for Europe. From before the inception of the European Coal and Steel Company (ECSC), Winston Churchill (1946) had called for the creation of 'a kind of United States of Europe'.

them there. Their reign is often spent in a constant battle to be perceived as indispensable to the future prosperity of the country they preside over: to validate their 'democratic legitimacy'. At the heart of this question on democratic legitimacy is whether or not a government adequately expresses their citizens' democratic *will*.

From a normative perspective, the concept of 'legitimacy' is concerned with the 'in principle' justification and acceptance of authority and with the rightful exercise of power.[12] Implicit within this concept is the idea that in a democracy, an elected government effectively abides by foundational democratic principles in terms of how it acquires and discharges governance—where power is always balanced against accountability. We use the term '*effectively*' because the processing of legislation through a parliament by coercive powers like the Troika is duplicitous. If a government's democratic legitimacy rests on the extent to which they represent the will of the people, and recognise their accountability towards them, then it comes as no surprise that the transferral of decision-making authority from the internal domain of domestic government to international organisations raises deep concerns regarding the legitimacy of *both*. On the one hand, national governments have surrendered their decision-making capabilities; on the other hand, external bodies have progressively sought to sequester them.

## Autonomy and the Challenge of Troikanomics

So, how can the phenomenon of Troikanomics help us to better understand what 'national autonomy' is, including how it can be fostered within communities such as the EU? Here, in terms of the depth and scope of heteronomy that it has engendered—observable in its antecedents, manifestations, and consequences—it provides a timely means of articulating not only the specific ways in which autonomy is vulnerable, but also the *value* that it holds for nations.

In order to more deeply convey this point, we can broadly differentiate between two forms of autonomy: 'local' and 'global'. Local autonomy

[12] This is drawn from Flathman (2007) and de Búrca (1996) *cited in* Schneller (2010). See also Beetham (1991).

relates to the situation-specific enactment of autonomous capacities: exhibiting control over behaviours in certain circumstances.[13] Troikanomics, however, compromised a far broader *historically* significant range of capacities. In this context, 'global' autonomy refers to more than just the ability to perform particular tasks, and instead encompasses a holistic description of the agent themselves, one that conveys their *being* rather than purely their *doing*.[14] Our depiction of autonomy (evident in our tripartite model) takes account of its 'global'-rootedness—offering, we believe, the fullest expression of both the requirements of autonomy and its rewards.

Drawing on insights from the relational perspective on autonomy, we become more acutely aware of the degree to which impediments to fostering autonomy manifest themselves in more than simply the direct curtailing of *actions*. Rather, nations' freedom of 'will' (as opposed to just their freedom of 'action')—for example, in the belief that they had both the potential *for* and right *to* realise their autonomous capacities—is an altogether truer testament of what autonomy demands and what Troikanomics undermined. Analysis that only focuses on a behaviour *at a certain* point in time fails to fully appreciate that autonomy is underpinned by *historical* reflection. Building on this perspective, the autonomy of an act therefore reveals itself more so through the deliberative processes underpinning actions than in the act's specific *content*. To put this point in context, in the lead-up to the Bailout, while countries like Ireland and Greece may have fulfilled criteria for autonomy in a *situation-specific sense* by self-endorsing their actions (e.g. Ministers signing their names to the official Bailout requests), it is surely the case that they nevertheless may have *still* acted in a heteronomous fashion because the decisional process underpinning their actions had been commandeered by the 'external' forces of the Troika.[15]

[13] Here, Meyers (1987) argues that the 'all-or-nothing' perspective on personal autonomy is misguided. She consequently differentiates between 'local' autonomy (as the capacity to decide in particular circumstances) and 'programmatic' autonomy (as the capacity to decide more major life choices).

[14] See MacKenzie (2014).

[15] Here, 'diachronic' perspectives on personal autonomy assert that we can only truly take ownership over the motivations and justifications underpinning our behaviours if they are subject to *temporally extended* critique. Christman's 'authenticity' argument is important to note here. It

This, we believe, is a pivotally important distinction because it pulls back the 'veil' of democracy from what is, in reality, a more brutal process: the pervasive erosion of a country's 'global' autonomy. In other words, it is entirely possible to exhibit instances of 'local' autonomy through carrying out certain goal-directed behaviours, while at the same time experiencing the loss of 'global' autonomy. Often, in this context, micro isolated actions can still be undertaken to serve macro heteronomous needs—placing their status as 'autonomous' in jeopardy when contextualised within the broader ambit of the agent's motivations. Again, within the context of Troikanomics, 'debtor' countries' actions may be considered to be heteronomous because they possessed a profound discomfort with their decisions and questioned how authentically representative they were of either the will of their people or indeed of *who their nation was.*

In itself, austerity—which is a narrower form of what we define as Troikanomics—may be seen as a necessary (if demanding) form of rebalancing a country's national income and expenditure in the interests of medium-term sustainability.[16] The decisions as to what form this rebalancing takes are properly regarded as the responsibility of the country's democratic legislature reflecting the Common Good. So, for example, the decision by Ireland some 20 years prior to the crisis to implement a painful rebalancing of the economy was undertaken by the government in circumstances which upheld both 'local' and 'global' autonomy: responsibility remained at all times within the hands of the Irish Parliament. This is radically different to events that transpired under Troikanomics, where for Ireland and Greece there was a *de facto* sequestering of governance; here, the rebalancing process was externally imposed by forces that were not accountable to a representative democracy. Nor were such measures

---

asserts that an agent's actions are only authentic if the agent does not feel a negative judgement or negative emotional reaction towards them, after having critically reflected on the historical processes leading to their desire (Christman 2009a). In a moment of weakness or vulnerability, a person may 'identify' with their action (see Frankfurt's (1971) analysis), but it may nevertheless fail to be authentic because it is in conflict with their historical self-narrative. In succumbing to the dictates of the Troika, countries such as Ireland and Greece exhibited behaviours that they may have 'identified' with at that particular moment in time (perhaps due to a prevailing sense of desperation or defeat), but which they would find very difficult to stand by when placed against the backdrop of the longer historical narrative of their nation.

[16] This perspective is discussed in greater detail in Chap. 4.

taken in the interests of the Common Good; instead they were subservient to a concoction of political and financial interests. Consider also, for example, the proposal by the Dutch Government in September 2011 for a specially created EU Commissioner who would be given the power to take over the economy of a distressed member country.[17]

Troikanomics, therefore, manifests itself as a form of oppressive adjustment under external duress. This perspective is reinforced by purported 'collaboration' on the part of the country—through, for example, enacting legislation to legalise actions that are rubber-stamped by parliaments with no discussion or scope for amendment. This pretence of legitimacy serves only to compound the emasculation of a nation's 'global' autonomy and sovereignty. This has been borne out in numerous ways during the era of the Troika—embedded in its architecture and mind-set. The Troika was mandated to displace all national decision-making on budgetary policy (undermining countries' self-governance); exclude countries from the deliberative process that should underpin communities (undermining countries' self-determination); and enforce a culture of deference to, and dependency on, the EU (undermining countries' self-affirmation).

This process was disempowering, a period in which nations were constrained from acting on an internal reasoned response to their more authentic dispositions or the demands of their circumstances, but, rather, often in contradiction to their wider set of values, goals, and beliefs. The Troika became the determining ground for their behaviours, the fulcrum upon which their motivations and justifications were balanced. It is said that autonomy reflects a fit between who one *is* and what one *does*; in contrast, heteronomy is marked by a dissonance between the two.[18] The oppressive regime under the Troika resulted in nations walking *away* from a healthy relationship with themselves and a sense authenticity towards their behaviours, and instead *towards* this state of inner conflict.

While the EMU was recognised as an opportunity for each member to develop their inherent competitive strengths and their capacities to contribute to the wider community, Troikanomics diverted it from this foundational aspiration. The organisational framework of the EU as it currently stands—

[17] A broadly similar suggestion was floated, and again withdrawn, by former German Minister for Finance Wolfgang Schäuble.

[18] As discussed by Westlund (2015).

with an unapologetic emphasis on autocratic oversight—perpetuates an image of the Commission as the *sole* agent of community sustenance and cohesion, therefore undermining countries' self-directive capacities. The paradox here is that, while member nations ostensibly commune with each other under the umbrella of the EU, it is the EU itself that impedes the reanimation of this purposiveness of community. The irony here is that the EU receives its legitimacy, and attendant authority, precisely from this community.

## Troikanomics' Influence on the Tripartite Model of Autonomy

We now turn to a discussion on how the experience of Troikanomics has left its mark on each of the three autonomous capacities that nations possess, namely: self-governance, self-determination, and self-affirmation. Taken together, these constitute a holistic set of capacities through which a country takes ownership over and expresses what it means to be autonomous within the wider hinterland of its peers.

Self-governance is a nation's capacity to critically engage with, and respond to, the range of characteristics that constitute its 'domestic identity'. Their ability to exercise ownership over their distinctive attributes can reveal itself in many ways: in their constitution, their legislation, their budget i.e. the range of ways that they seek to engage with their citizens and are responsive to their democratic will. This capacity is a means through which to exercise ownership over, and accountability for, matters within their own borders. Governments should thus maintain vigilance in critiquing the causes and consequences of their decisions, and examine whether they are in fact a coherent expression of their domestic identity. Self-governance engenders a sense of authority that ensures there is a consistency between the freedoms and responsibilities enshrined in a country's directives, laws, and constitution, and their capacity to exercise these in practice.

The Banking and Debt Crisis, and the injunctions imposed by the Troika, was demonstrably opposed to the self-governance of debtor countries. In the case of Ireland, for example, its banking sector had already behaved in a manner that severely compromised the nation's autonomy—acting against the best interests of the country's status as a small open economy and of its citizens. Troika-controlled countries were deprived of substantive control over their public services e.g. healthcare, education, and soçial welfare. While national governments recognised the diminution of their executive powers (and the aligned vulnerabilities that this provoked), their hands were tied both by a lack of resources and by the coercive and dependent nature of their relationship with the Troika.

Countries under the *fiat* of the Troika lacked the internal instruments through which to counter the crisis in an effective manner drawing on their own capacities, which they had ceded to a hegemonistic EU. Troikanomics systematically undermined the principle of subsidiarity, removing countries' capacity to exercise discretion over their own affairs (consistent with the intrinsically cooperative nature of the EU) and discharge their responsibilities towards their citizens. Since neither devaluation nor default were feasible, countries were effectively trapped in a situation that diminished the autonomy and standing of their nation and over which they had no control. This was reflected, as we have noted, in the displacement of the national parliament's role and status as the preeminent forum within which budgets were formed and debated—shifting this instead into a complex decision-making process subservient to the agendas and self-interest of creditor/surplus countries. What also merits taking into account, and has been too little acknowledged, is the impact of mass emigration in debtor countries—for which Troikanomics was the catalyst. The exodus of a young and highly educated labour force has contributed to a severe drain on countries' intellectual capital and, by extension, their capacity for self-governance.

Self-determination is a nation's capacity to critically engage with, and respond to, its transnational environment—which is, in turn, influenced by the agendas, priorities, and behaviours of those entities with which it interacts. Self-determination constitutes the primary means through which a country participates in legitimate and authentic dialogue beyond one's national borders. It enables these and other interactions to be underpinned by a *critical* stance—mindful of the importance of preserving their distinctive identity. It is, for example, exemplified, in diplomatic endeavours and bilateral/multilateral trade relationships with other countries—those occasions where nations reach out towards others. Navigating the demands of their external environment requires nations to *respond* with a sense of political independence and integrity—to assert oneself and have one's say, rather than acquiesce to others or become sublimated by the sway of consolidation.[19] Importantly, therefore, self-determination is exercised to the extent that countries exhibit freedom not necessarily *from* external constraints, but the freedom to fashion an authentic response *to* such constraints should they arise (uninhibited by latent pressures).

The structure of the Troika—*effectively* operating outside the remits of established EU practices and mandates—was not subject to the same degrees of democratic deliberation that would come with instituting any other transnational organisation. As an 'external' body, its relationship with domestic governments should properly have been grounded in a transparent and collaborative dialogue. The language and mode of enforcement of Troikanomics was, to this extent, disingenuous: it asserted that it was up to the individual members whether or not they wished to remain in the Eurozone, while at the same time, through its governance and its leverage over financial facilities, it made it practically impossible for them to exit without the imposition of the most severe penalties on its population. Manifestly, the deliberations and decisions of a country presented with a such a choice cannot be regarded as relational or symmetrical; they are intrinsically coercive.

This response to the crisis was configured around the marginalisation of weaker peripheral countries in decision-making at multiple levels—ensuring that their distance from the centre was maintained at all times (except for the photoshoots that perpetuate the illusion of solidarity and subsidiarity). Troikanomics demonstrated, in a manner never previously seen, the extent to which power differentials within the EU were rooted in a lack of willingness to adopt a dialogical disposition within the broader ambit of the community. From this perspective, capacities of national parliaments to which we have previously referred highlights the absence of any authentic collaboration—which itself signals the systematic emaciation of self-determination. It's problematic that not alone were such powers syphoned off in the first place, but that this was done in a manner that paid no regard to any substantive deliberative process on the content of budgetary or austerity measures.

Self-affirmation is a nation's capacity to trust in its legitimacy as an autonomous and sovereign entity—encompassing its right to affirm and be answerable for 'who they are' amidst a multitude of other nations. It is

[19] While autonomy may require a critique of one's environment, this need not necessitate standing *in opposition* to one's environment.

expressed in the extent to which nations recognise themselves as being both distinctive in their range of characteristics and capabilities, and yet also as holding an equal normative and political status to other nations—being worthy of a 'seat at the table' when occasions for transnational engagement arise. This capacity presents itself in the collective sense of identification that people experience for their nation, encompassed, for example, in a feeling of national pride or belonging. In practical terms, this is often expressed through symbolic gestures such as national anthems and their flags, as well as the broader showing of support for one's nation in its particular endeavours. In the present context, it was also expressed in marches and protests against the presence of the Troika in people's home countries, highlighting once again the Troika's status as an 'external' and intrusive entity when it came to their engagements with countries. Within the political arena, it is expressed in a calling to affirm and defend the nation and its values against forces that are perceived as undermining them.

Through the expression of this capacity, countries can react to moments of oppression not with passive resignation, but with a trust in their inner resources as having not only the *ability* to overcome such challenges, but the *right* to do so. Exercising self-affirmation enables countries to retain a sense of legitimacy in spite of potentially difficult circumstances. Without this, citizens and politicians may lack the courage or conviction to rally behind and support their nation in times of threat or coercion.

In both its content and character, the Troika's interactions with Bailout countries, were built on an expectation that nations should express a deference *towards* and dependency *on* them. During the Bailout, it was not simply that countries were effectively denied the opportunity to collaborate on the details of the 'Memorandum of Understanding', but it was the *reasoning behind* this denial that was important. The Troika knew that nations would not (indeed *could* not) be as oppressive and prescriptive in their conditionality for the Bailout as they themselves would be, and therefore they sequestered their say in the matter. It was made very clear to them that they simply had no other option, that *in and of themselves* they were unable to construct a path away from sovereign default. The profound sense of loss emerging from one's government's executive abilities being sequestered by an external entity swept like a wave throughout the bailout countries—an issue which emerges from our Case Studies of Ireland and Greece. Political autonomy, hard fought and carved out over centuries (such as was the case with Ireland), now appeared to be a malleable concept, subject to whatever was considered the most economically expedient course of action.

The weight of this experience was not given its due regard by the Troika. A country can engage in this form of asymmetric relationship for only so long before it begins to internalise its sense of powerlessness and ceases to question whether an alternative exists to the intrinsically unhealthy relationships that have been established. In other words, a state in which self-affirmation has lost its constitutive meaning and importance.

## References


Arnold, B. (2009). *The Fight for Democracy*. Dublin: Killynon House Books.

Beetham, D. (1991). *The Legitimation of Power (Issues in Political Theory)*. Basingstoke: Macmillan.

Christman, J. (2009a). *The Politics of Persons: Individual Autonomy and Socio-Historic Selves*. Cambridge: Cambridge University Press.

Christman, J. (2009b). Autonomy, Recognition, and Social Dislocation. *Analyse and Kritik, 31*(2), 275–290.

Christman, J. (2014). Relational Autonomy and the Social Dynamics of Paternalism. *Ethical Theory and Moral Practice, 17*(3), 369–382.

Christman, J. (2015). *Stanford Encyclopedia of Philosophy*. [Online]. Retrieved from http://plato.stanford.edu/entries/autonomy-moral/

Churchill, W. (1946). *Mr Winston Churchill Speaking in Zurich 19th September 1946*. [Online]. Retrieved from http://www.churchill-society-london.org.uk/astonish.html

Czaputowicz, J. (2014). Sovereignty in Theories of European Integration and the Perspective of the Polish Constitutional Tribunal. *Yearbook of Polish European Studies, 17*, 15–36.

de Benoist, A. (1999). What Is Sovereignty? *Telos, 1999*(116), 99–118.

de Búrca, G. (1996). The Quest for Legitimacy in the European Union. *The Modern Law Review, 59*(3), 349–376.

Dworkin, G. (1988). *The Theory and Practice of Autonomy*. Cambridge: Cambridge University Press.

Flathman, R. E. (2007). Legitimacy. In R. E. Goodin, P. Pettit, & T. Pogge (Eds.), *A Companion to Contemporary Political Philosophy* (pp. 678–684). Oxford: Blackwell.

Frankfurt, H. (1971). Freedom of the Will and the Concept of the Person. *The Journal of Philosophy, 68*(1), 5–20.

Frigot, F., & Bonadonna, E. (2016). *Europe and Sovereignty: Reality, Limits and Outlook*. s.l.: Robert Schuman Foundation.

Kinsella, M. (2015). *Becoming Oneself Amongst Others: A Reconceptualisation of Autonomy*. s.l.: PhD Thesis. Unpublished.

Krasner, S. D. (1999). Sovereignty and Its Discontents. In S. D. Krasner (Ed.), *Sovereignty: Organised Hypocrisy* (pp. 3–42). Princeton: Princeton University Press.

Lindseth, P. (1999). Democratic Legitimacy and the Administrative Character of Supranationalism: The Example of the European Community. *Columbia Law Review, 99*(628), 628–738.

MacKenzie, C. (2014). Three Dimensions of Autonomy: A Relational Analysis. In A. Veltman & M. Piper (Eds.), *Autonomy, Oppression, and Gender*. Oxford: Oxford University Press.

Meyers, D. T. (1987). Personal Autonomy and the Paradox of Feminine Socialisation. *The Journal of Philosophy, 84*(11), 619–628.

Raspotnik, A., Jacobs, M., & Ventura, L. (2012, August). *The Issue of Solidarity in the European Union*. TEPSA BRIEF. [Online]. Retrieved from http://www.tepsa.eu/tepsa-brief-the-issue-of-solidarity-in-the-european-union/

Schneller, L. (2010). Conceptions of Democratic Legitimate Governance in the Multilateral Realm: The Case of the WTO. *Living Reviews in Democracy*, 1–18.

Spolaore, E. (2013). What Is European Integration Really About? A Political Guide for Economists. *Journal of Economic Perspectives, American Economic Association, 27*(3), 125–144.

Westlund, A. C. (2015). Autonomy and the Autobiographical Perspective. In M. A. Oshana (Ed.), *Personal Autonomy and Social Oppression: Philosophical Perspectives*. New York: Taylor and Francis.

# 7

# Case Studies: Exploring the Lived Reality of Troikanomics

## Introduction

Adequately portraying the consequences of the European Banking and Debt Crisis—in particular its ongoing social costs—requires moving beyond a purely quantitative analysis, however informative the metrics might be. No data can provide a satisfactory exposition of the *lived experience* of locking the door to your family home for the last time as it gets repossessed, or of waving off your loved one as they emigrate in search of employment, or of contemplating how to rejoin the workforce as your pension becomes decimated. No statistics can capture the frustrations of citizens attempting to internalise how, or indeed *why*, their government has been emasculated of their authority to deal with what is unfolding in their country. Undoubtedly 'the facts' have a necessary role to play in constructing a narrative of the crisis, but *in and of themselves*, they cannot adequately capture the deep trauma visited on the psyches of people and of nations in its aftermath. This lived reality is what has transformed these events from an economic crisis to an existential crisis.



R. Kinsella, M. Kinsella, *Troikanomics*, https://doi.org/10.1007/978-3-319-97070-7_7

Greece was the first country to enter the Troika's Bailout Programme, at a time when the Eurozone was in a borderline catatonic state of shock in the initial aftermath of the global financial crisis and deeply fearful for its own future. The epicentre of Greece's financial crisis originated in failures of oversight and management of its public finances. Ireland was impelled into its own Bailout Programme later that same year—exiting three years later, the first country to do so. The epicentre of Ireland's crisis was a delinquent banking system that funded a classic property 'asset bubble'. Both countries are small peripheral economies with strong cultural heritages and national identities; each has made significant contributions to the history of European civilisation. They deserved better of the EU.

Whatever about the pros and cons of participation in international institutions—or the forks in the road where these countries, and indeed every country at some stage, fail to choose the right path—in both instances, their autonomy was deeply undermined by their participation in these programmes. Autonomy is central to the *lived* experience of a democracy. From its inception, the EU has faced the challenge of balancing the national autonomy and democratic legitimacy of individual members against, ostensibly, the voluntary sharing of these capabilities—*so as* to create a space within which members can in turn exercise 'local' and 'global' autonomy. Their experiences during this chapter reflect an acute and critical failure to succeed in overcoming this challenge because of Troikanomics.

Both the Greek and Irish experiences demonstrate that the governance of the Eurozone is effectively under the control of Germany (alongside France). Other members, even the larger ones, are on the bench or play in the reserves. The governance of Europe is essentially a form of political duopoly permanently at odds with the presumption of an open, transparent, and shared governance.[1] The Troika consistently discarded or overrode the democratic will of the citizens and the politicians they had elected to carry out their mandate; the extent of their control was granular and all-encompassing. The question, in this regard, is how to decipher and interpret what Troikanomics tells us about the nature, and attendant sustainability, of the EU that expressed itself within and beyond this crisis.

[1] See Traynor (2015).

# The Irish Experience

## The Lead-Up to the Crisis

There was no singular 'definitive' cause of Ireland's Debt Crisis; rather, it was the consequence of a *series* of events and decisions that were made over a number of years.[2] The precipitants were primarily domestic, in the form of a delinquent banking system operating within a 'principles-based' regulatory and supervisory regime—the outcome of a political turf war earlier in the decade.[3] The impact of this domestic crisis was magnified by the highly open and trade-dependent nature of its economy and financial system, including a very large international financial sector.

The Irish economy grew rapidly through the 1990s and into the early 2000s. It was in fact the strongest performing economy in the EU, widely lauded as an 'exemplar' to be emulated. Shortly thereafter, an insidious restructuring of the economy transpired—shifting it away from its export-intensive model underpinned by competitiveness and low interest rates.[4] Almost invisibly—except in the data published in the Central Bank's Quarterly Bulletin—an economy driven by excessive credit expansion (which grew at an annual rate of more than 20% during the period up to 2006) was born. An issue that has attracted little attention relates to the extent of 'connected lending' that occurred across the construction and property sectors (accounting for more than 20% of GDP at the time). This had been identified in 2006 by the Bank for International Settlements (BIS) as one of some 26 'Core Principles' to be considered by Central Banks and reviewed with commercial banks; it wasn't, even as the excessive lending was triggering seismic disturbances. At least as important was the fact that lending by banks to the construction and property sector was largely sustained by short-term borrowing from

[2] Here, the Joint Committee of Inquiry into the Banking Crisis (2014) notes that '[t]he crisis cannot be characterised as a simple banking systems failure but rather a crisis borne of a wider systemic failure'.

[3] It should be noted here that, in its letter seeking a bailout, the Irish government identified the banking sector as the primary cause of the crisis.

[4] As Stein (2011) notes, in becoming a member of the Eurozone, Ireland experience a sustained fall in nominal interest rates.

abroad—including very significant intra-EU lending. This excessive expansion on both sides of the banks' balance sheets left them particularly vulnerable to the kind of systemic shock generated by the collapse of banks in the United States.

The counterpart to this was escalating household indebtedness, distorting the allocation of resources across the economy and fuelling a classic 'bubble'. The accusation that 'the people of Ireland lost the run of themselves' in this heady period is frequently asserted, and is often resented by those who riposte that '*ordinary* people didn't lose the run of themselves'. The argument, in this context, is that people were transfixed by the music of their respective pied pipers, all too willing to trust (*perhaps* naively) that they were being guided on a journey that had their best interests at heart. The people of Ireland had been led to the cliff's edge by bankers whose short-sightedness had emboldened a generation to over-leverage. A misplaced *optimism*-cum-*hubris* ran rampant; for many, the houses that were purchased at this time were never able to become the 'home' they had dreamed of, they became an interminable sentence of insurmountable indebtedness.

The collapse in house prices, beginning in late 2007, pushed hundreds of thousands of householders into negative equity. Concurrently, the exceptionally high dependence of the government on property-related taxes meant that this collapse led to a precipitous drop in government revenue—opening up a rapidly growing fiscal deficit. The wider economy went into shock, and unemployment rose to over 15% in what had been a full-employment economy (whose labour force was augmented by net immigration over the previous decade).[5] These same factors developed into a massive increase in non-performing loans for banks. The latent weaknesses in Ireland's overleveraged banking system were exposed by the implosion of the ethically flawed business model which characterised the US banking system at the time.[6] The highly networked global financial system acted as a vector for this crisis, which soon spread across the European and Irish counterparts of the United States. Ireland's structural and regulatory issues were exacerbated by its enmeshment in an incom-

[5] For further insights on this point, see Kinsella and Kinsella (2011).

[6] For further discussion on this point, see Kinsella and Kinsella (2009).

plete monetary union marked by institutional deficiencies and by imbalances in the adjustment process. These circumstances would have tested the resilience of *any* economy.

On 30 September 2008 the government extended a Bank Guarantee to depositors and bondholders as a way of relieving stresses on the banks. Across the Eurozone, countries were attempting to shore up their stressed-out banking systems in all manner of ways. As a small trade-dependent economy with a large external financial sector, Ireland felt impelled to send a strong signal to the markets. Preliminary analysis had suggested that the Irish banks were positioned to cope with liquidity pressures; and that it did—for a short while—until the Guarantee expired in 2010. The Bank Guarantee has been criticised as misconceived. But in 2008 the economy had not yet imploded; nor had the full scale of non-performing loans materialised. Both national and EU authorities were still looking ahead and hoping that reprieve would reveal it. In the process, it created a 'funding cliff' as liabilities expired and were not rolled over. The consequence was, however, the sovereign and banking problems coalesced. The Central Bank was constrained to seek the support of the ECB in providing liquidity to Irish banks. This left it wholly dependent and with no leverage in the tense negotiations, culminating in the imposition of the Troika's Bailout Programme.

What *did* reveal itself to the markets with which Ireland was engaged was the beginning of Greece's (seemingly interminable) Bailout Programme. This transformed market sentiment, especially for other peripherals. The ECB's perceptions of Ireland's capabilities—both present and potential—were filtered through what was emerging in Greece. The question thus shifted from 'how can we help the Irish authorities get on top of what's happening?' to 'who is next to be bailed out after Greece—Portugal or Ireland?' The economic and political catharsis that convulsed Ireland between 2010 and 2013 was of existential proportions. The lead up to the final week before bailout was a disconcerting and disturbing experience; a surreal resistance to the dying of the light. In Dublin, the Irish authorities were contending with the challenge of maturing bonds. New data had demonstrated greater losses on the part of the banks. In this volatile situation the Minister for Finance was attempting to maintain a credible presence within the domestic political environment, in different fora across Brussels, Washington, and the G20.

Could it have been foreseen? As early as 2006, University College Dublin economist Professor Morgan Kelly had demonstrated that an economy marked by the kind of escalation of house prices experienced in Ireland was set for a collapse. The international evidence cited by Kelly was incontrovertible. Initially, the political system turned its face away; they simply did not want to know. With revenues augmented by property-related taxes, they sheltered themselves behind the illusion of robust public finances. This delayed adequate policy responses until the decline in property values, the level of oversupply, and the extent of the banks' exposure could no longer be outrun. These matters could and *should* have been acknowledged and acted upon earlier; it was a classic example of denial—raising important issues on the blindness of Party Politics.

## Building Towards a Bailout

The collapse, unprecedented in its scope and impact, came suddenly and reached its nadir in November 2010 when Ireland was forced into a bailout by the ECB, less than three years after the economy peaked in 2007. For the next three years political autonomy and democratic governance in Ireland was quarantined by the Troika. The backdrop to the efforts by Ireland to avoid the fate of Greece was the October 2010 EU Council meeting which impacted materially not alone on the Irish bailout but, more generally, on EU governance. The 'headline' outcome was an agreement between France and Germany on a new bailout mechanism to 'backstop' sovereign pressures across the Eurozone. Embedded in Chancellor Merkel's initial proposal was the assertion that any new bailout mechanism should be able to impose losses on private investors. In principle, this proposal made sense—they had made their own considerable contributions to the crisis. It would also have facilitated debt restructuring in stricken peripheral countries. In the event, the two leaders dropped this in deference to the reaction from the financial markets—but not before it had caused a spike in bond yields across the peripherals, including Ireland. It was less the *extent* of the increase than the *uncertainties* it had created for Ireland at a pivotal stage of its efforts to avoid a bailout.

Importantly, the subtext to the Council's meeting bears directly on the way it was stage-managed by Germany and France. At a sudden, unscheduled, bilateral meeting between Chancellor Merkel and President Sarkozy—the so-called Deauville Summit which took place prior to the Summit—the two leaders agreed that the proposed new bailout mechanism should incorporate *automatic* fines on countries that exceeded their deficit targets as well as the threat of removing their voting rights in the Council. It was a step too far, but it highlights the prescriptive and presumptive way the Franco-German alliance sought to impose its will on the wider EU. It revealed the same mind-set as that imposed on Greece by German Finance Minister Wolfgang Schäuble. The proposals were—as noted—shelved while, at the same time, the Commission was granted even greater powers of oversight over the EU's members. But what is especially striking here is that the very same 'burden sharing' which Chancellor Merkel had initially advocated, but then withdrew under pressure, was coercively rejected by the ECB President when it was put forward by the new Irish Minister for Finance some months later as part of a wider package of reforms.

It highlighted the inconsistency and *dirigiste* stance taken by the ECB and it emphatically dispelled the polite fictions of 'cooperation' between the government and the Troika. In the increasingly frenetic environment of the time, market sentiment and the perceptions of large institutions were of critical importance in efforts to 'firewall' contagion. At a more fundamental level it demonstrated the expediency with which they 'tacked to the wind' of Franco-German interests in keeping a flawed Eurozone afloat. Less than three weeks after the October Summit, Ireland was being impelled towards a bailout at the insistence of the ECB, still struggling to maintain its autonomy in dealing with the crisis.

The ECB's engagement with Ireland in the final weeks leading up to its formal application for a Bailout Programme, and in its aftermath, was adversarial and politically coercive. It is important to acknowledge that by this stage the extent of the ECB's resources tied up with Ireland were very large—upwards of 25% of its loan book (Hennigan 2014). Then again, the counterpart of the trade deficits of the peripherals was Germany's surplus. Nonetheless, it was the ECB that summarily impelled Ireland into a bailout, which imposed pervasive damage on the economy and the national psyche. It sought to front-load austerity on Ireland beyond the point that the IMF—with vastly more experience of structural adjustment programmes—thought appropriate or prudent. It peremptorily insisted that Ireland not impose burden-sharing on bond holders as part of an overall resolution of the crisis and, instead, imposed costs of billions of Euros on Irish society. In managing the Banking and Debt Crisis across the Eurozone, the ECB never questioned the normative legitimacy of its own behaviours. In terms of our primary themes in this book, it did not adequately critique the position which it had taken. It demonstrated that, from the EU's perspective, the Common Good of vulnerable peripheral countries came second to the perpetuation of a flawed political Eurozone.

Unconscionable pressure was brought to bear on Ireland by the ECB not to burn senior bondholders *notwithstanding* that this was the stated policy of the new government as part of a wider strategy to stabilise the banks and the wider economy—a policy widely supported by internationally respected economists. The priority of the ECB was to inoculate the Eurozone, imposing a disproportionate cost burden on the Irish people. They were difficult days. For example, had the costs of maintaining and winding down Anglo been 'ring-fenced' by the EU its access to the markets would have been enhanced, mitigating the perceived need for a bailout—especially bearing in mind that Ireland had already funded over €17 billion from its National Pension Reserve Fund (NPRF).

The Commission and the ECB were insistent that Ireland surrender to their demand to apply for a bailout. Certainly, the paperwork had well been prepared. EU officials had begun to 'leak' against the Irish position which was, in itself, extraordinary and told its own story. In these circumstances, the Governor of the Central Bank, Professor Patrick Honohan, in an unscheduled and impromptu interview from Brussels with RTÉ's *Morning Ireland*, Ireland's flagship morning news programme, was quite clear that the Bailout was going to happen. There was confusion and shock; disappointment in government but an acknowledgement that this was a decision made in good faith and in the national interest.

Even so, the political environment remained confused, with politicians in denial of what was being forced unilaterally and unconditionally upon the country. A letter received by the Irish government from the ECB on

21 November 2010 demanded that Ireland immediately formally request a bailout, under threat that facilities for Irish banks would be withdrawn forthwith. This set an implacable tone that was at variance with what might have been expected in a 'Union' ostensibly marked by solidarity. The government bowed to the inevitable and on Sunday, 22 November 2010, it announced that it was acquiescing to these demands. On 28 November 2010, the illusion of Ireland's autonomy was shattered as it was formally impelled into a €85 billion bailout. The letter—effectively dictated to the Irish government by the ECB—formally seeking support from the EU institutions and the IMF in the form of a bailout began: 'Ireland faces an Economic crisis without parallel in its recent history. The problem of low growth, doubt about fiscal sustainability, and a fragile banking sector are feeding on each other … at the root of the problem is a banking sector which at its peak was four times the size of the economy and is now under severe pressure' (Lenihan and Honohan 2010).

The Irish public, including the Social Partners, had been conditioned to anticipate austerity. What they got was Troikanomics. There is all the difference in the world between an austerity programme designed to correct domestic and external imbalances in which the priority is the national interest, and one driven by a political agenda that is not aligned with these interests and has the leverage to arbitrarily impose its will by *fiat*. Considered in this light, the imposition of Troikanomics was an unprecedented shock to Ireland: nothing akin to such an experience could have been envisaged since its gaining of Independence. After all the analysis and all the negotiations and all the unavailing efforts, Troikanomics became a reality: it had been agreed in Brussels and signed off in the Chancelleries of Europe and in Washington. It remained only to be formally announced to the Irish people in Dublin.

## Ushering in an Existential Epoch

Every description of the 'Night of the Bailout' inevitably falls short of the reality. In short, the nature of the problems confronting Ireland, as it slipped into the gravitational pull of Troikanomics, cannot be comprehended other than through a 'being-in-a-moment', as the reality imprinted itself on the national psyche. Bearing this in mind, however, we can at least try to envisage that experience as the formal announcement of the imposition of Troikanomics was made. Lise Hand (2013), a journalist then with the *Irish Independent*, who had closely followed the events leading up to that moment, provides a compelling description of what was unfolding—one that goes far beyond all the technical jargon and platitudes of what was being signed:

> *Outside on Merrion Square frozen snow glittered on the streets. But it was nothing compared to the icy chill which hung in the air of the press centre in Government Buildings on the desolate night on Sunday, November 28, 2010, as the packed room watched a group of strangers from the IMF, EU and ECB settled into seats just vacated by the Taoiseach and two cabinet ministers. This Troika was our new government now – unelected, unwanted and absolutely indispensable. Three Kings bearing a bitter gift of €85 Billion for a broken nation tethering on the edge of a precipice. Thirty pieces of silver in exchange for our hard-won, precious sovereignty … Earlier an ashen faced Taoiseach had insisted that he and his team had 'carefully considered all available policy options' before signing on the dotted line. But in reality, they had no options. There is no wriggle-room when your back is to the wall.*

There are images too, which convey something of the surreal sense of dissonance at what Ireland had become and how it had been humbled by its 'European Partners' into a sudden dependence 'on the kindness of strangers'. The Troika, on their way to take up office, in government buildings as they pass a homeless man on the street holding out an empty cup for a few coins. A locked gate, meshed by wire, into one of the many half-finished 'ghost estates' which had proliferated, like a rash, across the country. Signage at the Anglo Irish Bank headquarters in Dublin being removed letter by letter. The sudden queues outside social welfare offices as individuals—who had considered themselves comfortable and conscientious—were now forced into unemployment and waited in line to sign on. These radiate the essence of the existential angst that the country was going through at the time.

No Irish government could have envisaged that the Debt Crisis would have taken the country to the brink. Nor could any government that had such a historical empathy with Europe, and pro-EU sentiments, have conceived that it would be the European Institutions of the ECB and the EC—and *not* the IMF—that would have been its primary proponents.

The bailout was an ideological, as well as an economic, inflection point in modern Irish history. Troikanomics demonstrated how the intrinsically negative politics of austerity can change the wider political and cultural trajectory of a country, over and above the more visible macroeconomic consequences. The experience evoked a mourning that enveloped the public and the establishment alike. The Editorial in the pro-European *Irish Times* (2010) eloquently acknowledged that 'We are not naive enough to think that this State ever can, or ever could, take large decisions in isolation from the rest of the world. What we do expect, however, is that these decisions will still be our own. A nation's independence is defined by the choices it can make for itself. Irish history makes the loss of that sense of choice more shameful. The desire to be a sovereign people runs like a seam through all of the struggles of the last 200 years…it continues to have a genuine resonance for most Irish people today'. It concluded that '[t]he true ignominy of our current situation is not that our sovereignty has been taken away from us, it is that we ourselves have squandered it'. This was not, in any sense, an expression of nostalgia for a vanished age of political innocence and economic naiveté. It was a perspective rooted in the domain of globalisation with which the Irish economy was very much engaged through inward and international investment.

Neither the country nor the Irish authorities ever *really* thought—even as the Troika booked their tickets for Dublin—that the threat of a takeover of the country's governance by the ECB would materialise. It was not in the Irish character to contemplate such a debacle. From a Civil War in the 1920s in early years of the State to the eruption of violence in Northern Ireland; from the ravages of massive emigration and stagnation in the 1950s to EU Accession in 1972; and, just a decade later, the establishment of the massively successful iconic International Financial Services Centre (IFSC)—Ireland's experience in the twentieth century had demonstrated its capacity to overcome obstacles and effect transformational change from deep within its own resources, impelled by a strong sense of national identity wholly at ease with Europe.

This bears careful reflection in any rounded critique of the significance of what was unfolding in Ireland. Irish civilisation extends back millennia—the Neolithic tombs at Newgrange predate the pyramids by over 400 years. Christianity in Ireland dates from the return of St Patrick to

Ireland in 432 AD. In less than 200 years the monastic settlements of the early Christian Church had extended across the island and Europe. From the late eighteenth century the religious and political repression of Ireland impelled the drive towards political independence, closely intertwined with the revolutionary movements in France, especially in the wake of the failure of the 1798 rebellion where the 'United Irishmen' looked to France for military support. Between 1845 and 1849 Ireland suffered a devastating famine—an existential experience for a country already impacted by poverty and oppression. The death toll of over one million people was the catalyst for one of the great waves of European migration and imposed a deep wound in the Irish psyche. Concurrently, it continued to contend with the United Kingdom for political independence.

Following a political uprising in 1916 which was brutally suppressed by the British, it engaged in a guerrilla war for independence. The Anglo–Irish Treaty was signed in 1921, and with it Ireland had finally gained a measure of independence. Even so, the first decades of independence were difficult: a bloody civil war was followed by a trade war with the United Kingdom—quaintly referred to as 'The Emergency'—which took Ireland, largely dependent on its agriculture industry, to the brink of catastrophe.

Through all the vicissitudes of Irish history across that era, two points directly relevant to our analysis stand out: firstly, the tenacity of Ireland's quest for political independence and national autonomy, for which many sacrifices were made; and, secondly, the deep vein of empathy running through Ireland's engagement with Europe.

Beginning in 1957 and through the 1960s Ireland transformed itself from an inward-looking, largely rural economy scarred by protectionism and massive emigration into an open economy powered by foreign investment, a revamped banking system, and increasingly focused on achieving membership of the European Community (EC)—all the while contending with growing political instability on the Island. In the lead-up to the bailout the question was then asked as to where exactly these aspirations had led the country. Every dimension of the lives of people, and of Ireland as an independent and sovereign country, was stress-tested by the experience. The then Minister for Finance Brian Lenihan spoke of the country being 'at the gates of hell' shortly before the bailout agreement was formally signed—and of his efforts to contend with a situation which, as he pointed out, his predecessors had never envisaged. Membership of the EEC, of the European Communion, of the EU—each of the iterations, like stops that glide past on an underground tube journey—wasn't supposed to take Ireland to that destination.

In spring 2011, in the aftermath of the bailout, there was a General Election which swept government from Fianna Fail, a Nationalist/Republican Party founded by the iconic former President Eamon De Valera. The concept of an independent Republic, united and autonomous, 'among the nations of the world' was fundamental to identity forged by the 1916 Uprising, the Declaration of Independence, and the Civil War. A subsequent leader, Sean Lemass, had transformed the economy and society in the late 1950s/1960s, impelling Ireland towards membership of the (then) European Community. The challenges confronting Lemass at the time were scarcely more daunting than those confronting his successor in the fraught months and weeks of the second half of 2010.

Fianna Fail was displaced by a coalition of Fine Gael (its perennial conservative opposition) and a junior Labour Party partner with a hard-left ideological agenda and the leverage to drive it, as the price for keeping the government in power. The Coalition had inherited the task of implementing the bailout agreement imposed on its predecessor. The new Minister for Finance, Mr Michael Noonan, a seasoned and wily politician, was the public face of Troikanomics both domestically and in its engagement with the Troika.

The public had come to terms with the need for austerity, but the reality of expenditure cuts in public services and tax increases was a different matter. Over €34 billion had been injected into the banks. General government debt had risen to over 100% of GDP and the general government deficit reached 31% of GDP by 2010 (CSO 2013)—equivalent to 10.6% on an underlying basis. The government was faced with the challenge of pushing back against the oppressive terms of the bailout while at the same time pushing through enormous cuts in, for example, healthcare—where over 5000 staff were shed and the scope of work of those who remained was increased. Opinion Polls contended with the targets against the backdrop of Quarterly Meetings of Irish officials with Troika. Salaries of what aspired to be a 'Consultant-led Health Service' were subject to drastic cuts, leading to arbitrary and quite bizarre relativities.

This highlights the reality that short-term cuts in healthcare are counterproductive. The impact on the health status of the population is corrosive and, at some stage, generates much higher costs than any short-term savings. Expenditure on healthcare is an investment with measurable economic benefits. In the world of Troikanomics short-term budgetary arithmetic is prioritised over longer-term health status, including the prevalence of disease and the quality of services. The European establishment, the force behind the Troika, never appeared to understand or engage with this reality, either in Ireland or in any of the other peripheral or Eastern European countries.

## To the Depths and Back Again

At the end of 2013, Ireland exited from the €85 billion bailout and successfully returned to the markets. Since then, it has again become the fastest-growing economy across the EU. Indeed, there is a surreal dimension to Ireland's recovery *albeit* that it is driven primarily by multinational companies. It is almost as if such a searing and existential experience never happened, and this raises the important issue of how far a country learns from even the most fundamental economic and social catharsis. This narrative—from the heights to the depths and back again—bears reflecting upon. The EU establishment proclaimed that the Irish post-bailout experience showed that Troikanomics works, and held it aloft as a poster boy for 'proof of concept'. Firstly, the 'Troikanomics works' mythology largely obscures the legacy of Troika: a debt burden of more than 100% of GDP, an annual interest cost of €1 billion for having saved the banks of larger countries in the Eurozone, a chronic problem of homelessness, and—what has been almost wholly overlooked by most analysts—a seismic change in Irish politics characterised, in particular, by successive expressions of left-wing social legislation.

Secondly, the causality from crash to recovery largely derived from the restructuring that had *already* been undertaken prior to the country being forced into the bailout: this included not alone fiscal consolidation but an acknowledgement on the part of the public and among social partners that such consolidation was imperative. The government had already set up National Asset Management Agency (NAMA), which was in the process of transferring bad loans from the balance sheets of the banks.

Progress had been made in estimating the likely total losses across all the banks. The main credit institutions were in the process of being restructured and additional capital had been injected. A new rules-based regulatory and supervisory system with serious powers of enforcement had been put in place. In the event, the bad loans across the balance sheets of the banks proved to be significantly greater than anticipated.

Importantly, €35 billion of this related directly to the Anglo Irish Bank—accounting for the biggest single component of the costs of the bank collapse. This was not a systemically important bank in terms of money transmission and payments. It had, in fact, evolved from a specialised investment bank into a vehicle for speculation in an overheated property market. It could—and should—have been allowed to fail. The European Institutions, under the mandate of the Troika, coerced a stricken country to bear the cost of winding it down instead of allowing it to fail. Had this enormous loss been 'ring-fenced' the Irish authorities could, almost certainly, have navigated their way through the crisis. The ECB refused to countenance any such burden-sharing.

For the EU establishment, all that mattered was the Stability and Growth Pact. The principal beneficiary of Ireland's experience of Troikanomics was the Eurozone as a political and economic entity and, more specifically, its wider banking system. The burden of adjustment was not equally shared: the counterpart of the deficits of peripheral countries was the enormous surplus of Germany and the centre and yet the burden of adjustment fell heaviest on the deficit countries—on their labour markets and public services. Just as the Franco-German axis had initiated and shaped the Economic and Monetary Union to serve their interests, so too the resolution of the crisis was shaped by the interests of that same axis. Smaller countries were caught between the rock of their commitment to a kind of Europe that encompassed respect for national autonomy and the (very) hard place defined by even greater dependence.

It is one of the nostrums of the banking profession that a primary lending criterion is the character of the borrower. Had the ECB's response to the emerging crisis in Ireland been informed by a greater understanding of the qualities that form the character and ethos of a country—its historical resilience and capacity to adjust—then Troikanomics might have been perceived at a much earlier stage, as it later came to be, as oppressive and responsible for great damage. There are, for example, at least two propositions that can be made: firstly, had the IMF been operating on its own account it would not have 'frontloaded' the degree of austerity that in practice was imposed on Ireland. Secondly, the IMF would not have opposed 'burning the bondholders' which would have saved Ireland significant resources.

The Troika imposed a repressive internal devaluation on an Irish Economy that had already taken significant steps towards fiscal consolidation and the rebuilding of its banking system. The initial terms and conditions applying to the bailout were onerous, particularly in relation to countries such as Portugal. Mediterranean countries, both individually and collectively, had greater bargaining power compared with Ireland and, especially, Greece. Ireland was pressurised into absorbing a disproportionate amount of the total cost of stabilising the Eurozone's banking system.

The net effect of all of this was the erosion of Ireland's autonomy—by way of the precedent that had been established by Troikanomics, the policies that had been enforced, and the amendments to the European Treaty by which Troikanomics had been legitimised. This unfolded within an EU which was *ostensibly* committed to 'social solidarity', but which had conspicuously failed to embed such instruments as transfer payments within the Eurozone itself. The full weight of this institutional deficiency meant that the peripheral countries like Ireland had not only ceded an independent Central Bank—which would have helped mitigate the damage—but were also reliant on ad hoc and oppressive support by the European institutions.

Again, the question arises: was it necessary that such a pro-European member nation should have been put through this catharsis? This is the paradox: an essentially technocratic European elite, which constantly appeals to the history of the EU to vindicate its policies, demonstrated such a lack of political and cultural insight during the crisis.

In retrospect, the better option for Ireland, as it was being drawn into the crisis, was to have engaged unilaterally with the IMF in 2008 when it was a practical possibility. The IMF, after all, was very familiar with the imbalances that had built up within the economy from its regular Article IV consultations with Ireland. The Governor of the Central Bank, Professor Patrick Honohan, has pointed out that the IMF indicated informally to him that it might arrange a 'stand-by' facility for Ireland, as a segue to stabilisation. Such agreements are normally offered only to those countries which the IMF believe are being managed responsibly—in effect, providing a 'good housekeeping' seal of approval. This is, of course, conjecture. Events were moving frenetically both within the markets and at a policy level. We would take the view that, in retrospect, engagement with the IMF in 2008 was the best—or certainly the least worst—option for Ireland.

Having said that, there is a contrary perspective. The view taken by the government was that this would have raised questions within the financial markets on whom the Irish sovereign was dependent. Also, Dr Michael Summers, formerly Head of Ireland's innovative National Treasury Management Agency (NTMA)—one of Ireland's most distinguished public servant in the post-Whitaker era—in his presentation to the 2014 Parliamentary Inquiry into the banking crisis, gave expression to the view that an IMF Programme would be the worst kind of political catastrophe at that point in time. As noted, we take a different stance. What is clear is that the IMF's engagement with a vulnerable Irish economy, and subsequently during the Bailout, was more empathetic, supportive, and nuanced than was that of its 'European friends and Partners'.

An IMF 'stand-by' Programme would have kept Ireland out of the increasing gravitational pull of the European Institutions which were, by comparison, out of their depth. Instead, the government continued with reforms—recapitalising and restructuring the banks, reforming the regulatory system, establishing a 'Bad Bank' (NAMA) to acquire non-performing loans from the banks at a discount as a means of cleaning up their balance sheets and commencing the drafting of what was to be a National Recovery Plan. These initiatives constituted a significant austerity programme—not least for an economy where expectations within both the government and household sectors had so recently been excessively and unrealistically high. The era of Troikanomics changed Ireland—the lives of the people, its national autonomy, and its sense of self. What remain largely unchanged are the political system and the business model of the banks. Some things never change.

# The Greek Experience

## Introduction

The decision by the Eurogroup of Finance Ministers in June 2018 to endorse Greece's formal exit from its Bailout Programme has been portrayed as a milestone for Greece and, by extension, for Europe. The decision hardly represented a triumph—although inevitably it was cast in those terms by the Eurozone Ministers and the government of Prime Minister Alexis Tsipras. It was the culmination of an exhaustive process. A resolution that could have been reached much earlier had not Germany opposed the IMF's recommendation for debt relief. Ultimately, it reflected a perceived need by the EU establishment to 'clear the decks' for a post-2019 political and administrative order.

The economic and political experience imposed on Greece remains a defining indictment of the Eurozone and its response to the Banking and Debt Crisis. Greece's experience goes beyond economics or politics; it is intrinsically *existential*—a nihilistic *cul de sac*.[7] The era of the Troika is now part of Europe's history, but its impact remains very much a part of contemporary Greece. Almost from the outset, the Greek experience of Troikanomics was deeply subversive of the Common Good and of economic principles informed by social justice.

Greece is, of course, a resilient nation—there is little that it has not experienced since achieving its independence in 1822. Notwithstanding a succession of kingdoms and coups, of dictatorships and democracy, the DNA of Europe's founding civilisation still resonates across the historical hinterland of Europe. What unfolded in Greece between 2010 and 2018, therefore, diminished a nation who had bequeathed to the West foundational concepts in virtue-based model of political governance. It amounted to the imposition of a hegemonistic EU culture that emerged from of an essentially secularist consensus from the mid-1980s.[8] It was the very opposite of what the European Project aspired to be, that is, a democratic entity within which the identity and autonomy of member nations was

[7] There is a vast body of literature analysing the Greek experience of austerity, at multiple levels. Our analysis aims to avoid restating established facts and numbers as much as possible. See, for example, Doxiadis and Placas (2018).

[8] See Bénéton et al. (2017).

acknowledged at every level, and where governance was shared and not sequestered.

## Change Pressures on Greece

Before looking in detail at the chronology of events that constitutes the Greek crisis, it is important to put it in some kind of context (see Fig. 7.1). Reflecting on developments from 2010 to 2018, there were a number of 'forces' impacting on the engagement of Greece and the Troika:

1. At the outset of the crisis, Greece was impacted by a toxic mix of flawed fiscal policies and by viscerally opportunistic financial markets.[9] Unsustainable public-sector spending practices exacerbated the problem of fiscal consolidation aimed at adapting to the asymmetric shocks brought about by the broader European Banking and Debt Crisis.
2. Both Greece and the wider EU were impacted by developments in the global economy. It was part of the tragedy of Greece that the impact of its fiscal data debacle, whereby it understated the true status of its public finances, overlapped with the start of Eurozone's existential crisis.
3. There were systemic weaknesses and inequalities in the architecture and governance of the Eurozone.
4. There was an oppressive and adversarial engagement between the EU and Greece following the election of an anti-austerity government under Mr Tsipras in 2015.
5. The EU refused to countenance debt relief—even though the IMF had made it clear that such action was imperative.
6. Greece will continue to be subject to 'enhanced monitoring', even now that it has formally exited the Bailout. It is required to generate a significant primary budget surplus. Debt alleviation will be dependent on 'performance'. The scope for growth, employment, and a rise in living standards will be limited and the Debt/GDP ratio will remain significantly higher than when the whole tragic saga began. By any measure therefore, Greece's capacity for autonomous functioning has been corroded.

---

[9] See, for example, Story et al. (2010), Schwartz and Dash (2010).

**Fig. 7.1** Change pressures on Greece. Source: Authors' own

## Inflection Points in the Greek Crisis

Defining the primary impact of Troikanomics on the Greek economy and on the morale of the Greek people—bailout after bailout, conditionality piled on conditionality—is a challenge. First, there is the context. On the one hand, there is the hegemonistic EU dominated by its centre and, on the other hand, there are multiple manifestations of instability—from the Debt Crisis to an accelerating migration tragedy of enormous proportion. It is difficult to separate cause and effect in what were multiple 'feedback' mechanisms.[10]

[10] A most eloquent starting point is Galbraith (2016).

Table 7.1 provides an overview of the key events and the turning points along the road to crisis from the time that Greece joined the EEC and, more specifically, signed the Maastricht Treaty in 1992. Perhaps it is simply hindsight, but it is difficult to avoid an eerie sense of foreboding that, as events gather pace, they were only heading in one direction.

Reflecting on these developments from 1991 to 2018, the starting point of any narrative is this: Greece had a decade (more, if one considers the preliminary work involved in getting to that point) between adopting the Maastricht 'Convergence Criteria' and getting its public finances and fiscal policy to the point where it could formally implement these criteria by 2001. It did not do so. One can only hypothesise that a (politically rooted) sense of optimism prevailed in the run-up to, and aftermath of, the Athens Summer Olympics. For Greece, as for Ireland, there was a sense that 'it will be alright on the night'. Neither country envisaged—or perhaps could have envisaged—the scale and rapidity with which nemesis, in the form of the global banking crisis incubating in the United States, was approaching. Or, for that matter, the single currency to which they so enthusiastically aspired would morph into a catastrophic 'trap'. It remains deeply disconcerting that Goldman Sachs—the paragon of the US banking system—profited from facilitating the Greek government in presenting misleading information on its true fiscal status in order to gain admission to the Eurozone. The consequence was that efforts that might have otherwise been made to address the budget deficit were in stasis—until the worst possible moment, when the global banking crisis had metastasised across Europe.

A key inflection point was when newly elected Socialist Prime Minister Papandreou announced major revisions to Greece's public finances, so as to initiate a fresh start. The outcome was that the markets turning on them.[11] The window of opportunity to address the issue had been well and truly slammed shut and the prospect of generating a willingness on the part of stakeholders to agree to necessary fiscal consolidation and reforms was lost. Ireland, by contrast, had not alone largely developed its blueprint for austerity before the Troika arrived in Dublin, it had also largely gained the agreement of the Social Partners to reforms. It had not,

[11] As Stiglitz (2016) points out.

**Table 7.1** Greece on the road to Troikanomics

| | |
|---|---|
| 1991 | Greece joins the EEC |
| 1992 | The Maastricht Treaty is enacted—establishing the EU and paving the way for the Economic and Monetary Union (EMU), the Single Currency (Euro), and incorporating fiscal benchmark requirements (Convergence Criteria) for participating in the Eurozone |
| 1999 | Introduction of the Euro as an accounting currency with 11 of the 12 EU member countries. Greece fails to meet criteria relating to budget deficit—3%—and debt/GDP ratio (60%) (EU Commission tasked with monitoring Greece Public Finances) |
| 2001 | Greece joins the Eurozone while misstating the true status of its public finances[a] |
| 2004 | The Athens Summer Olympics take place, costing over €7 billion and contributing to a rising budget deficit—officially reported as 6% of GNP and a reported Debt/GDP ratio of 110%. The EU Commission is tasked with monitoring Greek public finances |
| 2007 (February) | Onset of Global Financial Crisis and credit contraction, leaving Greece unable to service its rising debt |
| 2009 (October) | Socialist Prime Minister Andreas Papandreou reveals that the Greek budget deficit will exceed 12%, later revised up to 15%. Greek borrowing costs escalate, and the Greek sovereign bond rating is reduced to 'junk' status. Prime Minister Papandreou publishes austerity proposals which are met with a general strike by trade unions |
| 2010 (May) | The first EU/IMF bailout of €110 billion over three years in exchange for austerity measures—which include €30 billion in spending cuts and tax increases. This results in outrage in Parliament and on the streets of Athens |
| 2010 (May) | ECB announces €750 billion bond-buying programme, enabling it to purchase sovereign bonds on the secondary market to ease market pressures on the sovereign |
| 2011 (October) | Prime Minister Papandreou calls a referendum on a proposed second bailout agreement, which is then cancelled after centre-right parties support revamped EU/IMF arrangements. Papandreou's administration is replaced by a 'Unity Government' led by Papademos |
| 2012 (February/ March) | Second bailout of €130 billion including a 53.5% write-down for private Greek bondholders, committing Greece to a reduction in its debt/GDP ratio from 160% to 120% by 2020 |

(*continued*)

Table 7.1 (continued)

| | |
|---|---|
| 2012 (March) | EU approves the 'Fiscal Compact' Treaty requiring EU members—excluding the United Kingdom and Czech Republic—to impose stricter budget controls including a 'balance budget rule' together with an automatic correction mechanism for countries exceeding the 0.5% target rule |
| 2012 (April) | Pensioner shoots himself outside of Greek Parliament, saying he did not want to pass debts on to his children |
| 2012 (May/ June) | Greek voters reject the political consensus and support parties opposed to bailout programmes and any further austerity. In a follow-on election voters support centre-right parties, enabling Antonis Samaras to form a coalition that commits to existing EU bailout plans |
| 2012 (6 September) | ECB bond-buying programme mitigates the impact of volatile markets on the borrowing costs of peripheral countries |
| 2012 (26 September) | 200,000 people march in Athens in anti-austerity demonstrations |
| 2012 (November) | EU/IMF revise the Greek programme. Continued austerity leads to further massive protests with security forces responding, including tear-gassing of protesters |
| 2013 (July) | Greek Parliament approves further austerity as a condition for gaining access to bailout funds. The conditions include a requirement to lay off 25,000 public servants, further wage cuts, tax reforms, and additional budgetary measures. Trade unions call a general strike |
| 2014 (April) | Greece raises €3 billion from the markets in the form of five-year bonds |
| 2015 (January) | Greek General Election won by Anti-Austerity Syriza party led by Mr Alexis Tsipras who says the election marks an end to the 'vicious circle of austerity'. Mr Tsipras appoints Economist Professor Yanis Varoufakis as Finance Minister and announces he will push for renegotiating on the bailout, debt cancellation, and public-sector spending |
| 2015 (March) | Greece defers to German pressure to adhere to the goals of the bailout arrangements. Subsequently, Professor Varoufakis, having retired as Finance Minister later that July, reveals that the 'negotiations' were always doomed to failure and asserts that Germany had no intention of entering serious negotiations |
| 2015 (June) | Negotiations between Greece and its official creditors break down, leading to the expiry of the bailout and a major Eurozone crisis. Prime Minister Tsipras unilaterally proposes a referendum on EU proposals and imposes Emergency Financial Controls |

(*continued*)

**Table 7.1** (continued)

| | |
|---|---|
| 2015 (End June) | The tipping point: Germany divided on whether, directly or indirectly, to force Greece out of the Eurozone. Chancellor Merkel, with the support of France and some of the smaller countries, circumvents efforts by German Finance Minister Schäuble to force Greece out of the Eurozone.[b] However, the terms and conditions imposed on Greece to allow them to remain are draconian, impacting directly on Greece's sovereignty, its economic capabilities, and the sustainability of its economy (including debt repayment capacity). The Greek economic data relating to GDP, unemployment, and poverty levels point to a major catharsis across every domain of the economy, including the social economy[c] |
| 2015 (5 July) | Greek voters in their referendum overwhelmingly reject new austerity proposals. The result matters not at all since the conditions have already been enforced on and accepted by Mr Tsipras |
| 2015 (16 July) | In the Greek Parliament Prime Minister Tsipras supports additional austerity to avoid Grexit and access to €86 billion bailout funds |
| 2015 (August) | Official creditors require Greece to implement tax 'reforms', cut public spending, privatise state assets, and reform labour laws |
| | The IMF refuses to contribute to the bailout programme until the EU provides 'significant debt reforms' without which, the IMF states, Greek debt is unsustainable while the budget cuts demanded by EU creditors will constrain the capacity of the economy to grow and thereby service the debt. EU/Eurozone decline to consider debt relief |
| 2016 (December) | Eurozone Ministers endorse short-term debt relief measures |
| 2017 (September) | EU Economic Affairs Commissioner states that Greece will remain under supervision until it repays 75% of its loans |
| 2018 (January) | Eurogroup announces the start of 'technical work' on debt relief measures |
| 2018 (April) | Greek Finance Minister acknowledges that Greece will remain under 'enhanced surveillance' when its Bailout Programme ends in August 2018 |
| 2018 (23 June) | European Commissioner for Economic and Financial Affairs, Taxation and Customs Pierre Moscovici states that 'The Greek crisis ends here' |

(*continued*)

**Table 7.1** (continued)

| | |
|---|---|
| 2018 (23 June) | Greek Minister for Finance states that 'This Government will not forget what the Greek people suffered for eight years', and that 'Greece is once again a normal country, regaining its political and financial independence' |

Source: Authors' own

[a]'It is subsequently made public that the US investment bank Goldman Sachs helped Greece misrepresent part of its debt through complex credit swap transactions' (Committee on Foreign Relations 2018)

[b]Here, Speigel (2015) notes that 'had it been up to (Dr.) Schäuble, Germany would have shown the Greeks the Eurozone door long ago. His problem is that the Chancellor does not share his sentiment ... because she does not want to go down in history as the Government leader responsible for the disintegration of Europe'

[c]Traynor (2015) notes that it is the 'most intense, most fractious, and most heated debate ever held by those responsible to the European Economy'

of course, anticipated the extent to which the political masters of the Troika would pressurise and threaten Ireland into absorbing a wholly disproportionate amount of the costs of the EU Banking Crisis.

The period from 2012 to 2015 was tumultuous for the Eurozone and for Greece. The reality of Troikanomics permeated the lives of the Greek people against the backdrop of an unfolding Eurozone crisis. The scale and rapidity of the fiscal consolidation was without precedent: by every metric—unemployment, emigration, and indebtedness—Greece was impelled headlong into the deepest depression in modern Europe, played out against an extended political crisis. The chronology of events does not begin to adequately capture the reality of Troikanomics. There are too many economic absurdities, too much obdurate, even surreal politics, and too many acrimonious relationships, all of it overshadowed by what Galbraith (2016) describes as 'economic policy as moral abomination'.

The election at the beginning of 2015 of the radical left-wing Syriza party, led by Mr Tsipras, marked an almost incomprehensible phase of Greece's political debacle. The impact of austerity on the economy and living standards was, by any EU standards, nihilistically harsh. Every combination of traditional politics had failed. The country was already impaled on a bailout. The voters turned to the radical left under Prime Minister Tsipras and his

Finance Minister, an unconventional but brilliant Economist, Professor Yanis Varoufakis. The Greek voters mandated a fresh start. The six months of hostility and confrontation that followed revealed the defining bleakness of Troikanomics and, simultaneously, a collapse in domestic democracy.

As the face-off between the EU and the new government approached, the authors of this book argued in mid-June 2015—and we quote extensively, since it sets the tone for our wider analysis—that '*[t]he narrative of the Eurozone crisis, the epicentre of which is Greece, has been airbrushed. Germany's insistence that the 2012 bailout programme is a realistic reference point for current discussions is misconceived. Its assertion that debt relief can be discussed only after the completion of the current programme, rather than being the obvious starting point for a new agreement, is profoundly mistaken.*

*The tenor of the euro zone's criticism of the government of Alex Tsipras has shifted from the patronising to the denunciatory, from faux long-suffering indulgence with a brash upstart to near visceral condemnation. The message is that the grown-ups in the room are "exasperated" and "running out of patience" with Greece. Germany's minister for economic affairs, Sigmar Gabriel, argues that "Greece's game theorists are gambling the future of their country. And Europe's too".*

*This is revisionist rhetoric. Greece is more right than its critics. One does not have to agree with the politics of the far-left in Greece to vindicate the integrity of their economic case. What is true of a relationship is true of a relationship: dependence is never healthy. Continued membership (of the Eurozone) means continued dependence. Given the pressures being exerted on Greece, exit rather than dependence would be the better option*'[12] (Kinsella 2015).

The outcome of the clash was catastrophic. The German Finance Minister Wolfgang Schäuble made no secret of his wish to push Greece out of the Eurozone, at least until it had regained its competitiveness. He was overruled by the German Chancellor Merkel. In the absence of a fresh start for Greece on both economic and moral grounds—to which Germany would never agree—Schäuble was icily correct in his analysis.

[12] See Kinsella (2015).

His priority was saving the Eurozone from a Greek contagion. Greece's continued membership was a threat to that larger and overriding objective. Abstracting from all the caveats and all the 'what ifs', Greece should have exited. The 'saving of Greece' came at the cost of a nihilistic austerity package, humiliatingly imposed on Tsipras after he had rejected a less onerous set of proposals. It led, as many other economists argued, to the undoing of democracy in Greece, to total dependence, and to a relationship between Mr Tsipras and the Troika that was and remains deeply problematic. Fast-forward to June 2018 when EU Finance Ministers announced the completion of Greece's Third Bailout Programme and its formal exit (pre-announced for August 2018) from the austerity programmes begun under the Troika in 2010. We return to this pivotal event in the concluding section.

## Greece and the Hegemony at the Heart of the Eurozone

Having reviewed the chronology, there is much to be gained from attempting to look, as it were, behind the stage to discern the forces at play bearing down on Greece. Figure 7.2 represents in stylised, hierarchical form the set of countries, institutions, and agencies impacting on Greece and the manner in which power is mediated across the EU. Financial markets are, of course, ubiquitous—interconnected, driven by short-termism, and utterly self-serving. They serve those countries that have, and exercise, power.

Two substantive points can be inferred from Fig. 7.2, which provides some insight into the enormity of the pressures in the face of which the Greek anti-austerity democratic revolution capitulated in July 2015. Firstly, Germany dominates the European economy. Throughout the crisis it has sustained a robust fiscal and trade surplus while the peripheral nations were under consistent pressure. Cultural factors are important here—notably Germany's high savings rate, its political culture and productivity, as well as the strength of its manufacturing base. By extension, it dominates the governance of Europe, wherein France serves as a partial off-setting power. Other countries, starting with 'core' satellite

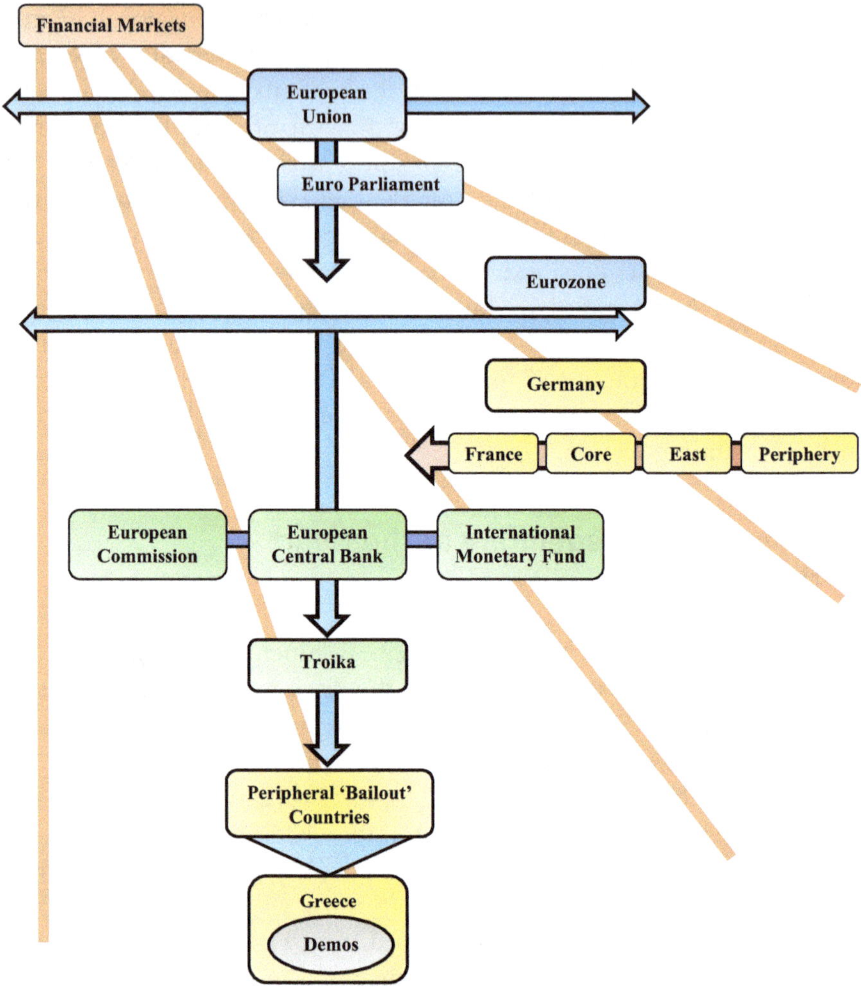


**Fig. 7.2** Greece: The anatomy of hegemony. Source: Authors' own

countries and extending out to include northern European and larger central Mediterranean countries, are configured around this. The eastern European countries, between them, have built a degree of autonomy from the prevailing Franco-German hegemony. Figure 7.2 illustrates how the weight of this power from Germany and the Franco-German axis bears down *via* the Troika on Greece. It is not, of course, quite as simple as this; there are many 'groups' and 'forums'. But it is a close approximation to the *realpolitik* of Troikanomics and how an unelected, unrepresentative, and unaccountable entity's 'influence' amounts to imposition.

The second point takes us deeper. There was little common purpose or vision amongst these various stakeholders on how best the Debt Crisis that had overtaken Greece might be resolved—certainly not enough to engender a workable sense of cohesion, consensus, or moral purpose. When entropy becomes endemic, effective resolution becomes much harder to attain. The Troika was conflicted in their engagement with Greece. The IMF and the European Institutions held markedly different views in relation to technical assumptions, forecasts, as well as on the necessity of debt relief. The ECB itself was conflicted between adhering to its own 'no bailout/monetary financing' rules and devising some form of monetary arrangements for getting around the issue. The EC was conflicted between its role as guardian of the Treaties and its growing executive function.

At the height of the crisis in June 2015, Germany was divided between the views of its Chancellor Merkel and its Finance Minister Schäuble, notably in relation to whether or not Greece should be forced out of the Eurozone, and on what the terms and conditions would be if it were to remain. France and Germany were conflicted on this same issue, with President Hollande supporting Chancellor Merkel in opposing (along with the Prime Minister of Italy) Schäuble. The wider EU was conflicted in how best to accommodate itself to the ongoing instability of the Eurozone while, at the same time, grappling with other crises—notably the migration crisis bearing down on Greece itself. Goldman Sachs, as noted earlier, was conflicted through selling Greece the complex financial instruments that allowed it to disguise the true status of its public finances.[13]

The whole set of players was riven by the refusal of Germany to entertain debt relief. But how can there be any coherent resolution

[13] Stiglitz has noted the manner in which the financial markets turned rogue and attacked the Greek sovereign when the new Socialist Prime Minister Papandreou disclosed the true size of Greece's budget deficit and debt burden.

when the dominant EU country exercised such hegemony over the very institution—namely the Troika—which it helped establish and invited the IMF to join, and *at the same time* refuses to engage with the IMF in an area in which the IMF had unrivaled expertise and experience?

There is an inherent contradiction in seeking to deliver rational conflict resolution when the process through which this is discharged is dominated, not by high-level principles and values but by the outcome of elections in the dominant countries—Germany and France—while ignoring the outcomes of elections and referenda in Greece. A judicial system, to take one example, could not possibly function in a situation where there were no harmonised principles directed towards a common end. The institutions and mandates impacting on a crisis-stricken Greece, at a time of unprecedented global instability, were not aligned because of conflicting, inconsistent political agendas and priorities. They interact, like particles in quantum theory, sometimes randomly and always with only probabilistic outcomes. The Troika were the vector through which this incoherence was transmitted to the Greek people.

## Beyond Austerity

For those versed in rational political economy, it is difficult to comprehend what possible sense there could have been for the Troika to lend so much money to an *already* highly indebted country, simply to repay earlier loans to itself—at least some of which should never have been made in the first instance (as the IMF itself tacitly acknowledged by making changes to its own terms and conditions to accommodate such loans).[14] What is even more resonant of the existential nature of the Greek crisis is that relatively little of the funds provided under the first two Bailouts found their way into the Greek economy. Rochell (2016), for example,

[14] A question that was raised by one of the authors in Kinsella (2015).

notes that the vast majority went to debt repayments, interest payments, debt restructuring, and bank recapitalisation.

The extraction by the Eurozone orthodoxy of a primary budget surplus from an economy in the equivalent of critical care was the price levied on Greece as opposed to engaging sensibly with debt relief.[15] The great British economist Keynes (2004) once asked what on earth was the point in imposing an impossible burden of reparations on Germany—and whether 'the great and the powerful' had actually thought through the consequences of this? Or, in terms of our argument, whether the processes and policies had been properly critiqued by the Troika. They had not, of course. Keynes' challenge remains relevant whenever a powerful orthodoxy imposes oppressive demands that sacrifice economic legitimacy for political leverage—as in the case here with regard to debt relief.

What all of this tells us is that decision-making within the EU over the period of Troikanomics was burdened by a failure to critique; to confront the elephant in the room, that is, a level of Greek debt that was simply unrepayable. And yet, for the EU, it appeared that while to be with Greece was difficult, to be without it was dread-inducing.[16] If one were to ask 'what's the difference then between austerity and Troikanomics?' one needs to simply point to the treatment of Greece by the Eurozone in late June/early July 2015. The 'take it or leave' conditions were imposed by the EU just before the announcement of results from a referendum called by Prime Minister Tsipras on the EU Proposals—which emphatically rejected them. For Greek voters and families, they meant less than nothing.

Former Greek Finance Minister Yanis Varoufakis has recalled the breath-taking extent of the control exhibited by the Troika. In the early days of his ministerial tenure he sought to address the challenge of how Greece might cope with Grexit—whether it be self-determined or impelled by Germany, as it could so easily have been in June 2015. This entailed drawing up a Plan B for how the national payments system might operate and serve as a platform for a parallel currency, should this be necessary. In attempting to carry this through, he was impelled to

[15] See, for example, Spiegel (2015).

[16] For a further analysis on this conflict, see Kuper (2017).

consider hacking into his own ministry to avoid being detected by Brussels—only to find that Brussels indeed *already* controlled the software running the taxation system, serving as an early warning signal to them of any government's contingency planning.[17]

It is difficult to comprehend how philosophically conversant institutions could justify engaging in a form of austerity whose social collateral was so normatively untenable—the migration of over half a million young people, homes subdivided to accommodate children who could never hope to own their own home, social support cut to ribbons, a debt of some €280 billion—the list goes on and on. This nags at the sensibilities of all who might be tempted to take the rhetoric of 'Europe' and its foundational values seriously. The use by the Troika of oppressive measures and interventions to enforce conditionality on a stricken country, its legislature, and its citizens, asks questions about the EU's legitimacy as an ethically viable institution conversant in the language of 'virtues', 'duties', and 'consequences'. This applies particularly where such interventions impact directly on living standards and vital public services and diminish democratic legitimacy to a form of *de facto* political blackmail.

Economic adjustment, including fiscal consolidation and rebalancing, is necessary across all countries at some point or another. However, we have discussed elsewhere the case against austerity as a 'go to' set of policies.[18] The Greek experience of Troikanomics went far beyond any technical definition of austerity. It encompasses the subversion of identity and autonomy within a country which had—in an extraordinary historical paradox—introduced to Europe and to the world the concept of representative democracy, including the role of the demos in the governance of the country.[19] It also poses the question of whether legislation that is intrinsically and measurably oppressive, and enforced under duress, can

[17] As it happens, the authors had been invited to participate in a conference call at which Professor Varoufakis revealed this example—to the great consternation, it should be said, of the co-Chairman of the session, former Chancellor of the Exchequer Normal Lamont and David Marsh of the *Financial Times*.

[18] As Blyth (2013) has pointed out, 'is not a well worked out body of ideas and doctrine, an integral part of economic or any other theory'.

[19] The 'demos' being, of course, what the EU orthodoxy would pejoratively define as 'Populism'.

be regarded as in any way legitimate. Is this what the EU really thinks? If not, then it is a short step from there to punitive and immoral governance, that is, to acts that offend against more than the legislative framework of an organisation or a country, *but go against the moral fabric weaving it together.*[20]

For a generation that lived through the seemingly never-ending Greek Crisis, stasis became 'normalised': a precedent has been set through years where it was *expected* to be unemployed, to watch one's loved ones emigrate, to be sick and yet not be able to avail of hospital access. The older cohort also remember how very different it was less than two decades previously when Greece joined the Eurozone on a wave of optimism. Simon Kuper (2017) distils what happened to Greece in reflecting on a visit he made to Athens in 2017: '*Outside Parliament, a few dozen people were waving Greek flags, protesting against something. But such scenes have become rare: most Greeks have given up. "For me, there is no crisis" shouted my friend from under his (motorcycle) helmet. "This is how we live. And we're learning to live with our fears". Athenians have adjusted to a forever crisis.*'

Between the rock and the hard place were the Greek voters in anguish over the meltdown of their politics and democratic heritage. Well over half a million young adults left since the onset of austerity, many of them paradoxically headed for the 'core' EU countries.[21] Pensioners had their pensions eviscerated. Medical facilities were left short of essential inputs, with a measurably negative impact on the health status of Greece.[22,23] The haemorrhage of young adults explains both the anger and the angst of Greek voters—of parents and employers—at the human impact of Troikanomics.

---

[20] There is compelling evidence of the subtle and incremental manner in which this can and has occurred. See, for example, Salter (2008).

[21] Lazaretou (2016) has pointed out that '[m]igration and poverty are undoubtedly the two most painful consequences experienced by a society in protracted crisis conditions'. She notes that in 2013, 100,000 people emigrated from Greece, tripling the yearly average up to that point with the same pattern continuing through 2014 and 2015. Cited in OECD (2018).

[22] In a recent analysis looking at the impact of austerity on pensions in the broader context of fiscal consolidation and longer-term sustainability, Angelaki (2018) notes that the introduction of significant cuts has led to an estimated reduction of pension benefits for current pensioners of close to 50% in certain cases.

[23] For an extensive literature on this issue, see, for example, Kentikelenis et al. (2014a, 2014b).

The experience of Greece highlights the moral as well as politico-economic dilemmas that have now become normalised, and the compelling case for the philosophic critique. In this context, it raised questions. To take just a few examples, is there a normative reference point, beyond all political expediency, for assessing whether the conditionality imposed on Greece in successive bailouts was oppressive to the spirit of the Treaty on European Union (TEU)? Can we regard as 'moral' a denial for so long of debt relief to Greece because of the unilateral decision of Germany *even though* the IMF, with its vast experience, argued that debt relief was essential to resolving the country's long-term future? Is it morally legitimate to impose a debt burden of such enormity across generations, even though the younger generation neither caused the crisis nor were responsible for the flaws in policy—both within Greece and in the design of Eurozone? Is it justifiable to continue to impose conditions on Greece in the *aftermath* of its exit of the bailout? More generally, how large does the difference in living standards between the EU core and the periphery have to be in order to acknowledge that there has been a breakdown in the moral template within which the EU ostensibly operated? The Troika had different views on how best to resolve the Greek crisis—as they did in the case of Ireland—so, by what principles and benchmarks are we to evaluate which of these views should prevail, given that they involve very different impacts, both on living standards and on the future trajectory of the economy?

These are difficult issues, and all the more important for that. The EU is more than a 'market economy'. Up to the mid-1980s there were normative principles, rooted in the Christian Democratic tradition, which shaped and informed ethical behaviours in terms of 'right' and 'wrong'. As these principles have been systematically displaced it is not clear what has or can replace them. One could robustly affirm that it was 'wrong' to sequester the homes or jobs of people, or to prevent another government carrying out its responsibilities to its people, because it was an affront to the Common Good. That analysis is no longer given credence within a system that speaks the language of moral values but of a kind of contractualism—'The Rule of Law'. That tells us little or nothing about whether, or not, Greece was decimated by the Troika and whether, or not, this was 'wrong'—in particular since it was imposed within what is canvassed as a 'community'. These and related questions take us into the domain of meta-ethics, which is beyond the scope of this book. Nonetheless, they deserve to be highlighted as a corrective to the pretensions of the EU elite in invoking the spirit of 'unity', 'solidarity', and 'subsidiarity' while demonstrating by its actions and its use of language that what counts is money—who pays most and who has the power to deploy it.

## The Illusion of 'Exit'

Perhaps the most telling criticism of the Troika's regime is that, in the end, different expressions of democracy—from successive elections and referenda to demonstrations (including the tear-gassing of pensioners on the streets of Athens)—failed to mitigate the assault of Troikanomics on Greece. The country was subdued into a kind of silence in the long-drawn-out process to a formal 'exit' from successive bailouts, all the while conscious that the EU orthodoxy that had imposed these developments would be likely to continue in 'monitoring their progress'. They were right. It is in the nature of bureaucracies to extricate themselves from debacles frequently caused by their own misconceived and failed policies. With a 'changing of the guards' by politicians/bureaucrats/technocrats—each moving on, moving up, or moving out—comes the hope of a kind of democratic amnesia, that is, that the demos will latch on to the aspirations of the future and forget the broken promises of the past. But the questions will endure.

When the Eurogroup announced an agreement on the conclusion of Greece's Third Bailout and its formal 'exit' from the EU/IMF Programme, it was greeted in the rhetoric typical of such occasions by the EU's Economic Affairs Commissioner Pierre Muscovici as 'an exceptional moment … the Greek crisis ends here tonight in Luxemburg'. It is difficult to see how this is borne out by its terms. The detail and scope are so demanding on the people of Greece, so discriminatory in its terms and conditions which extend upwards of 40 years into the future, that it provides an appropriate obituary for the Troika and the political mind-set underscoring it. It reduces Greece to a vassal state for the indefinite future, with no substantive budgetary autonomy.

The agreement permitted Greece to defer repayment of European Financial Stabilisation Mechanism (EFSM) loans of some €96 billion—40% of its indebtedness to the Eurozone—from 2023 to 2033.[24] It extended loan maturities by the same amount of time and provided funding of €15 billion to absorb debt repayments falling due over the short term and as a 'cash buffer' to facilitate a return to the markets. Profits made by Eurozone Central Banks on Greeks Bonds will be recycled back, with the prospect of additional relief for Greece in 2033 dependent on its 'performance'. The agreement made no provision for debt write-offs. It requires Greece to generate a primary budget surplus of 3.5% of GDP up to 2022 and an estimated 2.2% between 2023 and 2060. It also commits Greece to a wide range of actions, from social welfare and labour market policies to privatisation and public administration. It imposes quarterly 'enhanced surveillance' on Greece for the foreseeable future. All of this after three Bailout Programmes. And, it should be added, with the IMF unconvinced that the future is sustainable. If this is 'success', then Heaven forbid that 'failure' be visited on any nation.

There has been nothing remotely like this conditionality imposed on any other European country. From this perspective, the statement by the Greek Prime Minister after the agreement that 'Greece is once again becoming a normal country, regaining its political and financial independence' makes no sense whatever. Syrzia was mandated, at the polls and by referendum, to oppose Troikanomics. It failed—the hegemony was too powerful. In reality, the essence of Troikanomics has been perpetuated in an 'exit' agreement that leaves the Greek people with a caricature of political and financial autonomy.

## References

Angelaki, M. (2018). *Uncovering the Profound Effects That Pension and Health Care Reforms Have Had in Post-Crisis Greece*. [Online]. Retrieved from http://blogs.lse.ac.uk/europpblog/2018/02/23/uncovering-the-profound-effectsthat-pension-and-health-care-reforms-have-had-in-post-crisis-greece/

[24] See the Eurogroup (2018) statement. See also Khan and Brunsden (2018) for a useful overview.

Bénéton, P., Brague, R., Delsol, C., Joch, R., András, L., Legutko, R., Manent, P., Matlary, J. H., Pavón, D. N., Scruton, R., Spaemann, R., & Jan Spruyt, B. (2017). *The Paris Statement: A Europe We Can Believe in*. [Online]. Retrieved from https://thetrueeurope.eu/a-europe-we-can-believe-in/
Blyth, M. (2013). *Austerity: The History of a Dangerous Idea*. Oxford: Oxford University Press.
Central Statistics Office. (2013). *Government Finance Statistics – Annual*. [Online]. Retrieved from https://www.cso.ie/en/releasesandpublications/er/gfsa/governmentfinancestatisticsapril2013/
Committee on Foreign Relations. (2018). *Greece's Debt: 1974–2018* [Online]. Retrieved from https://www.cfr.org/timeline/greeces-debt-crisis-timeline
Doxiadis, E., & Placas, A. (Eds.). (2018). *Living Under Austerity: Greek Society in Crisis*. New York: Berghahn.
The Irish Times (Editorial). (2010). *Was It for This?*. s.l: The Irish Times.
Eurogroup. (2018). *Eurogroup Statement on Greece of 22 June 2018*. [Online]. Retrieved from http://www.consilium.europa.eu/en/press/press-releases/2018/06/22/eurogroup-statement-on-greece-22-june-2018/
Galbraith, J. K. (2016). *Welcome to the Poisoned Chalice: The Destruction of Greece and the Future of Europe*. Yale: Yale University Press.
Hand, L. (2013). *The Week Ireland Gave up Its Sovereignty*. s.l.: Independent.
Hennigan, M. (2014). *Ireland Accounted for 25% of ECB's Emergency Lending by Time of 2010 Bailout*. [Online]. Retrieved from http://www.finfacts.ie/irish-financenews/article_1028408.shtml
Joint Committee of Inquiry into the Banking Crisis. (2014). *Final Report to the Joint Committee*. Dublin: Houses of the Oireachtas.
Kelly, M. (2006). *How the Housing Corner Stones of Our Economy Could Go into Rapid Free Fall*. s.l.: The Irish Times.
Kentikelenis, A., et al. (2014a). Greece's Health Crisis: From Austerity to Denialism. *The Lancet, 383*, 748–753.
Kentikelenis, A., et al. (2014b). Austerity and Health in Greece – Authors' Reply. *The Lancet, 383*(9928), 1544–1545.
Keynes, J. M. (2004). *The Economic Consequences of the Peace*. Mineola, New York: Dover Publications.
Khan, M., & Brunsden, J. (2018). *Eurozone Creditors Reach 'Historic' Deal on Greek Debt Relief*. s.l.: Financial Times.
Kinsella, R. (2015). *Why Greece Should Choose Eurozone Exit Rather Than Dependence*. s.l.: The Irish Times.

Kinsella, R., & Kinsella, M. (2009). Ethical Causes and Implications of the Global Financial Crisis in Ireland: Political Contagion and Political Transformation. *Studies: An Irish Quarterly Review, 98*(391), 285–308.

Kinsella, R., & Kinsella, R. (2011). The Rise and Rise of Long Term and Youth Unemployment in Ireland: The Scarring of a Generation. *Studies: An Irish Quarterly Review, 100*(397), 83–102.

Kuper, S. (2017). *How Greeks Have Adjusted to the Forever Crisis*. s.1.: The Financial Times.

Lazaretou, S. (2016). *The Flight of Human Capital. Economic Bulletin*. Athens: Bank of Greece.

Lenihan, B., & Honohan, P. (2010). *Ireland: Letter of Intent, Memorandum of Economic and Financial Policies, and Technical Memorandum of Understanding*. [Online]. Retrieved from https://www.imf.org/external/np/loi/2010/irl/120310.pdf

OECD. (2018). *OECD Economic Surveys: Greece 2018*. Paris: OECD Publishing.

Rochell, J. (2016). *Most of Greek Bailout Money Went to Banks: Study*. [Online]. Retrieved from https://www.dw.com/en/most-of-greek-bailout-money-went-to-banks-study/a-19234391

Salter, M. S. (2008). *Innovation Corrupted: The Origins and Legacy of Enron's Collapse*. Harvard: Harvard University Press.

Schwartz, N., & Dash, E. (2010). *Banks Bet Greece Defaults on Debt They Helped Hide*. [Online]. Retrieved from http://www.nytimes.com/2010/02/25/business/global/25swaps.html

Spiegel. (2015). *Schäuble's Push for Grexit Puts Merkel on Defensive*. [Online]. Retrieved from http://www.spiegel.de/international/germany/schaeuble-pushed-for-a-grexit-and-backed-merkel-into-a-corner-a-1044259.html

Stein, J. L. (2011). The Diversity of Debt Crises. *Cato Journal, 31*(2), 199–215.

Stiglitz, J. E. (2016). *The Euro: How a Common Currency Threatens the Future of Europe*. New York: W. W. Norton & Company.

Story, L., Thomas, L., Jr., & Schwartz, N. D. (2010). *Wall St. Helped to Mask Debt Fueling Europe's Crisis*. [Online]. Retrieved from https://www.nytimes.com/2010/02/14/business/global/14debt.html

Traynor, I. (2015). *Three Days that Saved the Euro*. [Online]. Retrieved from https://www.theguardian.com/world/2015/oct/22/three-days-to-save-the-euro-greece

# Part IV

## Where from Here? Charting the Trajectory of the EU

# 8

# The EU as a Communal Endeavour: Ideal and Reality

## Introduction

Far-reaching changes within the EU and the Eurozone will occur in 2019/2020—Elections to the European Parliament, a new President for both the Commission and the ECB, as well as the implementation of extensive proposed reforms.[1] The EU's capacity to develop through to a new era of governance will, in large part, be dependent on the extent to which it can align its status as an *ideal* (encapsulated in its sociopolitical and economic aspirations, and the principles binding it together) with its *lived reality* (expressed in the experiences of the nations that function under its umbrella, and their citizens). Aligning the *ideals* and the *realities* of the EU experience over the last two decades is central to this transition. In its current form, there is a deep schism between them. This has led to the forfeiture of the foundational ethic of *community* that has been so anthropologically central to the EU, whereby the 'founding

[1] The next Elections to the European Parliament will be held in late May 2019. Following the withdrawal of the United Kingdom from the EU, a vote by the European Parliament in February 2018 stipulated that the number of Members of the European Parliament (MEPs) will be reduced from 751 to 705. These 705 members will represent around 500 million people from 28 Member States.



R. Kinsella, M. Kinsella, *Troikanomics*, https://doi.org/10.1007/978-3-319-97070-7_8

fathers' had a very deep, experiential, understanding of what community meant to the lives of people and the future of countries.

The first formal attempts at establishing a European Community were motivated by the belief that pooling common resources could produce a more peaceful and prosperous environment.[2] With respect to the question of emergent federalism, it has become increasingly clear that the EU is wrapped up in an ongoing integration process that fails to foster peripheral countries' autonomous ambitions, and instead *cedes* them to the will of the dominant countries. The question this raises is whether the 'Union' of the EU, in what it has now developed into, truly provides a space for countries and their citizens to live *in communion* within its larger ambit.

While there are common links, interests, and aspirations that unite this community, attempts to draw on a European *demos* often appear disingenuous—something that is largely contrived, periodically stage-managed, and at variance with the diverse sense of identity experienced within the EU at every level. Ask the people of Greece, from which the term 'demos' derives. Even as people 'approve' of Europe, it does not engage with them at the same primordial level as their 'own' national identity. How can this dichotomy best be expressed, and does it have to be a negative sum game—so that as Project Europe is impelled forward, the national domain is eclipsed? The EU has continued to build new institutions—and is set to build more—notwithstanding that there has been a failure to align the two paths which define what Europe is *about* and what it *is*.

## From the Ashes: European Ambitions in a Post-War Environment

From its beginnings, the European Project was premised on the ambition of becoming a co-directive force in the post-World War II rapidly evolving geopolitical climate. It was, consequently, opposed to any notion that

[2] These efforts were acknowledged by The Nobel Committee in 2012 with the awarding of the Nobel Peace Prize, noting that '[t]he union and its forerunners have for over six decades contributed to the advancement of peace and reconciliation, democracy and human rights in Europe'. Alongside this, they were keen to note that '[t]he EU is currently undergoing grave economic difficulties and considerable social unrest'.

it (or, more accurately, its member nations) should be acquiescent to more 'dominant' powers.[3] Of course, at the time, this endeavour may have appeared *overly* ambitious—self-assuredness inviting hubris, and naive regarding the considerable political and economic concessions that this would entail from individual members.

If anything, however, the project required a level of *humility* from its founding members, who had to acknowledge that their own sovereign prospects were best served within a communal context that required the shouldering of collective strengths and weaknesses—and a coming together, with shared political values informed by a common spiritual heritage, to build trust after an epochal war. Having passed the 60th anniversary milestone of the Treaty of Rome, it is clear that (notwithstanding its multiple crises) this Project has been indispensable in ensuring that the EU holds considerable standing *as a distinct entity*. Looking to the future, amidst growing sociopolitical dissent fuelled by events such as the manner in which the Banking and Debt Crisis was managed, we are increasingly left to question *whom exactly* this entity actually represents. Does it reflect and do justice to the increasingly diverse perspectives that now occupy the Public Square of intra-European politics?

The story of the EU—more especially in the wake of the recent US/EU divide in trade and security arrangements under President Donald Trump—has been woven amidst experiences that have tested the patience, resolve, and ambition of its member nations. It continues to encounter such trials—emanating both internally and from events in the wider geopolitical sphere in which it is embedded. Now making continued inroads towards further integration (read: federalism), it faces the challenge of having to align the autonomous ambitions of its members with an inclusive communal ethos. Balancing what appears to be—on the face of it—two polarities, is

[3] In 1956, following on from the Suez Canal Crisis and the corresponding end of Britain's and France's imperial influence in the region, the dominance of the United States over its Western allies had been left in little doubt. Consequently, German Chancellor Konrad Adenauer became emboldened to launch a European political initiative that could withstand other dominant global forces at the time. Here, he stated that while *individual* European countries would never be leading global powers *in and of themselves*, 'there remains to them only one way of playing a decisive role in the world; that is to unite to make Europe. ... Europe will be your revenge'. One year later, the Treaty of Rome launched the Common Market (The Economist 2006).

no small task. It requires constant vigilance in ensuring that, in its form and function, this project remains responsive to the autonomous needs of an ever-expanding and increasingly disparate populace, while also remaining a distinctly communal undertaking.

The first formal attempts at establishing a European Community were motivated by the belief that pooling common resources could produce a more peaceful and prosperous environment for a European people who had been irrevocably scarred by the trauma of World War II.[4] Simultaneously, there was a less obvious but no less important subtext, rooted in a sought-for political, economic, and military accommodation between France and Germany. Heads of national governments—Germany, Italy, and France—had witnessed the horrors that ensue when an absence of esteem for human life engages with an unquenchable thirst for power. Beyond seeking to make 'all things new' in the post-war environment, there was the more visceral and pressing motivation of *preventing* future war.

This sentiment was apparent in the Schuman Declaration (1950), which proposed that 'Franco-German production of coal and steel be placed under a common Higher Authority, within the framework of an organization open to the participation of the other countries of Europe'. In doing so, they created the mind-set, bolstered by a political and economic infrastructure, to ensure that conflict between these two nations was 'not merely unthinkable, but materially impossible'. This led to the first formal foundations of the EU being established in 1951, under the European Coal and Steel Community (ECSC)—which prized integration over divisiveness, and solidarity over the deeply negative forms of *nationalistic-cum-antagonistic* sovereignty that had come to darken Europe's doorway.[5] Brick by brick, the EU was slowly built from the (literal) ashes of war.

[4] Here, Weiler (1999) provides a discussion on three foundational ideals that underpinned the process of integration: peace, shared prosperity, and supranationality.

[5] The ECSC was formally established by the Treaty of Paris in 1951, and signed by Belgium, France, West Germany, Italy, the Netherlands, and Luxembourg. Its primary purpose was ensuring peace, which was achieved—amongst other ways—through the regulation of industrial production under a centralised authority. Based on the principles of 'supranationalism'—wherein member nations agree to delegate power to an authority (see Kiljunen 2004)—it helped set in motion the ethic of transnational dialogue and decision-making that would culminate in the foundation of the European Union. The Treaty of Paris expired in 2002, and with it the ECSC.

Given the events of recent years, one could be forgiven for thinking that the *modus vivendi* of European integration is economic—certainly, the post-2008 Debt Crisis has preoccupied our understanding of both *how* and *why* member nations are engaged within the union. However, it is important to note that from the outset the blueprint for Europe was predominantly political (with economic agendas emerging as a corollary). This position was asserted by German Chancellor Adenauer in the Bundestag in 1952, arguing that 'the political goal, the political meaning of the European Coal and Steel Community, is infinitely larger than its economic purpose'. In a more contemporary context, Article 2 of the Lisbon Treaty expresses the importance of *both* political and economic pillars in ensuring communal cohesion.[6] In fact, we can only truly appreciate the complexity of the EU's economic relations when we recognise how they are intertwined with, and often give expression to, the political will (for better or for worse).

Crucially, for its founders, the integration of political resolve and economic resources was not *in and of itself* the definitive deliverable for Europe; both of these were to give expression to its underlying normative goal of securing, amongst other things, democratic inclusiveness and social solidarity.

Project Europe sought to express shared values in a creative and transformational way. So, then, just as it is a day-to-day *lived reality* embedded in such things as trade relationships and labour mobility, it is also an *ideal* that imbues these activities with a higher purpose. What is often forgotten or marginalised is the fact that the 'founders' of the European Project Jean Monnet, Robert Schuman, Konrad Adenauer, and Alcaide De Gasperi—as people and politicians—acted within a distinct social culture and religious sensibility that was embedded in Christian Democracy.

We return to this theme later but it bears anticipating here: at the time of the ECSC's founding, Christian Democracy dominated Europe's sociopolitical order—it has thus permeated and animated its purpose,

---

[6] The Treaty of Lisbon (13 December 2007) states in Article 2. 1 that '[t]he Union's aim is to promote peace, its values and the well-being of its peoples', this is followed by Article 2.3 stating that '[t]he Union shall establish an internal market. It shall work for the sustainable development of Europe based on balanced economic growth and price stability, a highly competitive social market economy, aiming at full employment and social progress'.

and aligned principles, from an embryonic stage. The values derived from its system of thought provided a continuity with Europe's history, and have continued to shepherd it over subsequent decades. Briefly, according to the Konrad Adenaur Institute (2010) its founding belief is '...the Christian understanding of man as a creation of God – a creation of equal individuals who, while imperfect, should be treated with dignity'. Christian Democracy didn't seek to politicise its two conceptual pillars of Christian Social Teaching and Enlightenment Critique, but rather to apply these *in praxis* within the political realm. It helped to provide an answer to the question of how nations can be motivated to work together in a democratic manner, without having to completely rely on the (easily corruptible) incentives of either narrow nationalistic agendas or fear of reprimand. In the aftermath of the most existentially divisive war in Europe's history, Christianity's reconciliatory and redemptive ethic was drawn on to provide a rationale and motivation for dialogue that sought to transcend nationalistic allegiances—in as much as individual countries were in need of renewal, the European continent was *deserving* of it.

We can identify four prominent principles that underpin the Christian Democratic ethic, each making its mark on Europe's emergent identity at this time: (1) the inherent dignity of the person; (2) the innate sociability of the person; (3) the dysfunctionality and destructiveness of totalitarian regimes; and (4) the indispensability of a transnational moral compass (and in its absence, the related danger of moral relativism). In the absence of these shared principles, and the basis for a mutual vocabulary that they helped to facilitate, a very different template for Europe's post-war future may well have emerged. Other things being equal, these principles should have been central to any debate on the Troika's austerity mandate and how best to manage the post-crisis adjustment process. In practice, they were conspicuous by their absence.

The first two principles, dignity and sociability, are encompassed in the domain of Christian 'Personalism'.[7] Here, the Catholic tradition acts as a locus of moral thought, with the Pontifical Council for Justice and Peace (2005) explicitly arguing for 'the dignity of every human person, the

[7] Whose perspectives on these matters continued to be formalised in the years after the initial foundation of the ECSC.

respect of human rights, commitment to the common good as the purpose and guiding criterion for political life' (par. 407). In his discussion on this principle, Pope John Paul II (1995) argues that 'peace which is not built upon the values of the dignity of every individual and of solidarity between all people frequently proves to be illusory'. This stance implicitly parallels Immanuel Kant's (1785, p. 30) moral dictum that people should be respected as *an end in themselves*, noting that 'for, the ends of a subject who is an end in itself must as far as possible be also my ends'. This appreciation for the centrality of human dignity has helped give shape to the rights of the person, and the attendant duties of governments in upholding these rights.

Personalism also advocates for the inherently social nature of individuals, that is, how the experience of self-transcendence can (paradoxically) foster a sense of self-definition. People internalise the social relationships that they are embedded within, which have a pervasive influence on the internal competencies and relations-to-self that are central to both one's identity and aligned autonomy. Here, in terms of our broader analysis on the *relational* nature of autonomy, Pope Benedict XVI (2009) notes that people are defined through interpersonal relations, and that the more authentically a person lives these relations, the more their own personal identity matures. Charles Taylor's (1992) Communitarian critique also argues for 'dialogue' being the crucial feature of human life, and that an adequate understanding of the characteristics and capacities of the self cannot be achieved without attention to this foundational embeddedness. The process of personal discovery should not be seen as being worked out in isolation, but rather as a dialogical negotiation. To put this differently, interpersonal relationships are not just unavoidable or incidental, they are developmentally integral.[8]

Transposing these principles to our broader analysis—and with half an eye on the Troika's engagement with the people of Greece—we can say that they should find their expression in democracy. Recognition of the person's dignity and sociability is the seed from which democracy takes root within a nation, extending outwards and enveloping institutions and organisations. Democracy vindicates and cements their right to participate actively, equally, and responsibly in politics and society. By way of

[8] See also Wachtel (2014).

contrast—and because it was perceived in post-war European countries as a grave political threat—Soviet Communism is predicated on the subjugation of the individual and a deterministic perspective of history, one of its darkest embodiments being the Gulag forced labour camps within the Soviet Union.

To that extent, Soviet Communism is the very antithesis of solidarity amongst free people in democracies. For this reason, the transition of Russia to a new post-Soviet political paradigm should have been equivocally welcomed by the West that was, after all, shaped around the values towards which Russia was evolving. As we point out elsewhere, this didn't happen, leading to the present adversarial stance between the EU and Russia. It was a missed opportunity which might have vindicated Project Europe's democratic values progressing to closer cooperation—from trade and energy, to political and security cooperation. The argument can be reframed as a conviction that society *itself* (mediated through its political institutions) should be premised on upholding the dignity and sociability of the person—expressed, for example, through the egalitarian and participatory ethic of democracy. This view was also a definitive response to the political ideologies underpinning largely discredited nationalistic parties and an emerging Cold War in which Socialism was viewed with suspicion.[9]

Addressing the challenge of developing a European community entails defining a cohesive set of values through which to pool together and derive a sense of legitimacy. In the tradition of Adenauer, the teaching of the Catholic Church (2005) was emphatic in acknowledging the indispensability of transnationally recognised values, noting that if there is no general consensus on these values, the deepest meaning of democracy is lost and its stability is compromised.[10] Embedded in this is the argument which is central to our critique that relativism is not simply a moral quagmire—it is anathema to pooling the resources of different nations. Pope John Paul II (1991)—one of the most emphatic opponents of the invasion

[9] The true extent of this extraordinary historical dichotomy, played out in a divided Europe, is reflected in the purported justification on the part of a centralised Soviet Power to invade Hungary in 1956 and then again Czechoslovakia in 1968 to enforce '*fraternal* solidarity' (italics added) between a hegemonistic centralised authority of its vessel states.

[10] In this context, Pope John Paul II (1995) has stated that 'without an objective moral grounding not even democracy is capable of ensuring a stable peace, especially since peace which is not built upon the values of the dignity of every individual and of solidarity between all people frequently proves to be illusory'.

of Iraq—notes that '[i]f there is no ultimate truth to guide and direct political action, then ideas and convictions can easily be manipulated for reasons of power. As history demonstrates, a democracy without values easily turns into open or thinly disguised totalitarianism'.[11] Joseph Weiler (1999) has, here, also pointed out that the origins of European integration cannot be understood without an axiological dimension i.e. a commitment to 'the promise of Europe' that captivated and mobilised its leaders.

Building on this, there are many 'formal' means of holding nations together within the ambit of the EU. Constitutions, treaties, laws, trade agreements, all of these help to maintain an infrastructure within which countries can secure their membership. Countries elect their respective representatives into the melee of the European Parliament, they encourage their citizenry to participate in votes, and they contribute a percentage of their national budget to communal causes—all dutifully undertaken tasks. But are they sufficient? Still the question lingers: surely there must be something greater than institutional arrangements bonding people together? In its most extreme form the issue is not whether a citizen would vote for Europe but whether they would *die* for Europe, as they would for their nation. Even as the EU presses ahead with militarisation, this question has not been asked, much less addressed.

It is not just these mechanisms that matter, so much as the *mind-sets* that animate and motivate people. The European Project needs to be bound by more than simply an 'alliance of interests'; a kind of common internal empathy that underscores the acknowledgement that one's 'rights' as a member of a community must be complemented by a recognition of one's 'duties' towards the maintenance of community.

Shared foundational values were, and continue to be, indispensable to any form of integration process that seeks to align the autonomy of a nation with those services that are essential across *all member nations*. The EU's ability to survive amidst discord is rooted in the sense of *promise* that it brings to its participants. It is an ongoing journey towards peace and prosperity, but never *quite* its destination. The ever-elusive, but not intangible, striving for this realisation has in the past assisted in curbing swells of discontent that occasionally express themselves amongst the

[11] Weiler (1999) has also pointed out that the origins of European integration cannot be understood without an axiological dimension.

wider sociopolitical populace—being a central tenant of its status as 'democratically legitimate'.

Aspiration—the hope or ambition to achieve something—is a very powerful resource. Recall that the human psyche is itself inherently 'aspirational', reflected in our constant desire to understand more about ourselves and our world, to bound forward often into the unknown. This holds true not only in the relationships we form, the careers we embark upon, or the pastimes we occupy ourselves with, but in brief moments where a sense of existential curiosity takes hold. It vindicates the risks that we take, it justifies the challenges that we face, and it contextualises the failures that we endure. Our future self is thus an ongoing concern whose welfare can only be attended to in the present; if one's actions lack a sense of aspiration, then they may feel devoid of their deeper significance and therefore inconsequential.

The ethic of *communal* aspiration is relevant in this context. This aspirational ethic was a necessary remedy to the dissonance that had enveloped the European continent after World War II. The pursuit of peace within the continent was not simply about the recovery of stable transnational relationships, but about *discovering* a means through which to coexist in a manner that had never been so much as attempted, let alone achieved.[12] *En passant* this also applies to the largely politically contrived division across the European subcontinent today between 'the West and Russia'. The cohesion that aspiration provided has been eroded in recent decades, displaced by a secular culture that raises serious challenges regarding Europe's identity, precisely at a time when the EU is seeking to write a new 'post-crisis' chapter.

The biggest challenge facing Europe at this time therefore is not about Budgets or Brexit (important as they are): it is about normative principles through which it can be rebooted and reanimated as a *community* rather than an *empire*—how to rediscover substantive ideals without defaulting into revisionism and myths. Equally, how to reconcile what is demonstrably a fractured EU—from the North to the

[12] As de Areilza (2009) notes, this process necessitates 'sacrifice and a transformation of the politics of previous decades'.

Periphery, from the East to the Core, from Russia with whom it shares a continent and is estranged, from applicant countries with a different sense of 'self' to the original foundation members. This critique has been largely absent from conversations centred on the continued restoration of Europe.

## Communal Cohesion and Functional Interdependence

Turning again to our current theme, we can understand 'community' as a space in which the distinctive attributes and autonomous capacities of members are fostered within an environment that upholds their right to benefit from the 'good' of communal participation and their duty to contribute to the maintenance of that same 'good'.[13] Looking forward beyond 2019, this perspective is radically relevant to the content and character of reforms that are being proposed. Community does more than simply describe a 'shared space'. It is a *call to action*, the product of a collective resolution that has been made tangible through the pooling of shared resources—continuously in motion through the reciprocal engagement of its members. At one level, this forward momentum is necessary to stay responsive to a continually changing geopolitical climate. At another level, if the community loses sight of its embryonic values or overriding telos, then this process can, as we have seen, go askew and the bonds that connect members can come undone.

In spite of it being pivotal to the realisation of the European Project, the concept of community is also fundamentally contestable. Community is created through the coming together of distinct entities and yet it is also a distinct entity *in and of itself*. When members come together, they transcend national boundaries and create something more—something that is paradoxically both *derived from* and yet *distinct from* them. This

[13] Here Christman (2014a, 2014b) draws a distinction between 'respecting autonomy' and 'valuing autonomy', both of which can be transposed to the context of the EU. Respect, grounded in the principle of shared dignity, provides limitations on how another is treated and, in this context, would seem to be aligned with the right to negative liberty—*freedom from* oppression. Valuing autonomy is centred on promotion—upholding a positive *freedom to* act.

imbues community with both an ontological and a conceptual complexity. What it represents, and the ways and means through which it is considered to be given its fullest expression, is shaped by the experiences of its members (which, in the context of the EU, is embedded in each country's distinctive sociopolitical perspectives and motivations).

This point is pivotal. For example, Germany's idea of what is entailed in being an active participant in the wider community will be wholly distinct from that of Greece. While it is understandable that each nation occupies its own 'space' within the community and possesses their own experience of inhabiting this space, this becomes deeply problematic when members' experiences are not simply different but diametrically opposed. This vindicates the ongoing need to maintain transnational dialogue within the Union, so that consensus is reached in countries' understanding of such concepts and in how they can be collectively achieved.

A central characteristic of community is 'functional interdependence', in which each member must possess both the capabilities and the means through which to help sustain their wider community. Functional interdependence opens participants up to their distinctive attributes and provides a space within which they can work towards the attainment of their natural function. This perspective—drawing on the ethic of vocation—suggests that interaction provides the opportunity to contribute and develop capabilities in ways that are inherently meaningful, both for the nation itself and in terms of the concrete contribution such capabilities can make towards their community. More generally, as an ever-evolving field of interaction within which the purpose of countries is shaped and constantly worked through, communities have a central role to play in the formation, development, and affirmation of members' national identity (and their attendant autonomy).

Complete self-subsistence is, of course, not tenable. However, bridges built on communal aspiration, as a shared enterprise whereby nations' autonomy grows *in communion*, can engender optimal functioning.[14] This is a revelatory insight, too, since it has, directly and indirectly, been

[14] This has, throughout history, been made an explicit responsibility imparted on the individual, for example, in the Epistle of Barnabas: 'Do not live entirely isolated, having retreated into yourselves, as if you were already [fully] justified, but gather instead to seek together the common good' (The Epistle of Barnabas 4,10).

rejected by the Conventional Wisdom (Galbraith 1958) of the European establishment, which has become mired in a negative sum game: 'Europe can only grow by subsuming the autonomy of nations'. This is not true. Rather, through communal participation, countries individualise themselves through the contribution they make to their community and, in so doing, strengthen their communal bonds.

This is a demanding process. It necessitates a shift in the normative preconditions underpinning community's interactions—moving from the rights-based ethic of 'can do' that is afforded to members towards a duties-based ethic of 'should do' that is *expected* of members. The EU's sustainability is dependent on its members being both able and willing to actively transcend their national boundaries in the pursuit of transnational aspirations, which, at the same time, respect and help deepen their own autonomy. To this extent, participation is crucial not only from the pragmatic perspective (such as with economic integration), but also from a normative perspective in that such bonds are grounded in reciprocal recognition. In terms of the integration process, geographical proximity or members' individual competencies are therefore not an adequate criterion for legitimising community. A *relational cohesion* is required—which seeks to most fully strengthen and exercise healthy relationships within the community.

At the same time, rather than being a negative which must be overcome, national distinctiveness is a positive force, to be respected and fostered as a means through which the wider community grows and develops. The communal model which we advocate for is not, therefore, a push towards 'individualism'—the distinctiveness of countries should not detract from their capacity to possess both *shared aspirations and agendas*. The EU, designed as a 'union', is by no means entirely *unitary*. Its cultural, political, and economic diversity goes against the grain of any workable form of homogenisation.[15] But this does not mean that it cannot function effectively. The dichotomy is too simplistic and is semi-detached from the dialogical basis upon which communities survive and prosper. Even specific nations *themselves* are inherently pluralistic and dynamic—a fact which need not undermine their internal cohesiveness.

[15] For a further discussion on this point, see Innerarity (2014).

Community provides inherent 'goods' that express themselves in sustaining the community itself, as well as in the flourishment of individual members. This is imperative in combating the assimilation-cum-subordination that is indicative of federalist relations (in particular, when dealing with preexisting social, political, and economic diversities).[16] Community membership does not happen by accident. It is an *achievement* (Mason 2000)—a conscious endeavour undertaken with a cognisance of the risks and rewards that membership can endow. It is the ongoing culmination of a reflective process that reaches both inwards in search of one's national identity and outwards in search of transnational ideals and realities, drawing on commitments of the past to construct a future. It must be constantly worked at, reinforced, refined, and the foundations that underpin its original goals be revisited. Community therefore has a dual status for Europe: a concrete form of 'capital' as well as a normative endeavour that is central to the recognition and realisation of a shared ethos.[17]

## Upholding Community Values: Solidarity and Subsidiarity

While political and economic integration are necessary mechanisms through which the EU achieves its communal aspirations, neither are *in and of themselves*, the EU's final aim. Rather, their deeper purpose should lie in providing a means through which to express the foundational values at the heart of this community—among which are solidarity and subsidiarity. In spite of both these values having come under considerable threat during recent times of crisis, they remain central to the anthropology of Europe. As the existential threats continue to mount, there is now a need, more than ever, to rediscover and reanimate the values that had helped Europe overcome the post-war malaise it could so easily have become mired in, including its relational undercurrent. These same values can

[16] Here, Weiler (1991) differentiates between 'unity'-based and 'community'-based models of integration.

[17] For further insights, see Mason (2000).

serve as mechanisms—*relational dispositions*—through which the EU can provide nations with the opportunity to pursue their autonomous ambitions, secured under the European umbrella.[18] *In particular: solidarity in a manner that recognises autonomy as a relational capacity that is fostered within supportive reciprocal relationships; and subsidiarity in a manner that recognises autonomy as an inherent capacity that should be provided with opportunities to be exercised.*

Solidarity is the gravitational force around which members of a community orbit, an expression of their shared identification *with* and ties *to* each other. Robert Schuman defined solidarity as the meeting of 'fraternity and the instinct of enlightened conservation'—which was called upon as a response to the overt nationalism and cultural antipathy that had scarred intra-European relations.[19] Solidarity is not just about framing the duties of countries, but about fostering a *relational disposition* premised on the sharing of both the opportunities and burdens that membership entails. It is an inherently creative and transformational pillar for society—a means through which individuals/nations bring together their common capacities and resources in the establishment of something that, paradoxically, exists both *within* and *beyond* each of them, namely 'community'.

For more than 60 years, solidarity has animated Europe—an indispensable resource through which nations' dignity and belonging has been upheld, alongside a commitment to transnational dialogue.[20,21] At the core of solidarity is the 'unique and unrepeatable dignity' of the individual, and the existence of shared moral norms that are capable of transcending national borders.[22] These truths embody the ideals that have guided the community of the EU in its deepening: foundational values

---

[18] For further insights, see Raspotnik et al. (2012).

[19] Cited in Pimor (2017).

[20] The conceptual roots of the 'solidarity' are found in sociology, with significant foundational input from Emile Durkheim and Max Weber—who regarded it as being a fundamental principle of social integration.

[21] The Holy See (1992) notes that 'international solidarity is a requirement of the moral order; world peace depends in part upon this'.

[22] Iglesias (2001) provides an insightful critique into the nature, and attendant dignity, of the human person. Here, she discusses three fundamental aspects of the human being: (1) the human being is bodily, organic, physical; (2) the human being is also an integrated-unity-of-life, a living

from which the internal governance *of* and relationship *between* countries flow.

This principle has been repeatedly enshrined in the official literature of the EU. Having been given institutional expression in the Schuman Declaration (1950) and the preamble to the ECSC, it was not envisaged as a once-off commitment: it was crucial in the redemption and reconstruction of Europe's post–World War II trajectory. It was an ongoing *disposition* to be lived within communal relations through, for example, functional interdependence. It is a basic principle of European Law, written into the European Constitution (13 December 2007) as a common value and mission of the EU—whereby members seek to 'deepen the solidarity between their peoples while respecting their history, their culture and their traditions'. It is crucial to the European Social Model, which is based on the conviction that economic progress and social progress are inextricably bound, noting that 'competitiveness and solidarity have both been taken into account in building a successful Europe for the future'.[23] Here, Chapter IV (Articles 27–38) of the Charter of Fundamental Rights of the European Union (2012) is entitled 'Solidarity' and embodies a range of social needs.[24]

This concept of solidarity is fundamental to our argument precisely because, in spite of its pervasiveness within the EU analysis, it was almost wholly absent from any analysis of how the EU should engage with the Banking and Debt Crisis. Troikanomics was characterised by the implosion of 'solidarity'.[25] It was fractured not alone in the engagement of banks with

being, a living whole, a one, an individual; and (3) the human being is a being with a temporal continuity, a being with a history, a being in time.

[23] The Commission (1994) describes the 'European Social Model' in terms of values that include democracy, social protection, and solidarity.

[24] See also EurWORK (2011). Articles 27 to 34 bear directly on employment and industrial relation. The four remaining articles in the Solidarity Chapter are Health care (Article 35), Access to services of general economic interest (Article 36), Environmental protection (Article 37), and Consumer protection (Article 38).

[25] The authors discuss this point in Kinsella and Kinsella (2012). Here, newsreel footage comes to mind. It shows a middle-aged woman, in Middle America, in the immediate aftermath of having discovered that the pension on which she had relied had evaporated in the financial alchemy that defined the whole collapse. She turned to the camera and said, in a shocked voice: 'But they lied to me, they lied to me?' In this moment she was attempting to wrestle with the reality that perhaps the people whom she had placed her trust in did not have her own welfare at heart in their business

their communities but, importantly, in how responses to the crisis capitalised on this division between the core and periphery. The actions of the Troika in, for example, sequestering the pensions of Greek citizens or placing the burden of bank bailouts solely on Irish taxpayers (which, as the IMF has also argued, were properly the responsibility of European *community*) strike at the heart of solidarity.

Both Troikanomics and Brexit, in their different ways, reflect the same existential reality. The prevailing orthodoxy was less about how 'Europe' could shelter and support vulnerable peripheral countries—at least in part the authors of their own misfortune—than about how to quarantine delinquent member countries and prevent them infecting the Europe of the elite. The threat posed by the post-2008 crisis to the EU and, more specifically, to the Eurozone was therefore not so much addressed by invoking the *communal ethic of solidarity* as it was *repressed* by isolationism and the absence of a philosophical critique of (really) bad economics. The riposte, commonly along the lines that the wounds were self-inflicted, completely missed the point. A Europe that imposes such burdens, even on those who *were* in part culpable, cannot legitimately transfer this burden across generations. This runs contrary to the genesis of the ECSC. The same applies to strategies that bargain debt relief, which was and remains unassailable on economic grounds.

The point about moral norms is that they are not dependent on the calibre or political perspectives of individual politicians. At a political and societal level, redemption and a new start are their own vindication, and relief from indebtedness that has suffocated one generation and burdens the next is the perfect expression of solidarity *and*, as we know from history, redemption. More broadly, as the EU looks to the post-2018 era, it can be said that unless and until the true meaning of solidarity is rediscovered within the political leadership of the EU, there is unlikely to be economic stabilisation and sustainable recovery. To the contrary, a failure to move the Franco-German consensus away from the hegemony they have established in the wake of this crisis and towards a rediscovery of

undertakings. This visceral shock was of course replicated in a million different ways both across the United States and across the Eurozone.

solidarity runs the risk, as we have pointed out, of the 'Balkanisation' of Europe within a generation.

Solidarity is underpinned by the conviction that within communities there is an implicit egalitarian ethic that is vital in shaping and sustaining the relationships which comprise them. As is clearly evident across the EU, its members are not equal—certainly not in terms of their distinctive attributes. As discussed, calls for the EU to be grounded in equality require us to ask 'equality of what?' At first glance, there are several indications that inequalities pervade this relationship between, for instance, the core and the periphery. These bear on competitiveness, resources, scope for growth, and political clout. These are reflected in social metrics, such as average incomes, living standards (broadly defined), indebtedness, and health status. Alongside this, there is an observable asymmetry in terms of where the burden of adjustment arising from 'shocks' of different kinds should fall. There is little pressure to adjust on countries in structural surplus, there are onerous responsibilities on deficit countries. In a monetary union the capacity to use monetary policy, including the exchange rate, to facilitate that adjustment is removed. The terrain of the EU is shaped by these differentials. Consequently, if we are to ensure that solidarity does not succumb to asymmetries in power (whether real or perceived), then it is important to distinguish between two forms of equality.[26]

Firstly, 'ontological equality' (operating in a normative sphere) affirms each nation's rights, and the attendant responsibilities of other nations to uphold such rights. Equality is a foundational attribute endowed by countries' shared autonomy and sovereign status, and exists irrespective of the strengths/weaknesses that it may possess. It is, however, important to guard against a misinterpretation of ontological equality that entails homogeny, in that this may undercut our appreciation of nations' distinctiveness—and their attendant distinctive *value* to the wider community. Consequently, there is a second form of 'discrete equality' (operating, for example, in a socio-economic sphere), which affirms the distinctiveness of the attributes each nation possesses and allows us to recognise their differences. Equality in countries' dignity does not equate to equality in terms of their strengths or weaknesses. This reinforces the impor-

[26] This builds on a discussion by one of the authors in Kinsella (2018).

tance of solidarity as a *living* dynamic encompassing the mind-set, behaviours, and policies that are responsive to the distinctive character of each nation. This breeds greater awareness that, given such differentials, communal participation will entail both the sharing of successes in times of plenty and the shouldering of burdens in times of struggle.

Subsidiarity is a constitutionally enshrined principle that provides both a legislative and normative mandate with respect to *why* individual member nations' decisional and volitional capacities should be upheld, and *how* this can be most fully achieved. Specifically, it deals with 'the limits of the right and duty of the public authority to intervene in social and economic affairs'.[27] This principle has been progressively marginalised as the scale and scope of the EU has broadened and deepened. And therein lies a troubling truth: Europe continues to evoke foundational principles with one hand, while systematically undermining them with the other. Troikanomics is a notable example: its political dominance and economic leverage over highly indebted peripheral countries enabled it to emasculate their autonomous capacities, while at the same time calling forth the language of the 'Union' in order to justify their behaviour.

The principle of subsidiarity affirms that the EU should exercise its authority in a *subsidiary* manner—whereby its domain of competencies should not supersede those of members in issues that can be and are *more appropriately dealt with* at a local/national level.[28] This capacity to intervene on sovereign matters is deemed justifiable only if the nation in question is unable to adequately attend *of themselves* to the resolution of the particular need they are experiencing, or if the Union's intervention is considered to be of further benefit to nations' interests (Panizza 2018).[29]

[27] See Mulcahy and Massaro (2003).

[28] Specifically, Article 3b (European Union 13 December 2007) outlines specific mandates, with particular reference to the principles of 'conferral', 'subsidiarity', and 'proportionality'. Here, it notes that '[t]he limits of Union competences are governed by the principle of conferral. The use of Union competences is governed by the principles of subsidiarity and proportionality'. Specifically, it states that '[u]nder the principle of subsidiarity, in areas which do not fall within its exclusive competence, the Union shall act only if and insofar as the objectives of the proposed action cannot be sufficiently achieved by the Member States, either at central level or at regional and local level, but can rather, by reason of the scale or effects of the proposed action, be better achieved at Union level'.

[29] Under Article 5(3) (European Union 13 December 2007), three preconditions for intervention by the Union are laid out: non-exclusive competence; necessity; and added value.

The core ethic underpinning this principle is that sovereign governance is a right possessed by the citizens of a particular country, of which the nation *itself* should be the primary locus of decisions. This requires that decisions be made at a level that is as close as possible to the people who most directly bear the consequences of them, that is, national governments and their citizens.[30]

This principle is therefore not so much about the denial of the EU's capacity (and often responsibility) to operate in an 'interventionist' manner, but rather about the discretionary use of such interventions so as not to undercut the self-determining capacities of its members. The essence of participation in the Union is that it is a collaborative relationship, with members participating *in distinct ways*. While the primacy of national decisions is enshrined, this should not obscure the differences across countries. In a community—more so in a union—a key issue is how best to develop and utilise the capabilities and resources of all countries, mediated by institutional supports and trade, especially in relation to intellectual capital in a knowledge economy. This context changes the dynamic of the challenge: crisis management becomes less about 'the Eurozone being under threat' and instead about 'how best can the Eurozone be rebalanced in the interest of the people of member countries'. This is so that, for example, engagements with Greece are not seen as 'threatening', but rather as providing an opportunity to actually deliver on the principles and values that are so often evoked and evaporate out of the back door when challenges come knocking loudly.

It is important to take into account that 'deliberative influence' is a substantial means of cementing the contribution that each member of the community has, reinforcing their motivation to *remain part* of the community. The capacity to proactively participate in the governance of one's environment is integral to the sense that *one matters, of making a difference to a community*—and of the community mattering to its members. Without the capacity to influence, then, the wider community will become increasingly opaque, and decisions that *are* made may feel

[30] See de Benoist (1999).

increasingly oppressive. Subsidiarity helps open the door to acknowledging and accommodating the contribution that individual members can make to both their own national narrative and the trajectory of the wider European Project.

Alongside this, it fosters their recognition in *themselves* as both capable of and imbued with a right to make such contributions. Nations should therefore not become dependent on the interventions or functioning of the Union at a national level, but retain both the right and the responsibility (in as much as is possible) to resolve matters *at national level*. Thus, subsidiarity represents sovereignty that is shared. This allows for a model that is premised on supporting an egalitarian form of intra-communal interaction wherein, when most appropriate, participant members' capacities should be recognised and realised. This will ultimately create a more authentic and efficacious form of union.[31]

Solidarity and subsidiarity are thereby existentially present in the relationships that bind the community together; their contribution to the Common Good does not simply express itself in the sense of aspiration that they impart in nations and their citizens, but in the endeavours that are undertaken to make these aspirations a reality.[32] In the opportunities it creates and the challenges it helps overcome, community is *itself* a vital resource for its individual members most fully realising their capacities.[33] One of the strengths of the EU comes, paradoxically, in its recognition that it is through the sharing of both strengths *and* weaknesses which community entails that members can most fully attain greater peace and prosperity.

---

[31] Here, in his discussion on democratic leadership, Gastille (1994) argues that at the heart of democracy should be an ethic of 'deliberation'. The value of deliberation is that it enables both the challenges and opportunities that are encountered to be identified, explored, and resolved in a collaborative, congruent, and reflective manner. Leaders cannot, therefore, afford to be selfish with the power that they potentially wield, as doing so will cost dearly in terms of compromising members' longer-term capacity for growth.

[32] See Van Til (2008).

[33] For further insights on this point, see Frigot and Bonadonna (2016).

## References

Christman, J. (2014a). Coping or Oppression: Autonomy and Adaptation to Circumstance. In A. Veltman & M. Piper (Eds.), *Autonomy, Oppression, and Gender*. Oxford: Oxford University Press.

Christman, J. (2014b). Relational Autonomy and the Social Dynamics of Paternalism. *Ethical Theory and Moral Practice, 17*, 369–382.

Commission of the European Communities. (1994). *White Paper: European Social Policy – A Way Forward for the Union*.

de Areilza, J. M. (2009). The History and Foundations of European Integration: A Contribution to the Debate on the Future of the Union. In C. Arvanitopoulos (Ed.), *Reforming Europe: The Role of the Centre-Right* (pp. 9–21). s.l.: Springer.

de Benoist, A. (1999). What Is Sovereignty? *Telos, 1999*(116), 99–118.

European Union, C. o. t. R. o. t. G. o. t. M. S. (2007, December 13). *Treaty of Lisbon Amending the Treaty on European Union and the Treaty Establishing the European Community*. Volume 2007/C 306/01.

EurWORK European Observatory of Working Life. (2011). *Solidarity Principle*. [Online]. Retrieved from https://www.eurofound.europa.eu/observatories/eurwork/industrial-relations-dictionary/solidarity-principle

Frigot, F., & Bonadonna, E. (2016). *Europe and Sovereignty: Reality, Limits and Outlook*. s.l.: Robert Schuman Foundation.

Galbraith, J. K. (1958). *The Affluent Society*. New York: Houghton Mifflin.

Gastille, J. (1994). A Definition and Illustration of Democratic Leadership. *Human Relations, 47*(8), 953–975.

Grabow, K. (Ed.). (2010). *Christian Democracy: Principles and Policy Making*. Berlin: Konrad-Adenauer-Stiftung.

Iglesias, T. (2001). *The Dignity of the Individual: Issues of Bioethics and Law*. Dublin: Pleroma Press.

Innerarity, D. (2014). Does Europe Need a Demos to Be Truly Democratic? *LSE 'Europe in Question' Discussion Paper Series*, Volume 77.

Kant, I. (1785). *Groundwork of the Metaphysic of Morals*. s.l.: s.n.

Kiljunen, K. (2004). *The European Constitution in the Making*. Brussels: Centre for European Policy Studies.

Kinsella, M. (2018). Egalitarianism in Therapeutic Dialogue: A Catalyst for Client Autonomy. *The Irish Journal of Counselling and Psychotherapy, 18*(1), 5–10.

Kinsella, R., & Kinsella, M. (2012, July). The Implosion of Solidarity: A Critique of the Euro Zone Crisis. *Working Notes*, (69), 22–28.

Mason, A. (2000). *Community, Solidarity and Belonging: Levels of Community and Their Normative Significance*. Cambridge: Cambridge University Press.
Mulcahy, R. E., & Massaro, T. (2003). Subsidiarity. In *The New Catholic Encyclopedia* (p. 567). United States of America: Gale.
Nobelprize.org. (2012). *The Nobel Peace Prize 2012 to the European Union (EU) – Press Release*. [Online]. Retrieved May 31, 2018, from http://www.nobelprize.org/nobel_prizes/peace/laureates/2012/press.html
Panizza, R. (2018). *The Principle of Subsidiarity*. [Online]. Retrieved February 12, 2018, from http://www.europarl.europa.eu/ftu/pdf/en/FTU_1.2.2.pdf
Pimor, A. (2017). *Solidarity Was a Founding Principle of European Unity – It Must Remain So*. [Online]. Retrieved from https://theconversation.com/solidarity-was-a-founding-principle-of-european-unity-it-must-remain-so-74580
Pontifical Council for Justice and Peace. (2005). *Compendium of the Social Doctrine of the Church*. Vatican City: Libreria Editrice Vaticana.
Pope Benedict XVI. (2009). *Caritas in Veritate*. Vatican City: Libreria Editrice Vaticana.
Pope John Paul II. (1991). *Centesimus Annus*. Rome: Libreria Editrice Vaticana.
Pope John Paul II. (1995). *Evangelium Vitae*. Vatican City: Libreria Editrice Vaticana.
Raspotnik, A., Jacob, M., & Ventura, L. (2012). *The Issue of Solidarity in the European Union*. s.l.: TEPSA.
Schuman, R., & Monnet, J. (1950). *The Schuman Declaration*. [Online]. Retrieved from https://europa.eu/european-union/about-eu/symbols/europe-day/schuman-declaration_en
Taylor, C. (1992). The Politics of Recognition. In A. Gutmann (Ed.), *Multiculturalism: Examining the Politics of Recognition* (pp. 25–73). Princeton: Princeton University Press.
The Economist. (2006). *The Suez Crisis: An Affair to Remember*. [Online]. Retrieved May 19, 2018, from https://www.economist.com/node/7218678
The European Parliament. (2012). Charter of Fundamental Rights of the European Union. *Official Journal of the European Communities, C*(326), 391–407.
The Holy See. (1992). *Catechism of the Catholic Church* (2nd ed.). Vatican City: Libreria Editrice Vaticana.
Van Til, K. A. (2008). Subsidiarity and Sphere-Sovereignty: A Match Made in…? *Theological Studies, 69*, 610–636.

Wachtel, P. L. (2014). An Integrative Relational View. *Psychotherapy, 49*(4), 342–349.

Weiler, J. (1991). The Transformation of Europe. *The Yale Law Review, 100*(8), 2403–2483.

Weiler, J. (1999). *The Constitution of Europe. "Do the New Clothes Have an Emperor?" And Other Essays on European Integration*. Cambridge: Cambridge University Press.

# 9

# Troikanomics: Legacy and Lessons

## Synthesis and Overview

'Project Europe' has been an epic historical journey and its achievements are enormous. Notwithstanding this, as we have pointed out earlier in this book, all empires become fatigued. They lose touch with their foundational values, leading to crisis. The EU now contends with an existential crisis, largely of its own making.

Successive iterations of instability—from macroeconomics to migration—reflect a failure on the part of the establishment to discern and to critique the nature of the crisis now enveloping the EU. Austerity and, more specifically, Troikanomics has brought this crisis to the fore. With it, and at a great cost, has come the beginning of a much deeper appreciation of the centrality of the lived reality of autonomy. A seismic shift in the political landscape of Europe, initially driven by anti-austerity movements and, more recently, by the effects of the Migration Crisis raises new uncertainties about Europe in its present form. The EU establishment, tone deaf to the human costs of austerity and how it diminished the autonomy of member countries, has, so far, failed to properly acknowledge this dynamic—and how patriotism is invoked by countries



R. Kinsella, M. Kinsella, *Troikanomics*, https://doi.org/10.1007/978-3-319-97070-7_9

precisely when their autonomy and fundamental freedoms are threatened by pressures and coercion. The case for a fundamental critique as the EU is impelled into a new and uncertain era is compelling.

We begin with a few words about the context of this book and the argument which we spell out within it, which amount to this: the EU, as it has developed, is transfixed by a set of inter-connected crises. The most obvious, and the one on which we primarily focus, is the Banking and Debt Crisis and, in particular, the response by Europe to contain this crisis i.e. Troikanomics. But it's important to be clear that Troikanomics is part of a wider set of pressures which constitutes what is a deeper existential crisis.

Political and economic power within the EU was, from the outset, concentrated at its core within the Franco-German axis. This power is mediated through the European Institutions—notably the European Commission, the Council of Ministers, and the European Central Bank. The conventional narrative is that this power is 'shared' with other member states. In reality, the 'core' exercises a gravitational pull around which the wider membership must orbit—on a trajectory that habitually leaches their national autonomy and countervailing sovereign status. The upshot of this is that the political elite in smaller countries are motivated to participate in this relationship through the promise of standard welfare gains arising from trade and the synergies of regulatory, and other forms of, cooperation. But they are also impelled by the silken threads—unseen but very real—of dependency.

The further that Europe moves away from a 'community' model of egalitarian and participatory dialogue towards a fully federal political union, the greater this disparity is experienced. Hegemony displaces the communal good of collaboration, skewing political change towards the interests of the dominant core. Conversely, the national interests of other smaller sovereign states are progressively 'crowded out'—railroaded into a *faux* 'collaborative' process. This is regressive: voting is exquisitely weighted according to different formula that deflects from the *realpolitik* at the centre of decision-making.

The banking and economic crisis that assailed the EU was a fundamental catharsis that unveiled, as never before, this phenomenon through the imposition of austerity (via the Troika) on a set of smaller and highly indebted peripheral countries. This reinforced the extent of hegemony's status as both socio political and economic. The manner in which austerity was managed magnified the dependency on the core, diminishing 'debtor' countries' autonomy, that is, their capacity to construct an authentic and meaningful narrative for themselves that did justice to their distinctive national and cultural identity. In our 'global' model, autonomy is not just about a nation having the capacity to take ownership over *particular* decisions, but rather it is about coming to express a sense of self-definition in taking ownership over the broader trajectory that it carves out for itself. Here, the EU has been deeply lacking in an understanding of relational autonomy; it has not provided the space conducive to *'becoming oneself amongst others'*.

This is the phenomenon which we call 'Troikanomics'. We have attempted to harness philosophical critique focused on issues such as autonomy and political economy so as to examine this process and to reflect on what it demonstrates about the true nature of the present and future governance within the EU.

The DNA of 'Project Europe'—encompassing what it is, why it exists, and how it operates—continues to evolve. This is hardly surprising. The EU is, after all, a complex and ever-emergent entity: comprised of members who are both ontologically distinct and reciprocally intertwined. From its genesis in the form of the ECSC it has advanced through many iterations—from the EEC to the EC, and to the EU. Its character and its composition are enduring questions to be asked, which consistently elicit new and novel responses. This sentiment was, in fact, embedded in the Schuman Declaration (1950), which noted that 'Europe will not be made all at once. … It will be built through concrete achievements which first create a *de facto* solidarity'.

*And yet*, amidst the haze of ongoing changes, as well as various crises, it has become mired in an intellectual and moral stagnation. This goes against its own philosophical heritage and political trajectory—becoming especially evident in its reactions to the Banking and Debt Crisis. Critiquing these responses is an essential part of understanding the journey that the EU has undertaken from its original inception to the EU of the present day. This is essential so that it can seek to foster a way forward in which Europe can become more fully what it was called to be—and, importantly, in this process, encompass the autonomy of its member countries. There have been a number of developments that have highlighted the growing discord between the ideological aspirations contained in the EU's rhetoric and its actual capacity to provide a workable means through which these can be achieved.[1] In reflecting on these issues we pay close attention to the Banking and Debt Crisis, the measures, notably Troikanomics, that were deployed to firefight its immediate consequences, as well as what they tell us about the EU's long-term future. In doing so, we are mindful of the wider set of pressures that constitute what we define as the existential crisis.

These developments beg the question of whether the EU's founding fathers—impressed as they would be by its scale and international standing—would recognise the *character* of what it has now become. While they would no doubt see good in the individuals who work within this sprawling entity, it must also be acknowledged that within the bureaucratic milieu of democratically questionable administrative bodies and the technocratic sequestering of executive functions by elected officials, something has become lost in translation. Semantic gymnastics in an ever-increasing slew of Reports, *faux*-populist verbiage seeking to endear the elites to the masses—these indicate a conflict at the heart of the EU. The intergovernmental organisations that make decisions, semi-detached from the realities of national interests, are increasingly distant from democratic legitimacy and yet are desperate to remain part of a conversation that is quickly moving beyond them. Meanwhile, the executive branch is infiltrated by appointed 'experts' who arbitrate legislation and administer what are essentially government functions.

With the EU now facing a period of transformational changes, including the 2019 European Elections, these kinds of issues, and their deeper existential significance, require reflecting upon. The lessons we can glean from the burden of Troikanomics can help to inform the character of the path that the EU chooses to take as it continues to evolve. The existential crisis currently assailing the EU is an opportunity—grasped or lost—through which to reanimate what initially inspired and drove Europe forward.

[1] This tension is discussed by Schulz-Forberg (2012).

## Troikanomics: Mind-Set, Motivations, and Manifestations

Troikanomics took the cult of austerity to a wholly new level—repressive in the scale of its economic interventions and coercive in its political intrusiveness. It marked a decisive shift *away* from the fostering of countries' autonomous capacities and recognition of their sovereign status. Instead, it signalled a move *towards* the imposition of centrist hegemony. It was foisted upon Eurozone countries for whom internal and domestic rebalancing was essential and for whom devaluation as a means of enhancing their competitiveness was, by definition, no longer an option. This meant that the burden of rebalancing the economy fell entirely on the labour market (wages, pensions, and emigration) and on public services. The Troika ruled by *fiat* and was not accountable to national governments or legislatures—only to their unelected (and by inference unaccountable) parent bodies and to the political agendas of Eurozone creditor countries. There was a pretence of 'negotiation' with national governments in crisis, but that was effectively to save face—little more than empty rhetoric.[2] There was no doubt whatsoever who was in charge, as is borne out by the prescriptive obligations that were to be adhered to by these countries.

We have discussed two core inadequacies in the architecture of the Eurozone: the 'infrastructure' on which it was built and the 'environment' that it helped to stem the creation of. Both of these served as causal antecedents in the creation, perpetuation, and *exacerbation* of the crisis. The Troika, while being an administrative, legal, and ethical anomaly was in no way *anomalous*, given this strained architecture of the Eurozone and the environment within which it operated. If anything, it was an all-too-foreseeable expression. Indefensible market practices that reflected an ethical 'black hole' at the heart of financial markets and institutions; opaque financial reporting and 'rent seeking' which failed to signal what

[2] This issue was explicitly addressed in the European Parliament's Report on the Role and Operations of the Troika (2014). Here, they acknowledge that in spite of this explicit pretext of 'negotiation' which the Memorandum of Understanding between Member States and the Troika operated under, the manner in which these negotiations were conducted lacked transparency.

was unfolding but profited mightily from the clean-up process, unsustainable creditor–debtor relations; convergence metrics configured to wholly different circumstances in European and global financial markets; and an ECB mandate that was fixated on 'price stability' rather than on the kind of dual mandate of jobs *and* low inflation that informed the US response to the crisis: the warning signs were all there. The prevailing *zeitgeist* of subservience to corporate capitalism and to an emerging political hegemony across the EU, alongside deference to the Conventional Wisdom, hampered attempts to recognise each of the distinct yet connected forces that were building towards a perfect storm.[3]

The infrastructure and regulatory arrangements of the Eurozone were not sufficiently robust to weather the storm of economic and financial crisis, partly because they had not been adequately thought through in terms of institution-building and fiscal oversight.[4] The issue here is *not* simply that this crisis came knocking on the EU's door in the first place. A crisis such as this seemed fated to eventually materialise (albeit, not on such an unparalleled scale); its inevitability is symptomatic of deeply interconnected global economies. The issue is, rather, that the EU did not possess adequate expertise and resources to respond to the crisis proactively, nor did it critique this and its consequences.

Failures in the infrastructure of the EU were, thus, both structurally and functionally allied.[5] There were structural deficiencies to the extent that the EU did not possess the adequate resources through which to swiftly and effectively resolve the crisis as it emerged. Vulnerable countries were mired in an arrangement that, on the one hand, sought to bring diverse economies together while, on the other hand, could not

---

[3] See, for example, Hillebrand (2014) who argues that in addition to the failure of financial markets, there were also inadequate Eurozone institutions and a debt crisis with which to contend.

[4] A number of analysts have drawn attention to the institutional design failures underpinning the European Monetary Union, and the extent to which these failures instigated, perpetuated, and exacerbated the European Debt Crisis. For example, Bergsten (2012) notes the dearth in *economic* alignments (e.g. fiscal coordination) and Aizenman (2016) discusses the lack in institutional and policy backstops to asymmetric shocks—both issues seriously undermining the viability of this project. Lane (2012) also discusses the consequences of the Euro's initial institutional design inadequacies—both increasing fiscal risks during the pre-crisis period, and amplifying the fiscal impact of the crisis.

[5] By this, we mean that each composite part is functionally attuned to carrying out its distinctive tasks and ensuring the stability of the wider system.

provide mechanisms through which to respond to such diversities—operating, as they were, within a domain that fell short of an 'optimal currency area'. There were also functional difficulties because the resources they *did* set into motion were policy interventions that were not sufficiently equipped to perform their respective tasks.

Environmental precipitants included a high degree of interconnectivity between the EU's banking system and the wider economic environment; an over-reliance on banking credit; and a vulnerability of the mainstream model to behaviours that incentivised excessive risk-taking, leading to 'asset bubbles'. The environment encouraged both deference towards, and dependency on, debt between centre and peripheral countries. Once the crisis struck totemic US banks (beginning with Lehman Brothers) and from there impacted on major EU banks, liquidity immediately contracted and interest rates rose sharply, making it difficult for businesses and households to refinance their debts. There was an inability within the Eurozone to counter with any real clout or follow-through the unsustainable building of public debt—which spoke to the whole issue of political ideology and deficiencies in the calibre of political governance.

Contagion posed a threat not only to the Eurozone and the wider EU, but—as both the IMF Managing Director and the German Chancellor acknowledged—to the global financial system.[6] Financial contagion was primarily transmitted via short-term money markets, infecting the banking sectors of the peripheral and, increasingly, larger Eurozone economies. Economic contagion was transmitted domestically via shifts in demand, investment, and, confidence—as well as externally across trade linkages. Both financial and economic spheres interacted to further erode policy credibility and market confidence. But there was also an even more consequential form of contagion transmitted across the Eurozone: political contagion, which expressed itself first in disenchantment with the EU and then in opposition to it.[7]

---

[6] The ECB (2009) argues that, alongside the unwinding of financial imbalances and the occurrence of severe macro shocks, contagion is one of the mechanisms by which financial instability becomes so widespread that a crisis reaches systemic dimensions. This necessitates placing the containment and mitigation of contagion as a crisis management priority.

[7] The intertwined nature of countries' economic and political infrastructure is discussed by Schwab (2012) and Fagan and Gaspar (2007).

Alongside this, political union/deeper integration was being pushed by Germany as the 'solution' to the travails of the Eurozone—impelling further movement towards full federalisation. This was not through any real commitment to achieve a participatory Public Square; it was the perpetuation of an orthodoxy that led to an *already* massively centralised EU. It reflected Germany's capacity to make unilateral decisions on a wide range of pivotal issues—from EMU to migration: an ascendency reflected in the fact that it had come through the crisis with robust fiscal and trade surpluses, alongside record levels of employment growth.

Throughout the crisis, the EU elite was marked by a mind-set that was alien to its foundational values. Alongside this, the value-based humanitarian sensibilities that originally shaped the EU, as above all else a 'community', had been diluted and leached. Troikanomics was the direct consequence—one part an ad hoc reflection of a lack of capacity to have dealt with the crisis, the other part condemnation of crisis-stricken countries who had jeopardised the stability of the wider economic community. This raises the fundamental question of whether it is still possible to speak meaningfully of the prospect of member nations exercising their autonomous capacities in the emerging political space.

There is a growing political strain between a culture of dependency that has infected the mind-set and constrained the motivations and ambitions of peripheral countries, and increased sociopolitical tension that is attempting to push back against the hegemony of the EU. Dependency—reflected, for example, in a form of political stasis—does not happen quickly; it emerges insidiously over time within national political orthodoxy and in the multilateral institutions on which they are made dependent. This can often occur in tandem with the desire to *pull away* from such relationships and cathartically move beyond the dependence. The explicit threats made by the ECB against the government of Ireland, for example, raise questions about their receptivity to any critique that is not in the image and likeness of the prevailing deferential paradigm. As we have discussed, we see manifestations of a 'pulling away' from this paradigm. These include Brexit, the increased electoral support for anti-austerity parties characterised as 'Populists', as well as the deep divide between member countries on the issue of migration. These are interconnected. In a recent Brookings Institute Paper, William A. Galston (2018) makes the point that: 'Early on, many analysts believed that the rise of populism reflected mainly the economic distress created by the protracted Great Recession. As it waned, they hoped, so would the populist challenge. But even as Europe's economic recovery has gathered pace and unemployment has declined, the populist surge has continued. It is now evident that populism draws strength from public opposition to mass immigration, cultural liberalization, and the perceived surrender of national sovereignty to distant and unresponsive international bodies.'

This reflects a deep sense of dejection among the wider populous—apparent in a rejection of a political order that has prevailed in the lead-up to and in the aftermath of the Banking and Debt Crisis, and more recently in relation to migration. It prompts the question: whose orthodoxy is this anyway—and against what values is it legitimised? On what basis does it assert that the existential experience of citizens in the countries impacted by Troikanomics, or their political expression, is not valid? Both political and macroeconomic failures were spawned by flawed strategies that were obdurately defended. Political and economic spheres were tidally locked, with each forming a backdrop to the other as the EU continues to be confronted by crises that metastasise from one form into another without ever being resolved.

Let us turn this around to express what was in the minds of those who initiated the EU: Markets are there to *serve* the community from which they get their legitimacy. Governments are there to serve, and to give expression to, the will of the demos and to advocate for the Common Good, not alone domestically but across the hinterland of the community of which it is a part. Where they intersect, in the current context, should be in the shared regard for a reciprocal form of relational autonomy—one that amounts to a positive-sum game for member nations and a transnational EU—which eschews forms of domination in favour of a communally focused engagement of equals.

This comes close to embodying what remains in the 'core' of the embryonic European vision. Throughout this book we have referred to the political philosophy of Germany's Christian Democracy movement—co-founded by one of the architects of the European foundational vision—as a *lived* and practical expression of what Europe was, what the experience of the last decade suggests it has lost sight of, and what it must re-engage in to renew its nature and its mission.

Therein lies the paradox of the Troika—an entity put in motion to address real socially significant economic concerns, but instead subservient to a wholly different set of principles and not accountable to those whose lives it impacted on. As we have previously noted, there have been 'reviews' of the experience of Troika, notably by the European Parliament (2014), as well as by individual countries. But these largely miss the point that the Troika's legacy is reflected in deep scars in the social infrastructure of stressed countries. Greece, for example, despite its 'exit' from the Programme in June 2018, remains in a debt trap and a seemingly endless series of 'reforms' and ongoing surveillance that impoverish the country on a scale hardly credible a decade ago.

The debacle of Troikanomics has changed our *experiential understanding* of the EU—what it is, the extent to which it has shifted away from its more egalitarian and communally-focused roots, and what its future holds as the EU heads into a post-Brexit environment. There has been a recovery across the bailout countries, but that does not necessarily point to a causality between austerity and recovery—much less support a view that Troikanomics was the only, and still less the optimum, mode of adjustment. It takes little account of the existential costs of the experience, not alone the economic costs including continued debt service but the scars of diminished national autonomy and the human and economic shocks which it engendered. Ireland, for example, has one of the fastest growing economies in Europe—but this requires looking determinantly past the graveyard of the casualties of the Troika era, including the pressing social problem of homelessness.

Behind the different trajectories being advanced by the EU establishment and the pronouncements by France and Germany there abides the question: what is the EU's final goal? Is this a goal known to and shared by its members? If it is progressively achieved, how will it manifest itself in the identity, autonomy, and intercommunity relations of the EU? How are we to explain the significant clash of cultures and polarisation of politics across the EU? What is needed is a renewed sense of common purpose, accompanied by a strategic vision for the path ahead.

Perhaps the most important outcome of our methodological approach to reflecting on the experience of Troikanomics comes in the form of this question: How far has Europe engaged in a systematic critique of its own relevance and sustainability? To put this differently, has the survival of EU institutions become more important—a greater priority—than the individual interests of the community of nations, the balance of whose individual and collective welfare it was originally intended to serve? Is the balance a healthy one or has it become excessively skewed in favour of the dominant countries? Troikanomics pointed to a behavioural abnormality in the mind-set of 'official' Europe which it has never previously demonstrated: who, with any awareness of what Project Europe was ostensibly all about, could have conceived of the treatment of Greece or the threats to Ireland at a moment of crisis?

These are troubling questions that demand a serious internal critique of Europe. They should be central to European Elections; it is unlikely that they will be—and this is the problem. Facing 'facticity', which we reflected on in Chap. 3, is central to a resolution of these questions, and enables the existential implications of its misconceived engagement with vulnerable national economies to be internalised and critiqued. These engagements have included the habitual application of defence mechanisms that have shielded it from facing some hard truths and from living up to its responsibilities.

## Searching for Reflection and Reform

While the Troika was effectively stood down in 2014, the European Stability Mechanism (ESM) has not yet been transformed into a European Monetary Fund-type institution—and so it is difficult to know if the lessons over the last 10 years have been internalised. Even so, the legacy of Troika and of Troikanomics lingers on in the countries which they impacted.

The legacy of austerity continues to play a role in levels of inequality across Europe, reflecting a lop-sided adjustment process that disempowers deficit countries. The fiscal selfishness of the surplus economies has left Europe only now reducing its dependence on the ECB's monetary policy. At one stage, this amounted to printing money on a vast scale and negative interest rates—effectively paying countries to borrow. These unprecedented policies have created vast distortions in global financial markets. Inequality runs like a fault line across the 'Union', and the imbalances in macroeconomic adjustment are very evident.

In reflecting on membership of the Eurozone in the light of the experience of the crisis, it is important to ask who benefits most from the system that is in place. Clearly, it is Germany and France.[8] Compared with the formal, as well as the newly assumed, powers of the ECB, the Central Banks of other members have been functionally stripped of their irreplaceable role in vindicating the monetary autonomy (including exchange rate) of their respective countries. The negotiations on the design, mandate, and governance of the ECB were an expression of 'power politics' within the EU. The Bundesbank has been of pivotal importance in Germany, at multiple levels: its 'reengineering' into the ECB—think of it in terms of merger and acquisition (M&A) deals—was a very big deal for Germany. Having said that, the cost to Germans of foregoing the Bundesbank as part of EMU was more than offset by insisting that its mandate be focused on price stability, unimpeded by facilitating—as in the case of the US Federal Reserve—employment growth.

This reality alone was decisive in determining the severity of austerity, including such issues as debt forgiveness. Trading, in effect, the Bundesbank for the ECB also conferred significant geopolitical and economic benefits on Germany—not least in the enhanced role of Frankfurt in global capital markets. Crucially, there have been gains arising at the time from the relatively undervalued Euro, as opposed to the Deutschmark, which, by itself, would have appreciated *vis à vis* other currencies, with negative effects on its powerhouse export capabilities. All of this has conferred enormous benefits on the German economy, benefits reflected in its massive fiscal and trade surplus even as the peripheral members were locked into Troikanomics. As the EU enters into the post-2019 era, the ECB has indicated that they will continue to constrain interest rates. Since 2008,

[8] The growing economic asymmetry between Germany and peripheral EU Members is discussed in further detail by Ash (2012). Here, Germany—capitalising on its trade partners discontinuing competitive devaluation efforts—has held significant competitive advantages in areas such as export markets. These current account surpluses led to large capital outflows from banks that inundated peripheral markets with credit. Menéndez (2014) also discusses the asymmetries more broadly between the 'core Eurozone states and the peripheral members which, while giving the impression of income and wealth convergence, were actually masking growing divergence. This sequence of events is made all the more ironic in light of the European Commission's Report (2008), which stated that the EMU had 'brought significant benefits to its member countries engaged in a catching-up process', thanks to 'the environment of macroeconomic stability and low interest rates coupled with the support of the cohesion policy and its Structural and Cohesion Funds'.

Germany has saved some €300 billion from lower interest rates. In 2017 alone, interest savings at the Federal, state, and local level were €50 billion. By comparison, consider the interest rate burden on Greece.

At the same time, Germany experienced strong economic growth and the highest levels of employment since reunification. Its budget surplus was robust and the extent of its trade surplus a source of international frictions—all of this with a debt/GDP ratio forecast for 2019. By way of comparison, Greece is required to generate a primary budget surplus of some 3% in the short term and 2% well into the future: its debt/GDP ratio is over 180% (Trading Economics 2018a) and its unemployment rate over 20% (Trading Economics 2018b).

The point here is not to suggest a facile causality—it is simply that the experience of what it means to be 'European' is very different in Athens compared to Berlin: different worries, different dreams. Oppressive imbalances are embedded into the system even though a symmetrical burden of adjustment, directly or indirectly, would reflect a commitment either by the EU or by the EU elite to fairness. Consider for a moment the imbalance embedded in a 'Union' where the counterpart of problematic indebtedness by a peripheral country, to a country in massive surplus and full employment, is a haemorrhage of well-educated young adults and an ongoing transfer of income and wealth. Voters across the Union see this inequality, even as it is ignored by the elite. It is the outcome of misconceived, centralised policies based on profoundly bad economics. The important point here is that this fundamental inequality was magnified by Troikanomics. It follows that a radically different adjustment process is a *sine qua non* for greater equality, especially between the core and the peripheral economies.

It is not economic inequalities alone. There are very real differences in the political capabilities of countries. There is, in football parlance, a 'Premier League' and its equivalents who garner by far the greatest revenues; and then there are the minor leagues who simply get by, year to year. Pre-Summit meetings are where the Premier Leagues play. Even large countries like Italy can be left on the bench.[9] The exception arises in circumstances, such as in the ongoing Migration Crisis, where attempts

[9] See Traynor (2015).

by Germany to impose refugee quotas on other members were rejected by the new Italian Government who had the leverage to extract concessions. If you do not have leverage—or are not part of a larger subgroup such as Eastern European nations whose distinctive national values contend with those of the 'core'—you accept what is imposed from that same 'core'.

It is difficult to look at all of this without reflecting: 'This cannot be right, this cannot be what "Project Europe" is about?' And, of course, it is not right—but in a culture and politic mired in relativeness, even the word 'right' is problematic. The real challenge here is less about fiscal transfers than about fully developing the capabilities of each of the countries, *so that* a convergence in living standards and social solidarity is driven from within the member country rather than in the form of a subsidy (which simply reinforces the mind-set of dependency). Dialogue on comparative economics—on economic equality—is now hampered by the absence of normative comparisons that would once have been taken for granted—a hugely regressive development.

Troikanomics reflected the orthodoxy within which concepts such as autonomy and community have become platitudes—to be called on when expedient, but which have no place in a living, breathing, and deeply stressed peripheral Europe. This is difficult to understand. A rigorous analysis of Christian Democracy published by the authoritative Konrad Adenauer Institute highlights the fact that '[t]herein lies the principle of subsidiarity. … Solidarity with those who are weaker as an expression of the commandment of responsibility and charity towards the poor'.[10] This vindicates our argument that the EU has failed to embrace this dimension of the political and economic tradition—one which was a *lived* and unprecedented successful philosophy. Troikanomics is the measure of this rejection. These values which were at the heart of Christian Democratic politics in Germany's post-war 'miracle' have little resonance in contemporary Europe, now dominated by that same Germany.

For the EU establishment, the existential crisis which now envelopes Europe demands a concrete resolution—a lesson to have been learnt, an insight to have been uncovered, a motivation to now rally behind. It presents an opportunity for the EU to 'reform' at the beginning of a new

[10] See Grabow (2011).

era in a manner, and with a generosity and openness, which was once a defining characteristic. The adversarialism that, one way or another, characterised the Brexit negotiations would suggest that the EU establishment has simply not internalised what this requires. Looking to the short-term future, proposed reforms that have been canvassed envisage new institutional initiatives that will be engaged with within a very different system of governance to that which existed during the crisis: a different European Parliament, a new Commission President, and a new President of the ECB. The political background is very different too, notably in Germany, France, Italy, and of course in the United Kingdom—each of whom are, in their own way, politically stressed and operating within a highly stressed EU. The challenge posed by our analysis is whether, or not, the mind-set which produced Troikanomics in the first place will remain the primary force in the ongoing evolution of Europe—or will lessons have been learnt, and if so how will they be expressed in policy terms and in a shift in the balance of autonomy versus centralism?

The assertion by the European Commission (2017) that '[a]ll reforms initiated so far have been driven by the need to combine solidarity and responsibility at all levels' does not stand up to scrutiny when viewed through the lens of what Troikanomics entailed—which after all is the segue to the proposed Juncker reforms (2017). In setting out the reforms, the Commission acknowledges that the architecture of EMU was incomplete and that 'the crisis…laid bare some of its institutional weaknesses' which we have reflected on earlier. The proposed reforms, however, go well beyond the institutional level. They reflect an inflection point in the governance of the EU that, unless addressed, threaten an irreversible subjugation of the autonomy and consequential responsibilities of national governance to the EU 'core'.

Finally, we emphasise that, this book is a reflective exercise. It is not intended as a grand 'plan'. We do, however, propose that, on the basis of these reflections, Troikanomics has had deeply negative consequences that did little justice to what Europe was called to be; and, it should be added, hold a mirror up to the root causes—and consequences—of its wider existential crisis. We believe that the experience points to an intention on the part of the establishment to press ahead with the Conventional Wisdom, notwithstanding the costs, because of the political capital invested in it by the dominant countries.

The key point is this: autonomy is central to the capabilities of a country and to a form of governance that empowers both its own capabilities and its capacity to share them within and through its relationships. Troikanomics emasculated the substance of member nations' autonomy that had once been taken for granted—it provided a nihilistic demonstration of the consequences of losing the moral compass guiding the socio-political and economic trajectory. It infected what the EU was all about and shifted the locus of responsibility away from the demos in individual countries and centralised it within the control of the dominant countries. It contributed to a set of individual crises—from migration and Brexit to the widening rift across the EU—swamping the smaller members and emboldening the stronger to resist what they witnessed in Troikanomics, did not like, and rejected.

But as we pointed out earlier, crisis can be the essential catharsis which opens up the way to change and, perhaps, redemption—a different way and set of values within which to live our lives and our relationship with others.

A core challenge is whether, or not, the Commission and those standing for election in the new European Parliament will focus on reanimating the autonomy of member countries (by, for example, giving real substance to solidarity and subsidiarity).

Peripheral countries, in particular, which were motivated to participate in the EU by a promise of stability and prosperity, are now daunted by a latent fear of the resultant political pressures, should they attempt to democratically extricate themselves from what the EU has become. This, together with the inevitable complexities of enlargement and also the paradoxes of increased militarisation, has contributed towards a disenchantment with the EU and a significant resurgence in affirming the primacy of national autonomy. The EU has not, as yet, engaged pro-actively in this issue; this is its ongoing challenge as it moves beyond 2019.

At the beginning of this chapter we referred to the new 'domain' from which the EU can consign to the past the adversarial stasis that defined the Troika. That is, one which reanimates 'Project Europe' on the basis of a shared vocabulary of values; that celebrates the foundational *character* of the EU, including the dignity of every citizen; that eschews hegemony and a deeply worrying militarisation; that gives real substance to an economy and financial system that is motivated by *service*; and that fosters the autonomous capacities of its members and their ability to contribute *to* and flourish *within* their community.

## References


Aizenman, J. (2016). *Optimal Currency Area: A 20th Century Idea for the 21st Century?* [Online]. Retrieved from http://www.nber.org/papers/w22097.pdf

Ash, T. G. (2012). *The Crisis of Europe: How the Union Came Together and Why It's Falling Apart.* [Online]. Retrieved from https://www.foreignaffairs.com/articles/europe/2012-08-16/crisis-europe?page=4

Bénéton, P., Brague, R., Delsol, C., Joch, R., András, L., Legutko, R., Manent, P., Matlary, J. H., Pavón, D. N., Scruton, R., Spaemann, R., & Jan Spruyt, B. (2017). *The Paris Statement: A Europe We Can Believe in.* [Online]. Retrieved from https://thetrueeurope.eu/a-europe-we-can-believe-in/

Bergsten, C. F. (2012). *Why the Euro Will Survive: Completing the Continent's Half-Built House.* [Online]. Retrieved from https://www.foreignaffairs.com/articles/europe/2012-09-01/why-euro-will-survive

Council of the European Union. (2017). *Council Decision Establishing Permanent Structured Cooperation (PESCO) and Determining the List of Participating Member States.* [Online]. Retrieved May 12, 2018, from http://www.consilium.europa.eu/media/32000/st14866en17.pdf

Czaputowicz, J. (2014). Sovereignty in Theories of European Integration and the Perspective of the Polish Constitutional Tribunal. *Yearbook of Polish European Studies, 17*, 15–35.

European Central Bank. (2009). The Concept of Systemic Risk. *Financial Stability Review*, 134–142.

European Commission. (2008). *European Economy No. 2/2008 – EMU@Ten: Successes and Challenges After Ten Years of Economic and Monetary Union.* Luxembourg: European Commission.

European Commission. (2017, December 6). *Press Release: Commission Sets out Roadmap for Deepening Europe's Economic and Monetary Union.* [Online]. Retrieved from http://europa.eu/rapid/press-release_IP-17-5005_en.htm

European Parliament. (2014). *Role and Operations of the Troika with Regard to the Euro Area Programme.* Brussels: The European Parliament.

Fagan, G., & Gaspar, V. (2007). *Adjusting to the Euro.* Frankfurt: European Central Bank.

Galston, W. A. (2018). *The Rise of European Populism and the Collapse of the Center-Left* [Online]. Retrieved from https://www.brookings.edu/blog/order-from-chaos/2018/03/08/the-rise-of-european-populism-and-the-collapse-of-the-center-left/

Grabow, K. (Ed.). (2011). *Christian Democracy: Principles and Policy-Making.* Berlin: Konrad-Adenauer-Stiftung e. V.

Hillebrand, R. (2014). *Germany and the Eurozone Crisis: Evidence for the Country's 'Normalisation'?* Discussion Papers in Business and Economics, Fulda University of Applied Sciences, Volume 10.

Juncker, J.-C. (2017). Authorised Version of the State of the Union Address 2017. In E. Commission (Ed.), *State of the Union 2017* (pp. 5–22). Brussels: European Commission.

Lane, P. R. (2012). The European Sovereign Debt Crisis. *Journal of Economic Perspectives, 26*(3), 49–68.

Menéndez, A. J. (2014). The European Crises and the Undoing of the Social and Democratic Rechtsstaat. In J. E. Fossum & A. J. Menéndez (Eds.), *The European Union in Crises or the European Union as Crises?* (pp. 387–489). ARENA Report No. 2/14.

Schulz-Forberg, H. (2012). On the Historical Origins of the EU's Current Crisis or the Hypocritical Turn of European Integration. In E. Chiti, A. J. Menéndez, & P. G. Teixeira (Eds.), *The European Rescue of the European Union? The Existential Crisis of the European Political Project* (pp. 15–36). Oslo: ARENA.

Schuman, R., & Monnet, J. (1950). *The Schuman Declaration.* [Online]. Retrieved from https://europa.eu/european-union/about-eu/symbols/europe-day/schuman-declaration_en

Schwab, K. (2012). *The Re-emergence of Europe.* s.l.: World Economic Forum.

Trading Economics. (2018a). *Greece Government Debt to GDP 1980–2018.* [Online]. Retrieved from https://tradingeconomics.com/greece/government-debt-to-gdp

Trading Economics. (2018b). *Greek Jobless Rate Edges Up to 20.2% in April.* [Online]. Retrieved from https://tradingeconomics.com/articles/07122018092042.htm

Traynor, I. (2015). *Three Days That Saved the Euro.* [Online]. Retrieved from https://www.theguardian.com/world/2015/oct/22/three-days-to-save-the-euro-greece

# Index[1]



[1] Note: Page numbers followed by 'n' refer to notes.



R. Kinsella, M. Kinsella, *Troikanomics*, https://doi.org/10.1007/978-3-319-97070-7

FSC
www.fsc.org
MIX
Papier | Fördert gute Waldnutzung
FSC® C083411

Kolibri 360 GmbH
Ferdinand-Jühlke-Straße 7
99095 Erfurt, Deutschland
produktsicherheit@kolibri360.de